Teresa Moorey has written over thirty books on witchcraft, astrology and related subjects, including the best-selling *Witchcraft, A Beginner's Guide* and *Spellbound!* She is a practising counsellor, hypnotherapist and astrologer, and is also tutor for the Faculty of Astrological Studies, having gained their Diploma and Gold Medal in 1989. For her entire adult life she has explored the mysterious and the mystical, following the ancient paths of Goddess worship and witchcraft.

She lives in the Cotswolds, England, drawing inspiration from the beauty of the landscape, with her husband and four children.

SILVER MOON

Your Magical Guide to Working with the Moon

TERESA MOOREY

RIDER

LONDON · SYDNEY · AUCKLAND · JOHANNESBURG

1 3 5 7 9 10 8 6 4 2

First published in 2003 by Rider,
an imprint of Ebury Press, Random House,
20 Vauxhall Bridge Road, London SW1V 2SA

Random House Australia (Pty) Limited
20 Alfred Street, Milsons Point, Sydney,
New South Wales 2061, Australia

Random House New Zealand Limited
18 Poland Road, Glenfield,
Auckland 10, New Zealand

Random House South Africa (Pty) Limited
Endulini, 5A Jubilee Road,
Parktown 2193, South Africa

The Random House Group Limited Reg. No. 954009

Papers used by Rider are natural, recyclable products
made from wood grown in sustainable forests.

Printed and bound by Biddles Ltd, Guildford and King's Lynn
Designed by seagulls
Illustrations by Jane Brideson

Every effort has been made to trace all copyright holders but if any
have been inadvertently overlooked the author and publishers will be
pleased to make the necessary arrangement at the first opportunity.

A CIP catalogue record for this book
is available from the British Library

ISBN 0-7126-5715-0

CONTENTS

Acknowledgements

With gratfeul thanks to Claire Nahmad for permission to use her fairy spell.

INTRODUCTION

 Welcome to a book about our good neighbour – the silver Moon.

Much closer to us than any other celestial body, the Moon was once considered to be a resting-place for the soul on leaving Earth, and was a portal to other realms. Today the Moon still offers a place of repose, and is still a 'portal' in many ways. There is something about the Moon that invites us to question, to wonder, to look above and beyond ourselves – and to dream.

The Moon is distant enough to be a mystery, yet close enough to be familiar to us. Something about the Moon invites us to 'conjure', to speculate and to create. She is a reminder that existence has many levels – from the practical, through the symbolic to the sublime. Oh yes, we know with one part of our minds that she is a lump of rock, but with another part of our awareness we know she has so many other meanings.

We are not just passive observers, shut inside the cages of our skulls. We are not 'ghosts in the machine'. Rather, our minds reach out to structure our lives in a subtle fashion. Collectively, our minds form the cosmic web, which is the basis of existence. We can make of the Moon what we will, but however we regard her, she is still powerful – powerful enough to pull the tides, and powerful enough to work magic – which is about the movement of unseen tides.

In the following pages we shall be looking at the Moon in many ways. These include astronomy, lunar observance, the astrology of Moon phases and signs, Goddesses and Gods, the working of magic and practical living in harmony with the Moon. There will be many ways to think of the Moon and many things to do in relation to her. And we shall also be looking at why I call the Moon 'her' – which has cultural significance, as you will see!

Most important, however, just by being there the Moon reminds us of the beauty and balance of the natural world, and helps us to appreciate it.

Shine on, and blessed be!

Teresa Moorey

CHAPTER 1

MEET THE MOON

The Moving Moon went up the sky
And no where did abide:
Softly she was going up
And a star or two beside.
COLERIDGE, 'THE RIME OF THE ANCIENT MARINER'

✦ Our Friend the Moon

The Moon is a special feature in our skies. Nothing else has her glamour: she is ever-changing and yet is a creature of habit, whimsical yet predictable, enchanting yet homely. Her cycle is unique; never two days the same, she nevertheless repeats herself and next month she'll do similar things in a similar order.

The Moon has many facets. She is a queen riding high in the starry sky; a huntress chasing the wild clouds; a crystal within which poets and seers find their muse; a witch and a temptress; a source of mythology and folklore; a dispenser of dreams; a clock for kitchen and garden; an inspiration for nursery rhymes – and even (according to some) a block of cheese! What do all these things have in common? They all have links with a basic, instinctual and even child-like part of us. Of course this doesn't mean that the Moon is 'childish' in any way, but simply that certain traits that are often most active in childhood may be stimulated by the Moon.

Astrologers believe that the movements of the Sun, Moon and planets have links with life on Earth and with human personality and activity. Notice that I say 'have links' and not 'cause'. Astrology is based on observation over millennia.

Few astrologers believe that heavenly bodies make us do things – there is simply a correlation and no one is sure what this is, although there are many theories. In fact there may be several elements that connect the heavens with life here on Earth. In the case of the Moon, our nearest neighbour, some effects are easy to measure and some are obviously causal, notably the tides. However, we all react to the Moon in ways that may be either obvious or subtle. In this chapter we are going to look at the cycle of the Moon, discuss some facts about her, and find ways of attuning ourselves to her as individuals.

The Lunar Cycles

The Moon's Phases Firstly we need to understand the basics of the lunar cycle. The Moon has several cycles but the one that is the most obvious and that concerns us principally is that of the Moon's phases. The light of the Moon is reflected from the Sun. Although from a more subtle perspective it is evident that moonlight has its own special properties, the Moon herself has no luminescence. The phases of the Moon are caused by the light of the Sun being reflected in a different way, owing to the changing relationship between Earth, Moon and Sun.

The phases of the Moon are *the same all over the Earth*. When it is Full Moon in Britain it is also Full Moon in Australia, China and the United States. Full Moon occurs whenever the Sun and Moon are opposite each other, so the Moon reflects the Sun's light, and appears perfectly round. This will happen at a certain point in time, usually defined by Greenwich Mean Time, i.e. time by the meridian that passes through the Greenwich Observatory in London, England. So, for example, if the actual moment of Full Moon occurs at 12.00pm GMT, the Moon, when it is truly full, will be overhead at midnight in London. Five hours later it will be midnight in New Jersey and again the Moon will be overhead. People will look at the Full Moon, but strictly speaking this is now five hours after Full Moon. For practical purposes this makes little difference, but it is important if you wish to understand the basics of the phase cycle. The 'phase cycle' is also called the 'lunation cycle', and the time between successive New Moons being called a 'lunation'.

When the Moon is waxing in the first stages of her cycle, she appears as a crescent in the evening sky. This crescent can be cupped in a raised, curved right palm in the Northern Hemisphere, in a left palm in the Southern. The association with the right hand may be part of the traditional links between the 'right hand, Waxing Moon and good forces' and the 'left hand, Waning Moon and evil forces' concept. The fact that this is relative is demonstrated by the fact that in Australia and New Zealand the Waxing Moon can be cupped by the left hand! At the Equator the Moon appears as a bowl, either inverted or upright.

The Moon's First Quarter is when the Moon is seen as a semi-circle in the later evening sky. This is the point mid-way between New and Full Moons.

Around the time of Full Moon, the Moon is overhead at midnight, lighting up the sky with an opalescent glow. When the weather is clear, Full Moon is very obvious and it may be hard to sleep deeply for a few nights with that gentle yet relentless drenching of white light flooding through the bedroom curtains.

The Moon's Last Quarter is when the Moon is seen after midnight, appearing again as a semi-circle, the reverse shape to the First Quarter. This is the point mid-way between Full Moon and the next New Moon.

The Waning Moon can be seen in the small hours, shrinking as she disappears into the light of dawn. Now the Sun and Moon are approaching what astrologers call 'conjunction'. This means that the two heavenly bodies are together in the sky. At this point the Moon is invisible, and the time is called the Dark of the Moon. New Moon occurs as the Moon begins to pull away from the Sun in a fresh cycle, but the Moon still cannot be seen for about three days, until once more the silver sickle appears in the evening. Don't we all feel

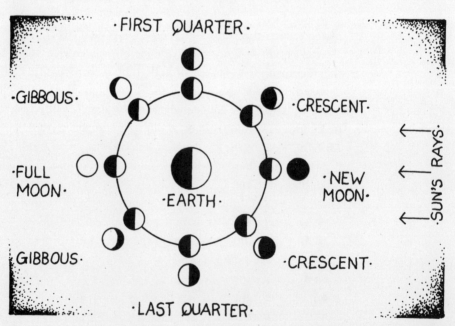

Figure 1: Phases of the Moon

just a small thrill of excitement when we see this, a feeling that something fresh is underway?

The passage of the Moon from New Moon to New Moon takes 29½ days, not an exact four weeks as many people assume. This 'phase cycle' is called the 'synodic month' and while its mean length is 29 days, 12 hours and 44 minutes, a synodic month can actually vary by as much as 13 hours because of the eccentricity of the Moon's orbit around the Earth. As there are 365 days in the year, most years have 13 New Moons or 13 Full Moons but never both. Occasionally a year will miss out and only have 12 of each.

Figure 1 illustrates the phases of the Moon.

The Zodiac Cycle The Moon has another cycle that is less immediately obvious but of great importance to us, and that is the Zodiac cycle. Most people know about the signs of the Zodiac. Over the course of a year the Sun travels through all the signs, and the sign the Sun was in when you were born is what makes you a 'Pisces' or a 'Taurus'. The word 'Zodiac' literally means 'circle of animals'. The Zodiac forms a belt in the sky on either side of the Sun's apparent yearly path. However, the Moon and all the planets also travel through the signs and have an effect on us. The Moon moves the fastest, passing through an entire sign in just over two days.

The Zodiac cycle means the Moon's passage from the beginning of the sign Aries, for example, through all the other signs and back to the start of Aries again. This takes slightly less than 28 days. There are 13 of these cycles in a year, and this is one of the connections between the number 13 and 'witchy' things, which are also connected to the Moon. The Zodiac cycle is strictly speaking referred to as the 'sidereal cycle' although there is a difference that we shall soon explore. One of the interesting statistics about the Moon is that the number of sidereal months in the year is exactly one more than the synodic (or phase) months, being 13.369 as opposed to 12.369.

The difference between the phase cycle and the Zodiac cycle accounts for the fact that the Full Moon appears in a different sign of the Zodiac each month. This is because while the Moon is flitting around the Zodiac, the Sun is also moving, although much more slowly. So the Moon 'catches up' with the Sun a little later each time, and the Sun has generally moved on a sign. The Moon is always opposite the Sun when it is full, so it is easy to tell the sign of the Moon at Full Moon, if you know which sign the Sun is occupying. For instance, if the Sun is in Pisces, Full Moon must be in the opposite sign, Virgo. You can check this out by looking at the Zodiac wheel in the diagram.

Figure 2:
Zodiac wheel

Blue Moons Very occasionally a Full Moon will occur right at the start of a sign of the Zodiac and again at the end of it, because it takes the Moon about 29.5 days to go from Full to Full and it takes the Sun just over 30 days. For instance in June 1994 the Full Moon fell in the second degree of Capricorn (each sign has 30 degrees) and then again in the thirtieth degree of Capricorn in July. This happens more frequently, however, in the months that have 31 days, namely January, March, May, July, August, October and December.

Every two and a half years the Full Moon occurs twice in a calendar month (although not necessarily in the same sign of the Zodiac). For example, we had a Full Moon in Cancer on 2 January 1999 and then a Full Moon in Leo on 31 January. Such second Full Moons are called 'blue moons'. Hence the saying 'once in a Blue Moon' doesn't mean 'never', but 'rather rarely'.

Another more literal 'blue moon' is when the Moon appears blue owing to pollution. This can happen when dust particles filter out the light at the red end of the spectrum and the shorter wavelengths of blue, indigo and green intensify. This is especially noticeable when the Moon is low on the horizon, appearing larger due to magnification by the atmosphere and also subject to the greatest refraction of light. Massive forest fires in Canada gave rise to a dramatic blue moon in September 1950, and a similar effect occurred in 1883, associated with the eruption of Krakatoa. Therefore some associations with 'blue moons' may be sinister or alarming.

The Sidereal Cycle

'Sidereal' means 'of the stars' and the sidereal cycle refers to the movements of the Moon relative to the fixed stars. For practical purposes this cycle is the same in length as the Zodiac cycle, since the difference is minute. However, it is important for gardening – which we shall examine in more detail in the final chapter – to note the exact position of the Moon relative to the stars in their constellations. If you wish to make a study of the Moon in your life you may also wish to identify the Moon's position by the stars. However, it is important to be aware that the physical constellations no longer correspond to the symbolic signs of the Zodiac that are named after them.

Figure 2 shows the 12 signs of the Zodiac. The Zodiac wheel begins with Aries, the Ram, and goes through all the signs until Pisces, the Fishes, is reached, and so back to Aries again. Each of these signs has many meanings and these are broadly connected to their position in the Zodiac. For instance, Aries is about pioneering, new beginnings, enterprise, energy and all the things we associate with getting going. People who have the Sun or Moon in Aries, or have the sign in any other way prominent in their chart will display these characteristics to some extent. The next sign, Taurus, the Bull, is about the establishment of territory; next is Gemini, which is about communication of where one is at; sign four, Cancer, is about starting a family, and so on... until we reach Pisces, who sees the links between all things and is often connected with sacrifice. And so we move to a new cycle beginning with Aries again. Of course, this is a great over-simplification of the signs – we all know that Pisceans can be pioneers (Einstein was a Pisces). However, this gives a basic idea of the development of the concept that is the Zodiac.

Like all the signs of the Zodiac, Aries is also a shape formed by the stars in a certain part of the sky – a constellation. It is natural to link the sign of Aries with spring, and the Sun does indeed enter the astrological sign Aries at the Spring Equinox, around 21 March. However, the signs no longer coincide with the constellations because of a phenomenon known as the Precession of the Equinoxes. The constellations weren't always different from the signs of the Zodiac. In the year CE221 (CE stands for Common Era, the equivalent of AD but not welded to Christianity) they were the same.

There are many factors that affect the movements we see in the skies and one of these is a wobble of the Earth on its axis. If you imagine the Earth skewered by a gigantic knitting needle around which it spins, and you now also imagine the point of this 'knitting needle' very slowly, over thousands of years, tracing a circle against the stars, you will get some idea of why the constellations move in relation to the seasons.

The first point of Aries is marked by the time when the Sun crosses the Celestial Equator on its journey North. The Celestial Equator is merely the Earth's Equator projected out into space and conceived as an imaginary line. This crossing happens at the same time each year, give or take a day. But because of the wobble of the Earth's axis, the point in the sky where the Sun makes this transition is continually moving, very slowly, against the background of the constellations. So the first point of Aries has now gone backwards through Pisces and is moving close to Aquarius – one of the reasons why people say we are at the dawning of the new Aquarian Age. It takes a total of 25,800 years for the equinoctial point to move all the way round, from the first point of Aries back to the first point of Aries again.

The signs of the Zodiac make 12 equal divisions of the Ecliptic, or apparent path of the Sun, 30 degrees each. This is mapped out from the first point of Aries in a belt around the Earth. This is called the Tropical Zodiac, because it is based on the seasons. Most astrologers use it and find it works very well. There are sound concepts behind this and even some scientific evidence concerning the solar wind, to back it up, but this is outside our scope here. The Zodiac signs were indeed named after the constellations. However, the constellations may well have been named after influences sensed by our more instinctual ancestors, rather than the shapes the stars are supposed to make – most of the constellations stretch the imagination to the maximum when we seek the figures they are supposed to represent! In other words ancient people may have been aware of 'ram-like' energies when the Sun was in a certain patch of stars and therefore named that 'patch' the Ram because of the way they felt rather than because of what they saw. At all events, the Tropical Zodiac is the most popular, at least in the Western world.

The Sidereal Zodiac is, in fact, the same Zodiac, but measured from a different point. This is the Zodiac that is tied to the fixed stars and the patterns they form – the constellations. This Zodiac may be important for certain aspects of life and it would appear that from the point of view of gardening, at least, it is the Moon's place in the Sidereal Zodiac that counts. According to many researchers, the Zodiac of antiquity was the Sidereal one, used by the Babylonians and the civilisation of the Tigris-Euphrates. The difference between the two Zodiacs is called the 'Ayanamsa' and is currently about 25

Table 1: Dates of the Zodiac

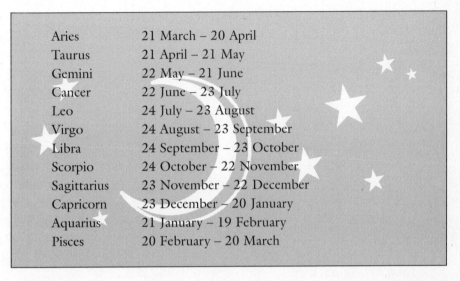

Aries	21 March – 20 April
Taurus	21 April – 21 May
Gemini	22 May – 21 June
Cancer	22 June – 23 July
Leo	24 July – 23 August
Virgo	24 August – 23 September
Libra	24 September – 23 October
Scorpio	24 October – 22 November
Sagittarius	23 November – 22 December
Capricorn	23 December – 20 January
Aquarius	21 January – 19 February
Pisces	20 February – 20 March

degrees. This means that when the Moon is in 0 degrees of Aries, sidereally it is in about 5 degrees of Pisces.

One very approximate rule of thumb is taken from Full Moon. As we have already seen, when the Moon is full – and the exact day can established from a newspaper or calendar – it will be in the sign opposite to the Sun, the positions of which are given in Table 1.

If the Sun is in Aries, then the Full Moon is in Libra, and so on around the Zodiac wheel. Unless the date is very close to the end of a sign, for instance, from 16–21 April, when the Sun is right at the end of Aries – you can be reasonably sure where the Moon is in the Sidereal Zodiac by counting one sign backwards. So your Full Moon in Libra is, in fact, in Virgo in the Sidereal Zodiac. The sidereal Full Moon equivalents are given in Table 2, but not in zodiacal order. You may test yourself if you wish by placing your palm over the answers in the right hand column. When you have the idea you will be able to tell the sidereal sign of the Full Moon without the aid of this book.

The Moon moves approximately one degree every two hours and changes sign every two or three days. The Sun moves about one degree a day. If you are good at arithmetic you will be able to work out the position of the Moon in a sign simply by knowing the position of the Sun. For instance, on 24 March you will know the Sun is about three degrees into Aries. A Full Moon on that date will therefore be in Libra. From there you can get a pretty good idea of the Moon's position. But for serious study you will need to obtain some planetary tables (see Resources).

Table 2:
Sidereal
Moon Signs

Full Moon with Sun in Pisces = sidereal Moon in Leo
Full Moon with Sun in Taurus = sidereal Libra
Full Moon with Sun in Aries = sidereal Virgo
Full Moon with Sun in Gemini = sidereal Scorpio
Full Moon with Sun in Leo = sidereal Capricorn
Full Moon with Sun in Sagittarius = sidereal Taurus
Full Moon with Sun in Aquarius = sidereal Cancer
Full Moon with Sun in Cancer = sidereal Sagittarius
Full Moon with Sun in Virgo = sidereal Aquarius
Full Moon with Sun in Scorpio = sidereal Aries
Full Moon with Sun in Capricorn = sidereal Gemini
Full Moon with Sun in Libra = sidereal Pisces

Tropical or Sidereal Zodiac – which is correct? The truth is, we cannot be sure! Probably both have a validity. The linking of the Zodiac with the seasons breaks down for Equatorial regions and the Southern Hemisphere. However, there is a mystery in astrology, because here we have the human mind moving within the cosmos, looking for patterns and deductions, while modern physics is establishing that the observer affects the experiment! Of course, this doesn't mean that you can believe anything and have it work! However, both systems, Tropical and Sidereal, are based on sound and time-honoured principles and there are successful and helpful practitioners of both disciplines. The greater part of this book is based on the Tropical System which I and many other Western astrologers have found unfailing in psychological astrology. Experiment for yourself if you wish!

★ ∴ ★ *More Moon Data*

Harvest The Harvest Moon is the juicy, golden Full Moon that rises in September, close
Moon to the Autumn Equinox. At around the time of the Equinox the path that the planets take around the Sun (i.e. the Ecliptic and Zodiac) is tilted at its smallest angle to the horizon, running low above it. The effect of this is to cause the Moon to rise only about 12 minutes later each evening, instead of its average of 50 minutes, throughout the year. Thus, at sunset around harvest-time, for several successive evenings, the ripe Moon hangs just above the Earth as a reminder of the bounty of Nature.

Hunter's Moon This is the October Moon. She behaves in a fashion similar to the Harvest Moon, lingering on the horizon, extending the light for hunters and stirring nature in a last flush of activity before winter. Stags rut, leaves begin to fall and it is the last chance to gather and to husband before winter begins to bite.

Eclipses We have seen that the Sun, Moon and Earth are 'in line' twice in the lunar cycle, at New and Full Moons. At New Moon the Moon stands between Earth and Sun, at Full Moon the Earth stands between Sun and Moon. However, they are not often in exact alignment. When they are, eclipses occur. An eclipse of the Sun occurs at New Moon, and an eclipse of the Moon at Full Moon. Because of the relative sizes and distances, total eclipses of the Moon are more common than those of the Sun. During an eclipse the Moon turns blood red in the shadow of the Earth, or may disappear completely. Solar eclipses may be annular, in that a ring of the sun may be left around the Moon if the Moon is at its farthest point away from the Earth in its elliptical orbit. Even in a total eclipse of the Sun, the area of the Earth in shadow is never more than 170 miles wide. The shadow sweeps across the Earth as it rotates and the Moon circles. Partial eclipses can be seen, however, for thousands of miles. Lunar eclipses, on the other hand, are visible throughout the entire night hemisphere, and may

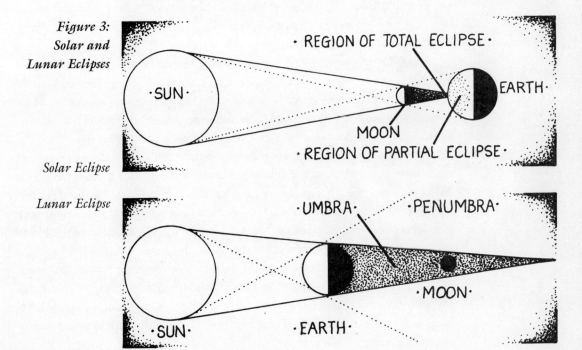

Figure 3: Solar and Lunar Eclipses

Solar Eclipse

· REGION OF TOTAL ECLIPSE ·
·SUN·
·EARTH
MOON
· REGION OF PARTIAL ECLIPSE ·

Lunar Eclipse

·UMBRA·   ·PENUMBRA·
·MOON·
·SUN·   ·EARTH·

last for up to two hours as opposed to the seven or eight minutes maximum for a solar eclipse. Eclipses occur at six-monthly intervals, solar eclipses and lunar eclipses taking place about a fortnight apart. Figure 3 shows what happens at an eclipse.

What happens in the sky at an eclipse is clear and simple, but what happens on more subtle levels is open to debate – and observation, to some extent. Ancient wisdom teaches us that eclipses are very negative, especially those of the Sun, which were believed to herald the death of the sovereign. Solar eclipses are dramatic and scary. In a total eclipse everything goes dark, animals and birds go quiet and there is a feeling that everything is holding its breath, as though fearing that the Sun will never come back. Astrologers do not always take so negative a view, and indeed there are many factors to be taken into consideration. For instance, the other planets in the sky are significant, especially in respect of the angles they make to the eclipse point (which is, in fact, the conjunction of Sun and Moon). Another important factor concerns the aspects made by the eclipse to an existing chart. For example, if your birthchart shows that you have your Sun at 20 degrees of Aries and a solar eclipse occurs at 20 degrees of Aries then you may expect to experience some effect. This may be a total 'wipe-out' of many things in your life that are connected to your expression of your Sun – for instance your creativity. However, this could be a good thing, leaving the way open for new movement. Another possibility is an intensification in creativity, which may take on increased depth.

The solar eclipse of 1999 was particularly feared because it was in square aspect, i.e. at 90 degrees, to several difficult planets, including Saturn, Uranus and Mars. The square aspect is considered challenging and oppressive. The countries where the eclipse was visible did experience some misfortune in the subsequent few months in the shape of earthquakes and turbulence. This was even more the case where the eclipse point made a difficult aspect to an important planet in the chart of the country. A country's astrological chart would be based on when the current government came into power. If, for instance, the eclipse point were to form a square aspect to that country's Sun, one might wonder about some dramatic occurrence, such as the assassination of the Head of State or a milder manifestation in the fall of the government.

Closer to home, from the point of view of our lunar awareness, trees planted at the time of a solar eclipse have proved to grow in stunted fashion and to yield bitter fruit. A lunar eclipse has a stifling feel, as if one's dreams have gone dead. Observe these feelings for yourself, bearing them in mind in the exercises at the end of the chapter.

Astronomical Facts Our nearest neighbour in space, the Moon is only 240,000 miles away. Until the twentieth century, there was continual speculation about the possibility of life on the Moon. The Apollo landings clearly established that the Moon has no life whatsoever, and probably never had. The lunar atmosphere is thought to be derived from the solar wind, that stream of ionised particles given off by the Sun and travelling through the solar system. However, it is worth noting that there is a body of evidence that calls into question the evidence of the Moon landings, which may have been at least partially a hoax. Readers who wish to explore this will find a reference to Marcus Allen's material and his publication *Nexus Magazine*, which deals with this, at the back of this book.

The orbital direction of the Moon around the Earth is anti-clockwise, which is why it rises later and later each day. Only half of the Moon's surface is ever seen, as the same face is always turned towards Earth, giving rise to speculations about the 'dark side of the Moon'. The Moon is 2,160 miles in diameter, in contrast to the diameter of the Earth, which is 7,927 miles. Although the Moon is much smaller than the Earth, it is big enough to exert a pull upon the Earth so that, albeit to a much more minor degree, the Earth also goes round the Moon, making a Moon/Earth 'system'. This is relevant when we come to consider the Moon as Goddess and her relationship to the Earth Mother – it is as if they are 'sisters' and the Moon is the celestial counterpart of Mother Earth.

The gravity of the Moon is 0.165 that of the Earth, and the surface temperature ranges from a sizzling 130°C by day to a paralysing -153°C at night, due to the fact that the Moon has no atmospheric blanket to protect it. Contrary to former belief, it now seems that the Moon may originally have been captured by the gravity of the Earth, rather than having separated from it, because of the differences between lunar rock and rock upon Earth. Despite the fact that certain areas of the Moon are called 'seas' there isn't, and hasn't been for millennia, any water on the surface of the Moon.

The Moon and our Culture

The facts about the Moon sadly fail to support our experience of her. But then, what sort of an idea might one get of a person just by being told the details of their height, weight, colouring, genetic background and postal address? This would give you little idea about whether they were kind or cruel, active or passive, creative or analytical. In the same way, the Moon is much more than a collection of statistics, although many of these are important to life on Earth when examined.

The phases of the Moon have been observed and recorded since the Stone Age and possibly earlier. Lunar phases have been found marked on bones from as far back as 35,000BCE. The well-known ancient figure, the 'Goddess of Willendorf' (dating from about 19,000BCE) shows seven strata of notched circles on her head that relate, in all probability, to the approximate seven days of each of the lunar quarters. The phases of the Moon are a metaphor for rebirth and the resurgence of life. Even in present times certain indigenous people mark their respect for the Moon. Laurens van der Post records how certain African bushmen dance all night to show how much they love the Waning Moon, so that she will return. It may well have been the Moon who taught the human mind to operate in the abstract, holding an idea of something that is not immediately present. The cycles of the Moon are more subtle in this respect than the Sun, which is connected to the alternation of day and night. The Moon is more easy to forget, yet back she comes as a reminder. Barrow mounds were often constructed to face moonrise, so that the souls of the dead might travel along the moonbeams. The Moon epitomised the tomb that was also womb, the unseen and fearsome place that was yet the cradle of life, the ancient and sometimes sinister crone who re-appeared as a beautiful maiden. In short, the Moon connected – and connects – life with death, in a continuous cycle.

The importance of the Moon's cycle is shown in words derived from the Greek word *mene* (meaning 'Moon'), such as month, di-*mens*-ion, *mens*truation, com*mens*urate, me*as*urement, *mens*uration, and many others. The complex cycles of the Moon needed more deliberate working out than the day/night, winter/summer movements of the Sun, so the Moon was a teacher – although she is linked to the instincts, she also made our forebears think. She was also an agricultural reminder. Her rapid changes in size are a clear way of working out the passage of days and the times for harvesting and hunting. In most cultures the earliest calendars seem to have been based upon the Moon. These performed far more serious functions than the pragmatic order of life. They connected human beings to the cosmic order of which they were a part and which formed the basis for their agriculture, religious observance and spiritual experience. The Babylonian month began when the first crescent appeared in the evening sky. The Hebrew calendar was also lunar, with major feasts occurring at Full Moon, specifically the Passover which occurred when the first Full Moon after the Spring Equinox rose over the Eastern horizon. Easter Sunday is in effect a lunar festival, as it is fixed on the first Sunday after the first Full Moon after the Spring Equinox. Dire consequences were believed to follow any violations of the lunar calendar, and while this may seem ignorant and primitive to us today, it is based on an appreciation of the importance of the rhythms of nature. Part of the purpose of this book is to re-learn something of this.

It is interesting to note that, as the instinctual ways were lost, so the Moon effectively disappeared from the calendar. While our modern months have a lunar derivation, they are no longer linked directly to the phases of the Moon. Some writers have connected to the calendar a 'battle' between solar knowledge (which is rational and conscious) and 'lunar knowledge' which is instinctual and magical. This struggle focuses especially on the numbers 12 and 13. Twelve is an even 'rational' number, capable of neat division, while 13 is not. However, the Moon makes 13 rounds of the Zodiac per year and it would be quite reasonable to have these 13 lunar months preserved in our calendar, with a spare day to catch up. Remember, the Zodiac or Sidereal cycle is almost 28 days, 28 x 13 = 364, and there are 365 days in a year. The adoption of the 12-fold division may have links with the patriarchal take-over of more ancient Goddess-worshipping cultures, and the suppression of things female and intuitive. Much of this is speculation. However, the linkage of 13 with the magical, mysterious and sinister is preserved in our culture, folklore and superstitions.

Calendars, Festivals and Observances

Around the world there are numerous lunar observances, feast days and calendars. Here is a small selection.

African Lunar Rituals
Certain African tribes have a lunar ritual that only involves women. The Moon is regarded both as mother and the protector of ghosts (in keeping with the womb/tomb theme!). Just before the rainy season starts, a rite is celebrated at the New Moon. Clay and the juices of vegetables are used to make the women's skin lighter. Bananas are fermented to make a drink and the women dance and pray that the souls of the dead may rest and that the tribe will be fruitful and well-fed. Then they refresh themselves with the brew. (In Western lore, bananas are 'governed' by the Moon.)

American Tribal Calendars and Rituals
Native American peoples often followed a calendar allied to Sun and Moon, and had a special name for each Full Moon. Many of these were later adopted by the white settlers. Here are some examples:

January — Wolf Moon, Ice Moon, Play Moon
February — Snow Moon, Black Bear Moon, Elder Moon
March — Crow Moon, Big Clouds Moon, Earth Cracks Moon
April — Seed Moon, Big Wind Moon, Pink Moon
May — Milk Moon, Hare Moon, Flower Moon
June — Honey Moon, Rose Moon, Strawberry Moon
July — Thunder Moon, Mead Moon, Corn Tassel Moon
August — Corn Moon, Woodcutter's Moon, Red Moon
September — Harvest Moon, Fruit Moon, Spider Web on the Ground at Dawn Moon
October — Hunter's Moon, Blood Moon, Basket Moon
November — Beaver Moon, Initiate Moon, No Name Moon
December — Long Night Moon, Oak Moon, Big Freezing Moon

You may like to use or adapt some of these names to suit your own ideas about the Moon in the different seasons.

The Hopi Indians refer to the lunation around the Winter Solstice as 'Dangerous Moon' because this is the time when all life comes to a standstill, the affairs of humans become secret and spirits walk. Fires are kindled to keep alive the powers of light and life and to conjure back the Sun.

The Cahuilla observed certain lunar rituals at the time of a girl's first period. She was placed on a bed of herbs and bushes in a heated trench. For three days and nights she remained there while the members of the tribe sang and danced in honour of the Moon. This first menstruation was expected to take place at New Moon and the young woman received special care until the end of the lunation.

The Chinese Calendar This calendar synchronises Sun and Moon, including intercalary days on certain months. Each Moon has a special name and function. The Chinese New Year occurs at the first Full Moon in February and the ritual year is based on the Moon.

The Hebrew Calendar This calendar also synchronises the solar and lunar cycles, using a system of leap years in which an extra month is added to every nineteenth year.

The Islamic Year As this system depends on the cycles of the Moon, the Islamic New Year appears to move backwards each year in comparison with the standard Western way of measuring the years.

The Mayan Calendar   The synchronising of solar and lunar cycles was crucial in the complex calendar of the Mayans.

Megalithic Monuments   Well-known sites such as Stonehenge, Avebury, Callanish, Carnac and possibly the North American Medicine Wheels have lunar associations, built to mark and predict the phases and phenomena.

Rhythms of Life

The Tides   The Moon causes almost 70 per cent of the tidal pull and the Sun accounts for the remainder. High tides occur when the Moon is overhead, and when it is at its opposite point. At New and Full Moons tides are higher because the gravitational pull is greater; these are called Spring Tides, when the Moon is closest to the Earth in its orbital ellipse and also near the Equinoxes. Tides where the highest and the lowest points only differ slightly are called Neap tides and these take place when the Sun and Moon are at right angles, at the first and last quarters.

The Moon and Life on Earth   Much argument and speculation exists about the effects the Moon has on life on Earth. Some have stated that because the human body, like the Earth, is about 70 per cent water, the Moon's pull must be felt within our bodies too. Others have countered with the argument that any such movement must be minute. However, if something as tiny as a virus can affect us, surely the Moon may be felt? Besides, there is more to the presence of the Moon than mere gravity. From observation you may notice all sorts of lunar effects – on you, as well as on your plants, animals, home and dream life. Here are some reasonably well-established lunar effects.

★ Menstruation takes its name from the Moon and is obviously linked to the lunar cycle. In fact, many women find that their periods tend to occur at New or Full Moon. Even those who do not normally have a 29-day cycle may find their periods are 'pulled' by the cycle. For instance, a woman who has a 35-day cycle may find that she menstruates at 33 days when this coincides with Full or New Moon, or that the cycle is extended to 37 days for the same reason. You can establish the effect on you by plotting a menstrual mandala (see page 21).

★ The light of the Full Moon may stimulate ovulation in humans (although certain studies have shown that this can also be stimulated by artificial light).

Because many women ovulate at the Full Moon, this is a good time for conception. It is also a time of increased sexual activity.

★ More births occur at Full Moon. This was observed by my own midwife who said that she and her colleagues always observed the lunar phases and expected to be busier at Full Moon.

★ Fertility in other animals is also affected. Although the oestrus cycle of the horse is three weeks, conceptions are more likely on or just after Full Moon. This is just one example of the Moon's effects on animal and plant reproduction.

★ Bees are more active at New Moon, in keeping with their function as fertilisers of plants. This was established by the biologist Oehmke, at Goethe University, Frankfurt.

★ Plant metabolism is at its highest around Full Moon. Factors relating to the storage of carbohydrates are most active at New Moon, and those relating to flowering and growth at Full Moon. This was confirmed by a study in 1989 at the University of Paris.

★ All life forms have an electrical charge and the electrical charge of trees peaks at New and Full Moon.

★ Seeds germinate more quickly and effectively when sown with a Moon waxing to full. (This is a separate issue from final crop or flower yield, however – see Chapter 7.)

★ The water content of plants is greater at Full Moon. Because of this a Waning Moon is far preferable for tree-felling. A French law in 1669 stipulated that timber should only be felled during a Waning Moon. Studies by Professor Frank Brown and Carol Chow in North-Western University, Illinois, confirm this aspect of plant metabolism.

★ A certain New Moon in the spring triggers the hormone thyroxin in salmon who need to swim down river to the sea. This is the best time for them to make the journey unseen by predators. This curious fact was discovered by zoologists in the University of California.

★ In an experiment at Long Island, oysters were brought in-land and observed. For a while they continued to open and close in rhythm with the tides at their place of origin, but gradually they adapted and then opened and closed in direct response to the Moon overhead.

★ There are more accidents, crimes and admissions to mental homes at Full Moon.

★ In surgery, the bleeding from wounds often increases at Full Moon.

In his agriculture lectures of 1924 Rudolf Steiner, the originator of the Steiner system of education, said that 'On the days of the Full Moon something colossal is taking place on Earth'. Something significant is also taking place in our lives.

Your Lunar Attunement

We all know there is no substitute for experience! If you have not been in the habit of observing the Moon, here are several ways to become aware of the effect of the Moon.

Lunar Altar   We shall be expanding upon the idea of a lunar altar in your home later in the book. For now, you need to create your altar in order to stimulate your awareness. All you need is a small shelf in a secluded place. You will need to buy or make four cards or pictures to represent Dark Moon, Waxing Moon, Full Moon and Waning Moon (see Resources). Check the lunar phases and change your card/picture to reflect the phase of the Moon in the sky. Once you are in the habit of doing this, you can move on to lighting a candle to mark these phases – a black candle for Dark Moon, a silver one for Waxing, a white one for Full and a purple one for Waning. Or other colours may seem appropriate – for instance the surge of life at Full Moon may be expressed by a red candle, you may prefer white for the innocence of the Waxing Moon, a gold candle may feel better for the Full Harvest Moon, etc. It is up to you. Place flowers, seeds and other artefacts there as seem right to you. Enjoy this.

Celebration   Why not make time to mark the lunar phases? Open a bottle of wine at Full Moon, make love, use a new perfume, have a long, leisurely bath, buy a pot of flowers or have a party. At the dark of the Moon spend time meditating, celebrate your quieter gifts (your powers of reflection and introspection), wear darker colours, keep more secluded (but only if these things feel right for you).

A Lunar Diary   Keep a diary that records your thoughts, feelings, impressions, experiences, moods, etc. Try to write in it on most days. Make sure there is plenty of space to write and that the lunar phases are clearly marked. This isn't a place to write your shopping list or your engagements, but to describe the inner you. Here are some of the things you might like to focus upon:

★ Physical energy: how lively do you feel?

★ Emotions: are you feeling unusually upset or tough, sympathetic or self-centred, passionate or detached?

★ Sleep patterns: are you sleeping deeply or lightly, comfortably or tossing and turning, falling asleep quickly or taking ages, sleeping late in the morning or up with the lark?

★ Dreams: are you dreaming a lot or very little/not at all? (Do not record specific dreams – that is for a separate diary.)

★ Sex: do you feel sexy and are you making love a lot? Or are you 'turned off'?

★ Menstruation: this is important for women and there is a separate section on a menstrual mandala below. Men may like to keep a record for the women in their life.

★ Foods: what do you yearn for? Chocolate? Fruit? Dairy produce? Alcohol? Are you more or less hungry and thirsty than usual?

★ Hot and cold: do you feel especially chilly or warm?

★ Restlessness: are you fidgety or settled?

★ Creativity: do you feel raring to go with lots of ideas or do you prefer to sit and dream. Can you concentrate?

★ Achievement: are you getting a lot done or very little – and do you care?

★ Personal habits, urinating and bowel movements: are these in any way altered?

★ Your health: keep a note of any infections or feelings of well-being.

★ Intuitions and impressions: are you feeling particularly psychic or quite blanked off? Keep a note of your feelings about places or people. If you do tarot or some form of divination, record this, how well it went, the outcome, etc. Record any kind of psychic experience.

★ Tastes: are you 'off' your favourite perfume or especially tuned to it? What is your favourite colour at the moment? What about music – do you feel a greater response to it, or less?

★ Your partner: make a note of anything remarkable they do.

★ Your children: keep a record of any achievements, scrapes or moods they have.

★ Your pets: what are they like? Are they more energetic, or less? Eating more or less? Awake at night? Lazy? Noisy?

★ Your plants and garden: notice your plants, their growth, take-up of water, pests that affect them, etc.

★ Wildlife and bird flight: is there anything happening?

★ The news: what are the headlines? What do you notice in your area?

This very long list is intended primarily as a memory-jogger. Use the items that are most important in your life. You will have the greatest success with your diary if you devote ten minutes a day to it – no more. If you devote any longer each day you may get fed up with it quite quickly, and unless you keep it for at least several months you cannot hope to get an idea of how the Moon is affecting you. In fact, the diary will tell you most if you can keep it over several years. So keep it manageable and write down the things that first occur. This isn't intended to be a chore – far from it. You will find it fascinating.

Your Dream Diary

Again, you need to keep this simple. In contrast to your general lunar diary, you do not need to write in it every day. Indeed, you may not have *anything* to write on many days, for we do not always remember our dreams. However, do not believe people who say they 'don't dream' for we all go through periods of REM sleep. REM stands for Rapid Eye Movement and it occurs when we dream. If we are repeatedly woken up when we are dreaming and deprived of our dream-life we can become mentally ill, for in dreams we work things through, resolve the conflicts of daily life and allow our subconscious to speak. Dreams can also be inspirational and even prophetic. In time you may come to use yours to give you an idea about a decision you have to make or a fresh insight or creative resource.

Your dream diary should also mark the lunar phases, but this isn't so necessary as you can link up with your main diary. Keep it beside your bed – dreams are fleeting things and you will forget them if you don't write them down immediately. Just jot down the major elements; a long account will bore you and you will probably forget important bits that come later. Just write down major things (such as running away, feeling sexy or looking for something) and major symbolic pictures (such as a red rose, a piece of jewellery or a dark cave). Also note the people you meet in your dreams.

Usually, as you begin to note down your dreams, the message gets through to your subconscious that you are registering them and you will begin to remember more and more. Explore this beautiful treasury within you.

Menstrual Mandala

We tend to regard periods as a nuisance at best, which is a great shame. The rhythm of her periods gives a woman access to different parts of her being at different times of the month. One of the reasons why PMS is so prevalent and tiresome is that women do not honour their cycle. Neither does our culture give them any room to do so, for our society abides by more linear time-observance. Indeed it might suit women much more to live by the Moon, working harder at Full Moon, when they may well be ovulating, and taking rest and seclusion when they are menstruating.

In olden times women in some cultures were segregated when they had their periods. *But this was not because they were thought of as being unclean!* It is more probable that women in tribal cultures were granted seclusion because they were magical and powerful at the time of the period, that 'wise wound' giving them the shaman's skill to travel into the spirit world to mediate unseen forces for the tribe. Women did not need to undertake the gruelling initiations of their menfolk for their connection with the forces of life; their monthly blood-loss, childbirth and creativity meant they were already close to the pulse of life. But the cleanliness taboo nevertheless became an unfortunate association, so it is pleasing to note that today periods are 'coming out' and we now have humorous adverts about sanitary protection. However, we are still a long way from giving due honour to the periods. We should try to refrain from calling our periods the Curse – maybe they could be a blessing!

In a patriarchal culture, where paternity is guarded and women are valued for their child-bearing gifts (but not their independence and 'feistiness'), the period may be seen as a threatening time of destructive barrenness, even linked in some subconscious way to the killing of children, as the unfertilised womb expels its contents. Some of this sort of anti-women feeling was behind witch-hunts in some quarters and the rules given in the Bible (namely the book of Leviticus) regarding menstrual blood. Also premenstrual and menstruating women can be very 'witchy' in most of the meanings of the word! These attitudes – and there are still traces of them around – devalue and denigrate an aspect of womanhood. However, there is some basis for regarding the period as a great contributory factor in the building of family life. Women do not have an oestrus cycle and behave like animals on heat, but sexual desire and interaction may have many manifestations at all the different times of the month, enabling a closer bonding. Also, because of the lack of oestrus cycle, women sometimes say 'no' to potential mates, encouraging social skills and subtlety in males. It is easy to overlook these factors.

Bearing this in mind along with the fact that periods are often linked to the Moon, let us look at making a menstrual mandala. A mandala is a circular symbol of wholeness, and you can plot your period in this shape. As you compare previous mandalas with your current one, you may notice developments. For instance if you are trying to conceive, your cycle may become stronger, if you are athletic you may observe surges in energy, your creativity may be stimulated and you may note other changes. Considering your mandala may make you feel more complete and more able to understand yourself and the ways the different parts of your cycle balance each other.

Draw first a large circle on a piece of A4 paper. Around the edge draw the Moon's four phases. Now quarter your circle. Divide three of the sections into seven, and one into eight, making 29 sectors in all (Figure 4). It is hard to get this exactly even, but don't worry (also, it won't matter if a day or two is missed out). Aim to have as many sections as your average cycle covers, if you can. Each of these wedge-shaped sections can be sub-divided so you have room for a word or two about dreams (you can draw a symbol, write 'scary', 'sexy', 'confused', or whatever), note your mood, energy level and any illnesses, mental acuity, etc. You can use colours too if you wish. If your cycle is irregular you can continue around the edge, like a snail's shell, if you wish. The weather can also be noted around the edge.

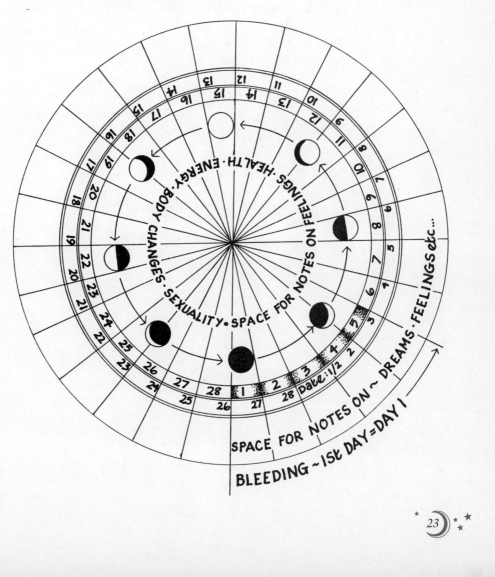

Figure 4:
A menstrual
mandala

Often noting and appreciating the cycle can serve to regulate it and ease some of the ills that come with PMS – but not all! The mandala isn't a menstrual panacea but a process of self-help, self-discovery and attunement to a force that affects your periods – the Moon. Observing your menstruation can enrich your life – so go with the flow!

For Men Men also find that their energy levels and feelings fluctuate along with the Moon. All the above exercises equally apply to men, apart obviously from the section on menstruation, but it may interest you to see how your partner's menstruation dovetails with your own feelings – and not just because you feel you are walking on eggshells when she has PMS! Often observing the Moon can help men in particular to contact their more instinctual side.

Take the first step – check the phase of the Moon right now – and add a new dimension to your life.

CHAPTER 2

YOUR MOON SIGN

It is the stars
The stars above us, govern our conditions
WILLIAM SHAKESPEARE, *KING LEAR*

...The fault, dear Brutus, is not in our stars,
But in ourselves, that we are underlings
WILLIAM SHAKESPEARE, *JULIUS CAESAR*

Sun Sign, Moon Sign

In the previous chapter we looked at the movements of the Moon in her cycles. In this chapter we shall be considering the meaning of the position of the Moon at the time of our birth.

Many people quite rightly raise the objection that although there are only 12 Zodiac signs, individual people are endlessly varied. How can astrology have any meaning, they ask, when it attempts to narrow people down into only 12 types? The answer is that true astrology is far more complex, taking many other factors into consideration. For instance, it isn't only the sign the Sun occupies but also the signs that hold all the other planets that are considered. Almost as important as your Sun sign is your Moon sign.

Moving far more swiftly than the Sun, the Moon goes through all 12 signs in around 28 days, meaning it makes 13 rounds of the Zodiac per year. So the Moon changes sign every two days or so. Because of this, two Virgos, born in the same year but only three days apart, will have different Moon signs, meaning there will be a great difference between their personalities.

Often the Sun sign says something about our self-awareness and growth. We may be conscious of behaving 'like a Virgo' and we may be aware that we value and embody certain Virgoan traits. As we are growing up we may become more like our Sun sign as we become well-integrated, start to make decisions and organise our lives. We are not always automatically like our Sun sign, but our ambitions and self-image may be bound up in it to some extent. However, the Moon sign is quite different, far less conscious, and often more evident in childhood, although it continues to be very important all through our lives.

What Your Moon Sign Conveys
Your Moon sign describes the automatic, instinctual part of you. It reflects the way you react when you aren't thinking, your knee-jerk responses, your habits, what makes you feel at home, your 'comfort zone'. It is also related to the body, in the sense that the body reacts to our emotions and our sense of security or safety. So the Moon is connected to health, or the kinds of things we need to stay healthy, the therapies to which we respond, the food we like, and so on. The subconscious mind is linked to the Moon, our dreams and, most importantly, our intuitions. Your Moon sign determines what sort of intuitions you have and how you are likely to register them and respond to them.

The Moon sign is powerful in small children who are still at the very instinctual stage, and this is especially in evidence before they can talk clearly. For instance, a baby with Moon in Sagittarius may be fretful if it cannot stretch and kick, whereas one with Moon in Virgo may get quickly distressed if they are wet or dirty. Little Moon in Taurus may not be able to tolerate the slightest hunger pang. However, our Moon sign isn't something we 'grow out of'. It is true that the influence of our Moon sign can become overlaid by other developing characteristics, but it is always there, and continues to be in evidence in domestic situations with our family and close friends, or indeed at any time when we are relaxed or vulnerable.

Our lunar nature is often playful and instinctual and we may have been taught to suppress it. However, if we are to be whole people, in tune with our own needs and able to access the natural wisdom of our intuitions, we need to respect that Moon. Reconnecting with our lunar natures can make us healthy, wealthy and wise!

The Phase of the Moon

The phase of the Moon has nothing to do with the sign she is in – you can have a Full, Waxing or Waning Moon in any of the signs of the Zodiac, depending on where the Sun is. Moon phases depend on the relationship between Sun and Moon, as seen from the Earth.

At New Moon the Sun and Moon are 'conjunct'. This means they are close together, in the same sign of the Zodiac. So if you were born at New Moon then you are likely to be even more like your Sun sign because the Sun and Moon are both in the same sign. Of course, they may also be in the same sign when the Moon is reaching the end of her cycle, just before New Moon, when she is catching the Sun up again. Also, the New Moon period actually continues for a while after the Moon has moved on into the next Zodiac sign and so it is no longer conjunct with the Sun. During the month the Moon, which is moving much faster, pulls away from the Sun. After a few days she can be seen in the evening sky as a silver sickle, which grows to a hemisphere. This is the first quarter and a time of challenge. The Moon becomes increasingly round until the Full Moon. At this time the Moon is in the opposite sign of the Zodiac to the Sun, so if you were born with Sun in Virgo at Full Moon your Moon would be in Pisces. Full Moon comes about $14\frac{1}{2}$ days after New Moon. As the Moon shrinks she again becomes a hemisphere at the last quarter, and this may be a challenging time, too, but often the challenges are more subtle and internal. $14\frac{1}{2}$ days after Full Moon, the New Moon occurs again, but by now the Sun has also moved on considerably in the sky, and the next New Moon will fall in the following sign. To use the example of New Moon in Virgo, the following month's New Moon will be in Libra, which immediately follows Virgo. Each time the Moon makes a complete tour of the Zodiac it takes her another couple of days to catch up the Sun, which is why the phase cycle is longer than the Zodiac cycle.

These two 'luminaries' make an interesting dance in the sky, and the 'energies' at the different stages of the cycle are very different, meaning that people born at different phases have subtle differences in their reactions. Those born at Waxing Moon tend to have more dynamic and active responses than those born when the Moon is waning, for these will be more reflective. People born when the Moon is full may have strong intuitions and clarity of vision but they may feel pulled two ways as the tug of the inner realms vies with outer reality. For instance, a Waxing Sagittarian Moon is likely to be very adventurous and something of an explorer, whereas a Waning Sagittarian Moon is probably more of a philosopher and armchair traveller. Of course a Waning Sagittarian Moon could never have the Sun in Cancer, Leo, Virgo, Libra or Scorpio – see Figure 5.

Figure 5:
The Moon's
phases and the
Zodiac wheel

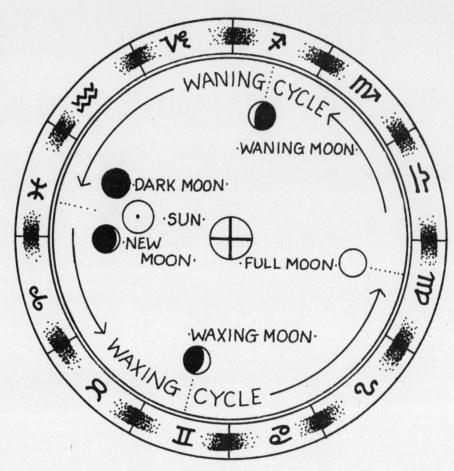

When you have looked up your Moon sign on the tables provided on pages 31–3, you can easily check your Moon phase by looking at Figure 5 above. You can copy it on to a sheet of paper and mark the positions of your Sun and Moon. If the Moon is *ahead* of the Sun in an *anti-clockwise* direction, then the Moon is Waxing. If it is roughly opposite then it is Full, and if it is catching the Sun up, closing the gap (always anti-clockwise) then it is Waning.

The important thing to remember is that this is a cycle. This means that there aren't any definite boundaries. The New Moon becomes Waxing, then Full, then Waning, and you may feel that you have a bit of both types influencing you if you are born on a borderline. This is fine – it's the way things are. The main stages of the cycle for each Moon sign are described below, to help you become even more aware of that inner 'you'. However, you may need to 'blend' two descriptions if you are between two phases, because this is a process of unfolding. Also, please remember that although I have selected four points in the cycle to interpret, one could take a freeze-frame of the cycle in a multitude of places. In my book *The Moon and You* I interpret the phase cycle in nine types (see Further Reading).

Aspects Between the Sun and the Moon

'Aspects' are the angles that astrologers note between planets in the chart. The aspects are calculated from the relative positions of the planets around the 360° of the zodiac. For instance, planets that are 90° degrees apart are in a 90-degree aspect called a 'square' aspect. Aspects can be smooth or challenging – the square aspect is considered difficult, but constructive, whereas the 120-degree aspect, or trine, is harmonious. Planets that are in aspect to each other will often be 'locked together' in the life of the person, in a way that can be either pleasant or tense.

It is not hard to see that as the Sun and Moon go through their monthly *pas de deux* they form every aspect possible to each other. When the Moon is in her first and also her last quarter, Sun and Moon are in square aspect, and this can be challenging. At Full Moon they are in opposition (180° apart), and this also is not without its stresses and strains. The 120-degree and 60-degree aspects are flowing and easy.

Aspects between Sun and Moon show how well your conscious mind is in harmony with your instincts. To be completely sure of all of this you need to consult an astrologer (see Resources). However, if your Sun and Moon are in the same element, e.g. both in Water signs, then they may be in trine. The actual 'orb', or number of degrees in which the aspect has an influence, is taken as 8°. So they could well be in the same element, but not form an aspect, but this will still make for internal harmony. Another flowing aspect is the sextile, i.e. an aspect of 60°, and this occurs when the Sun and Moon are in the next-but-one sign to each other. Water and Earth signs are in sextile, Air and Fire are in sextile.

If your Sun and Moon are in the same Quality, i.e. Cardinal, Fixed or Mutable, (see below), then they may well be in square (at one of the quarters) or opposition (at Full Moon); if they are in the same sign, they may be in conjunction (at New Moon). Even if the aspect is not 'in orb', there will still be a feeling of challenge. This isn't necessarily a bad thing – in fact this can be very good because it means you will make more of an effort and may become more self-aware than someone who feels more at ease. But you will probably find that at times you feel pulled two ways.

★ ∴★ The Signs of the Zodiac

Even if you know very little about astrology, you will probably be familiar with the 12 signs of the Zodiac. Each of the signs belongs to one of the four elements: Earth, Fire, Air or Water. The Fire signs tend to be bold, act on impulse and flashes of intuition and have lots of energy at some level. The Earth signs are practical, grounded and love comfort and security. The Air signs are 'head' people who like ideals and communication, while the Water signs are emotional, caring and intuitive.

The signs also belong to one of the Qualities: Cardinal, Fixed and Mutable. In respect of these, Cardinal means active, Fixed means stable, and Mutable means changeable. You may have planets in all of these, but the position of your Moon will be especially important. Here is an initial run-down.

Aries ♈	(Cardinal Fire)	Energetic, assertive, courageous, hasty, thoughtless
Taurus ♉	(Fixed Earth)	Affectionate, practical, steadfast, stubborn, materialistic
Gemini ♊	(Mutable Air)	Talkative, mobile, versatile, enquiring, inconsistent, superficial
Cancer ♋	(Cardinal Water)	Sensitive, caring, imaginative, tenacious, touchy
Leo ♌	(Fixed Fire)	Powerful, whole-hearted, dramatic, proud, dominating
Virgo ♍	(Mutable Earth)	Precise, analytical, conscientious, methodical, critical
Libra ♎	(Cardinal Air)	Refined, balanced, loves beauty, co-operative, indecisive, lazy
Scorpio ♏	(Fixed Water)	Intense, profound, focused, magnetic, vengeful, jealous
Sagittarius ♐	(Mutable Fire)	Adventurous, philosophical, confident, extravagant, careless
Capricorn ♑	(Cardinal Earth)	Ambitious, cautious, constructive, disciplined, inhibited, negative
Aquarius ♒	(Fixed Air)	Independent, idealistic, detached, liberal, humane, rebellious, awkward
Pisces ♓	(Mutable Water)	Imaginative, intuitive, changeable, dreamy, kind, confused, deceptive

Of course there is much more to each of the signs, and there are particular meanings when the Moon in each of them, as we will see.

Interpreting Your Moon Sign

In this section you will find the psychological characteristics of your Moon sign and phase, and how you go about relating. Table 3 shows the Moon sign for the beginning of each month since 1950, and the process of calculating your exact Moon sign.

Table 3: How to Find Your Moon Sign at Birth

Step One: Your Year and Month of Birth
Find your year of birth in left-hand column in the table below, then look across the table to find your month of birth. The tables give the Moon Sign at the beginning of the month. Make a note of this.

	Jan	Feb	Mar	Apr	May	June	July	Aug	Sept	Oct	Nov	Dec
1950	♊	♌	♌	♍	♏	♑	♒	♓	♉	♊	♋	♍
1951	♎	♐	♐	♒	♓	♉	♊	♋	♍	♎	♐	♑
1952	♓	♉	♉	♋	♌	♍	♎	♐	♒	♓	♉	♊
1953	♌	♍	♍	♏	♐	♒	♓	♉	♊	♌	♍	♎
1954	♐	♑	♑	♓	♈	♊	♋	♍	♏	♐	♑	♒
1955	♈	♊	♊	♌	♍	♏	♐	♑	♓	♈	♊	♋
1956	♍	♎	♏	♐	♑	♓	♈	♊	♌	♍	♏	♐
1957	♑	♓	♓	♉	♊	♋	♍	♎	♐	♑	♓	♈
1958	♉	♋	♋	♍	♎	♐	♑	♓	♈	♉	♋	♌
1959	♎	♏	♐	♒	♓	♈	♉	♋	♌	♎	♏	♑
1960	♒	♈	♉	♊	♋	♍	♎	♏	♑	♓	♈	♉
1961	♋	♌	♍	♎	♏	♑	♒	♈	♊	♋	♌	♍
1962	♏	♑	♑	♓	♈	♊	♋	♌	♎	♏	♐	♒
1963	♓	♉	♊	♋	♌	♎	♏	♐	♒	♓	♉	♊
1964	♌	♎	♎	♐	♑	♒	♓	♉	♋	♌	♎	♏
1965	♑	♒	♒	♈	♉	♋	♌	♎	♏	♑	♒	♓
1966	♉	♊	♋	♌	♍	♏	♑	♒	♈	♉	♊	♋
1967	♍	♏	♏	♑	♒	♈	♉	♊	♌	♍	♏	♐
1968	♒	♓	♈	♉	♊	♌	♍	♏	♑	♒	♈	♉
1969	♊	♌	♌	♎	♏	♑	♒	♈	♉	♊	♌	♍

	Jan	Feb	Mar	Apr	May	June	July	Aug	Sept	Oct	Nov	Dec
1970	♎	♐	♐	♒	♓	♉	♊	♌	♍	♎	♐	♑
1971	♓	♉	♉	♋	♌	♍	♎	♐	♍	♓	♈	♊
1972	♋	♍	♎	♏	♐	♒	♓	♉	♊	♌	♍	♎
1973	♐	♑	♒	♓	♈	♊	♌	♍	♏	♐	♑	♒
1974	♈	♊	♊	♌	♍	♏	♐	♒	♓	♈	♊	♋
1975	♍	♎	♏	♐	♑	♓	♈	♉	♋	♌	♎	♏
1976	♑	♓	♓	♉	♊	♋	♍	♎	♐	♑	♓	♌
1977	♊	♋	♋	♍	♎	♐	♑	♓	♈	♊	♋	♌
1978	♎	♏	♐	♑	♓	♈	♊	♋	♍	♎	♏	♑
1979	♒	♈	♈	♊	♋	♍	♎	♏	♑	♒	♈	♉
1980	♋	♌	♈	♎	♐	♑	♒	♓	♊	♋	♍	♎
1981	♏	♑	♈	♓	♈	♊	♋	♍	♏	♐	♏	♐
1982	♓	♉	♉	♋	♍	♎	♏	♒	♓	♈	♉	♊
1983	♌	♎	♎	♐	♑	♒	♓	♉	♊	♌	♎	♏
1984	♐	♒	♓	♈	♉	♋	♌	♍	♏	♑	♒	♈
1985	♉	♊	♋	♌	♎	♏	♑	♒	♈	♉	♊	♋
1986	♍	♎	♏	♑	♒	♈	♍	♊	♌	♎	♏	♐
1987	♒	♓	♈	♉	♊	♋	♍	♎	♐	♑	♓	♈
1988	♊	♌	♌	♎	♏	♐	♒	♈	♉	♋	♌	♍
1989	♏	♐	♐	♒	♓	♉	♊	♌	♍	♏	♐	♑
1990	♓	♉	♉	♋	♌	♎	♏	♒	♓	♈	♉	♊
1991	♋	♍	♍	♏	♐	♒	♈	♓	♊	♋	♍	♎
1992	♐	♑	♒	♓	♉	♊	♋	♌	♍	♐	♑	♒
1993	♈	♊	♊	♌	♍	♏	♐	♒	♓	♈	♊	♋
1994	♍	♎	♏	♐	♒	♓	♈	♊	♋	♌	♎	♏
1995	♑	♓	♓	♉	♊	♋	♌	♎	♐	♑	♓	♈
1996	♉	♋	♋	♌	♎	♐	♑	♓	♈	♊	♋	♌
1997	♎	♏	♐	♑	♓	♈	♊	♋	♍	♎	♏	♑
1998	♒	♈	♈	♊	♋	♍	♎	♏	♑	♒	♈	♉
1999	♋	♌	♍	♎	♐	♑	♒	♈	♉	♋	♌	♎
2000	♏	♑	♑	♓	♈	♊	♋	♍	♎	♐	♑	♒
2001	♈	♉	♉	♋	♌	♎	♏	♐	♒	♈	♉	♊
2002	♌	♎	♎	♐	♑	♓	♈	♉	♋	♌	♍	♏
2003	♑	♒	♒	♈	♉	♋	♌	♍	♎	♐	♒	♓
2004	♉	♊	♋	♌	♍	♏	♑	♒	♈	♉	♋	♌

	Jan	Feb	Mar	Apr	May	June	July	Aug	Sept	Oct	Nov	Dec
2005	♍	♏	♏	♑	♒	♈	♉	♋	♌	♍	♏	♐
2006	♒	♈	♈	♊	♋	♌	♍	♏	♐	♑	♓	♈
2007	♊	♋	♌	♎	♏	♐	♑	♓	♉	♊	♌	♍
2008	♎	♐	♑	♒	♓	♉	♊	♌	♎	♏	♐	♑
2009	♓	♈	♈	♉	♌	♎	♍	♐	♒	♓	♈	♊
2010	♋	♍	♍	♏	♐	♒	♓	♈	♊	♋	♍	♎

Keys to signs:

Aries	♈	Taurus	♉	Gemini	♊	Cancer	♋
Leo	♌	Virgo	♍	Libra	♎	Scorpio	♏
Sagittarius	♐	Capricorn	♑	Aquarius	♒	Pisces	♓

Step Two: Your Day of Birth

In the circular diagram at the foot of the page, place your finger on the sign that your Moon was in at the beginning of your month of birth. Consult the table above the diagram, then count round *anti-clockwise* the number of signs shown in the table. (Follow the arrows.)

Birthday:	1st	2nd	3rd	4th	5th	6th	7th	8th	9th	10th	11th	12th	13th	14th	15th	16th
No. of signs to count on:	0	0	0	1	1	2	2	3	3	3	4	4	5	5	6	6

Birthday:	17th	18th	19th	20th	21st	22nd	23rd	24th	25th	26th	27th	28th	29th	30th	31st
No. of signs to count on:	6	7	7	8	8	9	9	10	11	11	0	0	1	1	

Example: Birthday on April 7th 1983
Step One: Moon Sign at the beginning of April 1983 is ♐. *Step Two*: For the 7th, count on two signs.
Answer: ♒ The Moon Sign for April 7th 1983 is Aquarius.

Please Note: because of the variable nature of the Moon and the fact that it changes signs in the course of a day, these tables are only 70 per cent accurate. For an accurate birthchart, please contact the author (see Resources).

Moon in Aries

If your Moon is in Aries you may be quick to demand what you want, but you may not be so sure of what you truly need, at a deeper level. You tend to ask questions after the event, if, in fact, you bother to ask anything. You are a go-for-it, hell-for-leather individual, often with very little patience. You grab at life, often rushing in where angels fear to tread, but in the end finding that you have missed the real experience because you were never totally and consciously present! Your intuitive impressions come like a flash, but you may disregard them – always take a note of your first impressions but reflect before you act on them. You are a highly dynamic soul, but making a real connection can be hard for you. You may feel that you are always missing something. Your instincts are to initiate, and then having started something, to pass on. This doesn't mean you never finish anything, for especially in association with certain Sun signs, yours is a very effectual Moon. But somehow you rarely feel the sense of reward of a job well done because you are already heading off for something else.

This is not the easiest of lunar positions for the Moon is concerned with cosy habits and inner needs. Aries tends to scorn this, or at least not to stay around long enough to work out what this may mean. But you do have needs, nonetheless, and may feel resentful if these are unmet, without realising that this is really your own fault! Moon in Aries is a real 'individual' and you hate to be dependent on any person or thing. Being 'needy' makes you feel twitchy and you would rather seek adventure. You may get angry as a substitute for other, more vulnerable emotions. The thrill of the moment may take over from more profound needs. Moon in Aries purposely seeks challenges and obstacles in life, for you feel most secure when you are at liberty, captain of your own ship and enthused about something. Occasionally you may upset others because of your abrupt speech or actions, but deep inside you are a sensitive child and you can be terribly hurt by unfair treatment. There is nothing wrong with this! You do not have to expect strife in life, so try not to create it! You have a wonderful innocence and enthusiasm, and are always quick to pick yourself up, dust yourself down and try again!

Talents ★ Your judgement is quick and often spot-on.
　　　　　★ You are brave and have the courage of your convictions.
　　　　　★ You believe life is for living and get on with it.

Pitfalls ★ You can be too hasty in your actions.

★ Sometimes you are insensitive to the needs of others as well as yourself.

★ Be careful of turning your life into a battle-ground – it doesn't have to be that way.

Phases *New Moon in Aries:* This is the most exuberant, innocent and uncomplicated position. When it is an exact New Moon, both luminaries will be in Aries. You rarely weigh-up pros and cons. You see life as a collection of images and tend to launch yourself at one or the other in a series of power-drives. You have an immense need to experience anything and everything and you will charge through – or disregard – any barriers. Yes, you do tend to sow rather than reap, because you have little real interest in consequences – these are boring! Your relationships may happen to you while you're thinking about something else and you are often emotionally, mentally or physically absent. But you can be very exciting and compelling as a partner! If the Aries Moon has not quite caught up with the Sun there is a very different quality. You could be quite visionary and prophetic. Being grounded may be a problem for you, for you exist in the abstract, although you are too active to be seen as a 'dreamer'. Using your imagination in a positive way is essential, and will be very rewarding.

Waxing Moon in Aries: An exact first quarter Moon in Aries will have Sun in Capricorn. Probably you feel compelled to blaze your own trail and may sometimes be in conflict with the establishment. Sometimes you behave like a rebel without a cause, spoiling for a fight, and feeling frustrated because it seems to you there is so much standing in your way all the time. There is – it's just this boring old world! Deep inside you long to construct something innovative, but your urge is hard to satisfy because you feel forever called off to pastures new. You have a feeling of unfinished business hanging around, but you may blame this on other people. It is true that sometimes you can be a little selfish and this can mean you shoot yourself in the foot. If you can bite your lip and take full responsibility for your actions and what you don't achieve, you will feel better about things in the end. Count your opportunities rather than the ways you feel blocked. If you do this you can move mountains.

Full Moon in Aries: Relationships versus personal concerns is likely to be a dominant theme in your life. (An exact Full Moon in Aries will have Sun in Libra.) It is important that you try to balance your own needs with those of others. Sometimes this can result in a person who denies they need anything, yet is always trying to get other people to supply what they want – this can be unrewarding! The inner child in you can take over, being quite demanding yet never admitting to it! But the other side of the coin is that you are capable of putting everything into making relationships work. You will be at your best if you also put some of that energy into developing self-awareness, about which you may be contemptuous – or possibly very enthusiastic! Because you have an immediate grasp of hidden dynamics, yours may be a very intuitive Moon, quick to respond to stimuli. True self-love (as opposed to empty self-importance) is a vital step on the way to loving others and making satisfying relationships.

Waning Moon in Aries: You try to make some sense of your strong inward emotions so you can tell other people about this. (An exact last quarter Moon in Aries will have Sun in Cancer.) You can sometimes be bossy because you feel sure you know what's best for the other person, and possibly you do, but there are better ways of going about it! Your reasoning may well be correct but you may not always appreciate that you don't have all the facts. It is important to you to justify your own conclusions, and you may feel it is more important to be right than to be understood! Having strong opinions you may overlook differences in taste. Because you have vivid and clear imaginative powers, all you need to do is come to the realisation that people are different, and that this must be taken into account if you are to make the changes you dream about. With this in place you are set to make great changes for the better and to get appreciation when you 'mother the world' rather than just getting flak! Who needs it, after all!

Mixing and Matching

Because of your verve and enthusiasm you often seem to be a good mixer – and probably you believe that you are! Other people may seem rather two-dimensional to you, if you think about it, rather like projections on an internal screen. You love to greet guests and know how to make people feel really welcome with your warm manner. But you may find it hard to listen because it is hard to find the patience to let the other person finish! Tact could be something you need to work at. But if you get a reasonable amount of your own way, you can be the life and soul of the party. If you like someone, you get close quite quickly. The new relationship may not justify its initial promise, however, because your idea about the other party may be drawn from conclusions you jump to, rather than reality. But if you get things right to start with, the relationship goes like a house on fire! Aries Moon is full of passion and desire and makes strong bonds. In close relationships you may have a short fuse, and want things all your own way. Try to make your partner feel perceived as well as wanted, and don't be too quick to take offence – talk it through instead. With your Aries Moon there is never a dull moment; in fact, it can really be a walk on the wild side!

Moon in Aries with Sun Signs

Aries Sun: So fiery – be careful smoke doesn't get in your eyes!

Taurus Sun: You love quality and comfort – sit around and enjoy it sometimes!

Gemini Sun: Never idle, your active mind is always re-organising something.

Cancer Sun: You like to make sure your front door is locked, but you keep those car-keys handy!

Leo Sun: Onwards and upwards, but make sure your goals are truly relevant to you.

Virgo Sun: Is there anything you can't do? But let others help sometimes.

Libra Sun: Remember, peace and harmony must be allowed to prevail, not compelled to!

Scorpio Sun: Attack may be the best form of defence, but don't assume you need either!

Sagittarius Sun: Adventure is your middle name – up and at 'em!

Capricorn Sun: It's the things that stand in your way that truly energise you.

Aquarius Sun: You're a friend to all, but you follow your own star.

Pisces Sun: The person you get most impatient with is yourself!

Moon in Taurus

Easy-going is the word for Taurus Moon and people may think you are a complete pushover – until they oppose you! Then that gentle puppy who loves having its tummy rubbed turns into a great bulldog that can't be budged and bites if provoked! Yes, you are the most patient and kind of people, and people can rely on you utterly, but you do have your limit – others push it at their peril!

Each of the planets has a sign that it rules, i.e. a sign for which it has greatest affinity and in which it is strong; a sign where it is exalted, i.e. expresses its best qualities; a sign where it is in its fall, where more negative characteristics may surface; and a sign where it is in detriment, meaning it may be weaker. In Taurus the Moon is exalted. Therefore you folk tend to develop sound habits and have strong and well-grounded instincts. Often you are very good at making others feel nurtured. Best of all, you have the delightful ability to enjoy yourself thoroughly, because you become absorbed in the perfection of the moment. Just being near you can be reassuring, but your strongest instinct of all is towards self-preservation, and you can be terminally stubborn! As long as you have been well-nurtured yourself, you will accept the foibles of others quite placidly. Your intuition is felt in your body, so if you are uncertain about a person or thing ask yourself if your body is comfortable when near it or them. You're good-natured, your love of life is infectious and you are not easy to shock, being relentlessly matter-of-fact. Yes, you would far rather eat, drink and be merry than pick a fight, but if strife is the only way to protect your interests and those of your loved ones, make no mistake, you'll dust off the boxing gloves! Security is essential to you and you define it in very simple ways – money in the bank, food in the larder and good sex in the bedroom. While you can be very generous, this never goes beyond what you can comfortably give. Because you are extremely practical, you are often well-off, and it has to be said you can be materialistic and boring to more adventurous souls! There's no point arguing with you, though, is there? But given a reasonable amount of inner security you may eventually decide on your own changes – then watch the dust fly!

Talents ★ You are kind and patient.
      ★ Usually you can be relied upon – your word is your bond and not given lightly.
      ★ You find satisfaction in looking after other people.

Pitfalls ★ You can be incredibly stubborn.
      ★ Sometimes you are very materialistic and cannot see beyond your nose.
      ★ On occasion you can be very selfish.

Phases *New Moon in Taurus:* At the very beginning of the Taurean New Moon, the Sun is also in Taurus. To you the world is a pleasure-garden, just waiting for you to grab its delights. Sensuous and eager to experience everything physical, there is nonetheless a certain innocence about you. It is important to you to put down roots and to start creating something that is fresh, but well-grounded. Rarely do you want to change the world for purely idealistic motives but you do not like anything to stand in your way! Hands-on creativity may appeal, such as gardening, cooking and sculpting. You want to do something good with your life, but you aren't up for martyrdom. However, if the Moon is still approaching the Sun and it is Dark Moon, then, with your Taurus Moon, you will be much more inward-looking. Nature may appeal to you deeply and simple pleasures absorb you.

Waxing Moon in Taurus: The Sun will be in Aquarius, with an exact first quarter Taurean Moon. You feel that life has thrown down the gauntlet before you and that you must establish something lasting to meet the basic needs both of yourself and others. But this may seem very difficult because you tend to find yourself in conflict with your own ideals and future projects. It may seem as if the present must be sacrificed for the future, or vice versa. This may work negatively, making you feel compelled to ride roughshod over anything in your way but never for one moment admitting that you are being anything less than idealistic. However, a better possibility for you is that of truly creating something that serves both practical needs and deeper meanings, and so is really workable. (An example might be charitable work that truly supports those it purports to help rather than giving mere hand-outs.) If you can manage to face pain as well as embrace pleasure then you will be in a stronger position to build the security you need.

Full Moon in Taurus: The Sun will be in Scorpio when the Full Moon is exact in Taurus. Ownership and control are likely to be central to your life in some way. You certainly would not want your space invaded and realise full well that others have the same territorial rights. But your feelings run very deep and you fear vulnerability. Because of this it is hard sometimes for you to resist manipulating, just a teeny bit, seeking a measure of control over others, simply in order to make yourself feel more secure. Sometimes you know instinctively what others are feeling – possibly you feel it in your own body. You have the choice whether to use this insight to help, or to further your own ends. If you act principally for your own ends you run the risk of becoming a little obsessive and dissatisfied, maybe imagining that others are 'out to get you', but if you act for the general good you feel profoundly rewarded. You are potentially a very powerful person. The wise handling of all resources is very important.

Waning Moon in Taurus: The Sun will be in Leo when the Moon's last quarter is exactly in Taurus. You have a strong urge to be the boss. Because you are so practical and sensible, you feel that everyone should have the benefit of your opinion! Of course, much that you have experienced is extremely valuable, grounded as it is in reality, and you have a solid value-system. But however practical you are, this does not mean you are always right! However, you may be justifiably proud of what you have achieved because you have probably faced life head-on and still bear the scars. Experience will have honed your wisdom. Be careful of using dogmatism as a way to protect yourself from being rejected, which you actually find deeply hurtful. To get the respect you crave and deserve, you need to take just a minute to put yourself in the other person's shoes – then everything that you say can be relevant and helpful.

Mixing and Matching

A peaceful and gregarious Moon, Taurus nonetheless likes to be able to draw the boundaries. You feel it is very important to make people comfortable. A well-laden table is spread for guests and every effort is made to ensure that they are not too hot, too cold or in any way uncomfortable. It gives you real pleasure to see people having a good time, but you still like to keep to your own well-worn chair in the corner! You are a touchy-feely person who likes physical contact as a way of getting close. You are sensitive to the movements and physical presence of the other person at a subliminal level. Others may feel they have got close to you very quickly, but actually they may not know much about you, for you can be quite private. You have a relaxed and accepting presence, but your feelings run very deep. You do not readily give your heart and your passions can lie dormant. Often you confuse 'feeling' with familiarity. However, when you do fall in love, this may well be forever and you can be very possessive and jealous. Security in a relationship is very important to you and you do your best to create this by being supportive and organising the practicalities.

Moon in Taurus with Sun Signs

Aries Sun: You'll do what has to be done, but you won't forget tea-time!

Taurus Sun: Solid as an oak-tree, and you like your roots to go as deep.

Gemini Sun: You're interested in the facts, but only the useful ones.

Cancer Sun: Home, sweet home is your preoccupation.

Leo Sun: You may put on a show but you know what truly counts!

Virgo Sun: Tidiness and comfort please, but not necessarily in that order!

Libra Sun: A quiet life and a peaceful one – who could ask for more?

Scorpio Sun: Hang on tight – but don't hang on to a relationship that is past its sell-by date!

Sagittarius Sun: Your wanderlust is skin deep when the kettle's on!

Capricorn Sun: It's a must for you to have everything secure and well-insured.

Aquarius Sun: You prize all freedoms, but freedom from want above all!

Pisces Sun: You may chase rainbows but you don't forget your crock of gold.

.: *Moon in Gemini*

To the Gemini Moon, living is about satisfying your curiosity – as if that were ever possible! Life is one big question mark and you realise that there is always a multitude of ways of looking at anything. You analyse everything you see and feel but you are not looking for trouble – or indeed anything else. You have a thirst for information for its own sake and may not bother to interpret or make judgements. Like a humming bird you flutter from concept to concept and often from place to place – you are an eternal fidget! Your intuitions may arrive in the form of important concepts that you need to learn to apply correctly and sometimes you may even hear a voice in your head – don't worry, it's just your higher self communicating in a way you will pick up. The things that make you feel secure would have the opposite effect on most people. Variety is essential and boredom is torture. As a Gemini Moon, you are very good at creating change. Intellectual stimulation is of great importance to you and you must be free to explore, catalogue information – and chatter! When you are upset, your therapy is to talk about it endlessly, until all the hurt flows out with your words. What you really need to do is to get hold of your own deepest feelings and frame these in words, but sometimes you get lost in the trivial instead. Sometimes you play with words and natter endlessly in an effort to find out what you feel inside. At your best you have a very liberating presence because you are able to say what other people hardly dare to think, and to do so in a way that is not only acceptable but also amusing.

Talents ★ You are adaptable and lively.
★ Your gift of the gab draws people to you.
★ Often you are able to make sense of what others only dimly perceive.

Pitfalls ★ You can be too restless for your own good.
★ While you may be thirsty for facts, sometimes you do not fit these into a meaningful picture in your life.
★ You may avoid your feelings by intellectualising them.

Phases *New Moon in Gemini:* An exact New Moon in Gemini means the Sun is also in Gemini. You people ignore the phrase 'curiosity killed the cat' for you have more than nine lives when it comes to surviving the consequences of your impudence! 'Received wisdom' wins few prizes with you – you want chapter and verse from an unbiased perspective. If people want to wind you up all they have to say is

'Well, that's the way it's always been done round here!' You are very resourceful, active and full of inventions. You may flit around in a labyrinth of 'head stuff' and are likely to have a wide circle of friends and acquaintances, some of which may be quite superficial. If the Moon hasn't yet reached the Sun, the picture is slightly different and you are likely to be quite detached, sceptical and instinctively analytical. It will not be easy to pull the wool over your eyes.

Waxing Moon in Gemini: With an exact first quarter Moon in Gemini, the Sun will be in Pisces. Feelings are central to you, and your emotional life is multi-coloured and multi-levelled. You need to devote time to sorting out your emotions and framing them into words. Indeed it is very important that you work at being in touch with your true feelings because then these can be dealt with, rather than resulting in neurotic habits and worrying. If you try to be aware, then you can be skilful at noticing the feelings of others and expressing them for them – there is no better person for finding a voice for the emotions, and you may be poetic. You need time to unwind as you are continually torn between thinking and feeling. If you can avoid being over-anxious you will develop much psychological awareness.

Full Moon in Gemini: An exact Full Moon in Gemini will have the Sun in Sagittarius, and there is an urge to find meanings in life. You must have a direction, a place in the Big Picture, but you may get under your own feet by your compulsive gathering of facts and figures. To be satisfied you need to find a way of making information serve your purpose rather than getting bogged down or dissipating energy in trivia. You may be afraid that you are going to get carried away, and keep pulling yourself back from involvement, feeling that you have to check things out a bit more. You need the comfort of a degree of detachment but your intuition about your own path in life is generally good if you will listen to it. You need to give yourself permission to explore not only widely, but deeply.

Waning Moon in Gemini: The Sun will be in Virgo when the Moon's last quarter is exactly in Gemini. You must be very precise in what you deduce and you want others to listen properly to you so they can get your message clearly across. Sometimes you feel overwhelmed and discouraged because you want to know all there is to know about everything. It seems the more you learn, the more there is still to find out. Fulfilment comes from discrimination, and deciding what is truly useful and what is not. If you refuse to get side-tracked too often and keep a sense of proportion, you can find life endlessly fascinating, and be an absolute mine of useful information.

Mixing and Matching You are one of the friendliest people anyone could wish to meet and you are probably brilliant at the sort of small talk that circulates at parties. You are happy touching on everything while concentrating on little in depth, and this oils the social wheels. Gemini Moons can pep up the dullest of occasions with your ready wit, and you will talk to anyone from delivery boy to duke. People may get the idea that they are hitting it off especially well with you, while everyone else in the room thinks the same! It is not easy to get truly close to you, but a first step may be for people to express some of their own feelings for you to analyse. You need to know that the person you are with shares your interest in life before you spend extra time with them for you dread feeling held back and limited. Also you need to feel that any topic is fair game, even 'sensitive' issues. Gemini, as a sign, is not known for constancy but Gemini Moons will give their hearts where there is a 'meeting of true minds'. You only appear unreliable when you are forced into a mould of someone else's making. Your deep need is to be able to step back and analyse – not necessarily to flit on to another partnership, although this may happen if you are caged. Gemini Moon will always come back to the place where you feel free.

Moon in Gemini with Sun Signs
Aries Sun: You look before you leap – but usually jump anyway!
Taurus Sun: You need security, but may easily feel bogged down by it.
Gemini Sun: Who says eternal motion is scientifically impossible?
Cancer Sun: You'll look after anyone as long as they'll talk to you.
Leo Sun: You can't help laughing at your own sense of self-importance.
Virgo Sun: You would be lost without your *Encyclopaedia Britannica* and Encarta CD Rom.
Libra Sun: Friendship is the mainstay of your life.
Scorpio Sun: You love solving puzzles – and life's one big one!
Sagittarius Sun: Life is an adventure and you're going to tell the world about it.
Capricorn Sun: Perhaps you should take life seriously, but it's such a bore.
Aquarius Sun: You can think the unthinkable – and talk about it, too!
Pisces Sun: You love to talk about your feelings – it helps you find out what they are.

Moon in Cancer

This Moon is both infant and mother, and 'mothering' is often a primary theme in your life. The Moon rules Cancer and so it is especially strong in the sign of the Crab. You are intuitive about people and your dreams are often revealing but you need to be careful that you don't get your fears and negative fantasies mixed up with real subliminal messages. Really you need to come to terms with your own needs and to find positive ways of nurturing yourself. Needing to be needed, Cancerian Moon may sometimes manipulate others into being dependent upon them, so you can play the role of Big Mamma. Actually this is your way of feeding your own need to be close. Alternatively you may play the helpless child yourself – and in fact mothering and being mothered may alternate in your life. This may be fine if it is done consciously, for we all like to care for and be cared for. However, it is hard for you to be up-front about what you want, for your great sensitivity makes you fear rejection. So you may want other people to sense your feelings instinctively – quite useless if the other party has a Fire sign Moon or even an Air sign Moon! If subtle tactics do not work, Cancerian Moon may become very moody indeed, lapsing into self-pity and seeking consolation in food, drink, dreams and anything you can cling to. Cancerian Moon truly needs to belong. Once you realise that it is possible to relate without anyone being 'parent', you can then explain clearly what you want and need, and create the cosy and welcoming environment that is essential to you. This is a very kind Moon with a true talent for home-making. However, being 'at home' with your own inner nature is the most important factor in your comfort.

Talents ★ You are wonderful at caring for people and making them comfortable.
★ You have a dreamy, romantic charm about you.
★ You are very sensitive and gentle with the feelings of others.

Pitfalls ★ You can be very moody and over-sensitive.
★ You tend to mother the world, whether it wants it or not!
★ Alternatively, you may want people to mother you!

Phases *New Moon in Cancer:* An exact New Moon in Cancer will also have the Sun in Cancer. Needs are compelling with you. You actively seek deep and close attachments and inter-dependent relationships may be readily embarked upon. Parenting is likely to be central to your life in some form or fashion, although this may not be literally care of a child; a cause or even a place may be the focus of your nurturing. You can be a little manipulative for you like to be in control but do not like to be up front about it! You have a deep need to make others feel relaxed and at home and you are very kind and caring. If the Moon has not yet reached the Sun then relationships may be less easily made and privacy will be a priority. Instinct may be strong and comfort jealously guarded. Family will be of profound importance to you.

Waxing Moon in Cancer: The Sun will be in Aries with an exact first quarter Moon in Cancer. Here we have quite a demanding person, who can be very touchy. You can be just a little inconsiderate but take it to heart when you get a taste of your own medicine! You never really want to offend, and you throw yourself into a caring role with energy and determination, especially when fighting for those less fortunate. If you can learn to keep calm and think things out before launching into action you will find you are more effectual and so gain more satisfaction. Being sensitive, you sometimes rein yourself in, fearing that you may be hurt or lose what is dear to you. This is distinct from sensible reflection and may result in frustration, moods and even tears for you. Taking emotional factors into account before you act is the key to your wellbeing.

Full Moon in Cancer: An exact Full Moon in Cancer will have the Sun in Capricorn. You may find you are pulled between home and family. Your feelings for your relatives may be very strong indeed, but you also need to feel you are performing at work. Ambitions are important to you but because something has to be sacrificed to move forward in life you may feel caught in a dilemma. Generally you support the establishment – you like to see traditional values upheld. Building something of enduring value is a primary concern to this Moon. You are continually taking stock of where you are in life, where you are going and whether it all means something in terms of your roots. Usually you conduct family affairs with common sense, practicality and sensitivity.

Waning Moon in Cancer: The Sun will be in Libra if this an exact last quarter Moon. You are likely to have a talent for counselling and this may be especially developed in regard to partnerships and family matters. However, this operates best if you face your own needs and cater to them sensibly, rather than reasoning them away. Sometimes you may deny your own clinginess, saying you are in fact catering to the wishes of the other party. Rapport with people of like minds and a peaceful atmosphere are most important, and this Moon likes to encourage people to reflect on their own emotions and express them. You do not like to be alone and strife is anathema to you, so you may be a little too ready to agree with the views of others, at least on the surface. You can be a talented peacemaker if you are prepared to face the true emotional issues involved.

Mixing and Matching

You tend to attach rather than mingle. You always try to find out what makes others comfortable and to provide this as best you can. Usually you are very genial and tactile, eager to kiss and hug your friends and relatives, unless you are in a mood. However, you can be shy and retiring at first, and you may be secretive about your own affairs, although you are keen to know about those of others. You are a good listener, quick to find common ground and to identify with the concerns of the other person. 'Tea and sympathy' is your speciality. You know instinctively how others are feeling and do whatever you can to cater to this. As the relationship develops, it can become quite symbiotic, although you will keep withdrawn until you feel totally safe. Moon in Cancer invented the phrase 'joined at the hip' but to form really healthy partnerships you need to retain a measure of independence for both parties.

Moon in Cancer with Sun Signs

Aries Sun: Don't trample on anyone's feelings – especially your own.
Taurus Sun: Cosy, comfy, safe and snugly – that's the way you like life to be.
Gemini Sun: You wish you could reason away all those soppy habits.
Cancer Sun: What can compare with Home Sweet Home – especially with a family inside!
Leo Sun: Don't let your pride get in the way of meeting your needs.
Virgo Sun: Kind, modest – and just a bit of a worrier.
Libra Sun: Peace at any price? Internal peace comes from accepting your own needs.
Scorpio Sun: Follow your intuitions and remember – sometimes you need to let go.
Sagittarius Sun: Sometimes you feel you cramp your own style, but don't forget to value your softer side.
Capricorn Sun: Establishing a home and a place in the world is important.
Aquarius Sun: Your feelings are also entitled to freedom, you know!
Pisces Sun: Whimsical and sensitive, you escape into dreams!

Moon in Leo

Being noticed isn't quite enough for this Moon – you need to be loved and adored into the bargain. 'If you've got it, flaunt it' is your motto, but your innate pride ensures you always keep your dignity. To feel secure you need to feel extremely special – no half measures. You do tend to hog the limelight and your demands can be endless – admit it! But because you radiate such warmth everyone around you feels inspired and happy to give you what you want – usually! Your intuitions enable you to see the Big Picture and you can have an instinctive sense of how to order things. You can be a tad tiresome for you are never happy with the second rate, half of anyone's attention or indeed anything mediocre. You have a thirst for applause but deep inside you can be quite insecure and even feel hollow. You need to be continually reassured that you are special. Very playful and often dramatic, you are a vibrant person to be near, for those who have the stamina! Indeed you can come on like a bossy know-it-all and take umbrage when anyone tries to take you down a peg. Everything surrounding you – home, car and clothes – needs to be the best. This isn't showing off but a real, internal need. Because you are probably highly creative, it is likely that you will earn enough to live in the style to which you wish to become accustomed, although you can develop the attitude that the world owes you a life of luxury! And why not? You need a challenge and an occupation that truly is significant or your daily chores can turn into Star Wars for you! This Moon needs to feel luscious and wonderful – before this inspires resentment in more retiring Moons, let's face it, not everyone feels comfortable being the centre of the Universe! Leo Moon does, and you happily radiate this sense of wellbeing out to those around you. This is a generous Moon that loves life – and all the world loves a lover!

Talents
- ★ You are radiant and generous.
- ★ A colourful personality, you usually shine.
- ★ Your dignity and pride inspire respect.

Pitfalls
- ★ You can be utterly self-centred and demanding.
- ★ You can make a drama out of a crisis.
- ★ Sometimes you take things too personally.

Phases *New Moon in Leo:* When the Moon is just New in Leo the Sun will also be there. You are an ebullient person with lots of faith in life and in yourself, up to a point! If your bubble is pricked, however, you quickly deflate, although you bounce back fairly quickly and launch yourself full tilt at the next adventure. Endearingly childlike, you can also be highly exasperating. Full of sound and fury, it may seem you are getting nowhere until it transpires that you have accomplished the impossible. At your best you are wonderful to be near – when you come in you bring sunshine with you. If the Moon hasn't quite reached the Sun, the faith in life is likely to focus more on the spiritual. You may be a little more negative, although less demanding, and you are future-orientated.

Waxing Moon in Leo: With an exact first quarter Moon in Leo, the Sun will be in Taurus. Here we have a steam-roller pulling two ways at once, for you want to establish security but also create the maximum possible drama and grab all the attention. It is hard for this Moon to get the balance right between the practical and the imaginative – while you have one your need for the other feels thwarted. The sheer tension of this may result in tremendous creativity, and while you may never totally satisfy yourself, you may achieve great things. 'Life is the art of the possible' needs to become your mantra.

Full Moon in Leo: The Sun will be in Aquarius when this Full Moon is exact. A balance needs to be found between your inner need for drama and attention and your wish, on the other hand, to foster detachment and philosophical ideals. Sometimes you may manage to put the blame on others when you are in fact the one who is being emotional and demanding; at other times you may simply be an embarrassment to yourself! At your best, however, you can be something of a leader, able to blend your own impulse to shine with causes that are in the best interests of everyone. There could be elements of the visionary about you. The volatile Leo Moon needs to be acknowledged, not denied, or you could be tempted to take the moral high ground a bit too quickly. But to feel real internal peace you can never deny your need to be out in front – and why should you?

Waning Moon in Leo: An exact last quarter Moon in Leo will have the Sun in Scorpio. You have a great need to see deeply into yourself and your companions. You may become a champion of a suitable cause. Often you are very sure that that your cause is right, because you have insight and conviction, but you need to realise that there may be things you have missed. Your pride is equalled only by your courage. You are capable of cynicism if others stand in your way. However, for sheer guts and charisma you are probably unrivalled. If you main-

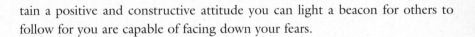

tain a positive and constructive attitude you can light a beacon for others to follow for you are capable of facing down your fears.

Mixing and Matching

Of all the Moons, this one may be the most of a socialite. You are a party animal and fun is the name of the game! Making other people feel welcome and radiating charm all over them gives you a buzz, but although the wine may flow and the plates may be laden, Leo Moon prefers it if someone else hands round the refreshments. Leo Moon is an entertainer, not a waiter! Being very warm, folk think you are getting comfy-cosy only to find that the Lion wants to go off and prowl again. You don't like to be tied down and dominated in any way, and you only stay around if you are inspired. However, having chosen a mate you can be very possessive indeed and it is a matter of pride to you to have the best relationship possible. You retain your playfulness and still need a challenge – an audience of one might not be enough. However, yours is an intensely loyal and honest Moon who is idealistic about love – nothing but the best for the best!

Moon in Leo with Sun Signs

Aries Sun: Active and energetic, or someone with vivid inner landscapes.
Taurus Sun: A life of luxury and sensual delight, if you can possibly get it.
Gemini Sun: Inventive and resourceful with imagination to back it up.
Cancer Sun: Don't let your fears stand in the way of your dreams!
Leo Sun: They're all cheering – what are you waiting for?
Virgo Sun: Unobtrusively you manage to be centre-stage.
Libra Sun: Your excellent taste is equalled only by your extravagance.
Scorpio Sun: 'Better to reign in hell than serve in Heaven?' – don't go there!
Sagittarius Sun: The whole world is a gigantic playground.
Capricorn Sun: Ambitious – but which comes first, fame or fortune?
Aquarius Sun: Don't embarrass yourself; express yourself!
Pisces Sun: You have a talent for drama – develop it positively.

⋆⋆ Moon in Virgo

If your Moon is in Virgo you probably have something of a retiring nature and 'less is more' could be your motto. Although you cherish friends that you can trust, you are most comfortable in your own well-ordered environment. Yes you do like tidiness and cleanliness, although you may define these in your own way. But of greatest importance to you is a feeling of self-possession and being able to keep tabs on your belongings, going about things in your own way. Your intuition works well with plants and animals, and you should take note of your body. If something isn't right physically, while you may reason yourself out of it, you are likely to feel ill if you do not get it sorted – this is true of everyone but especially of you. Yours is not the easiest Moon placement because just where you might be expected to be most spontaneous and instinctual you tend, in fact, to respond practically and precisely. However, you can be very helpful to those who understand you. It is not really possible to catalogue fantasies or to dissect a fairy under a microscope but you may try to do this, resulting, sadly, in the destruction of your own dreams. So you may find you yearn for something you cannot define, while analysing even this yearning to the point where you deprive yourself of the possibility of finding what you want. Probably you want, like all of us, to feel part of something greater, but you reason this away and become preoccupied with details. However, that only happens in the worst of cases. In fact you have finely-tuned senses that respond to music and to art with gentleness and exquisite taste. You may be very capable domestically, having green fingers and a lot of skill in the kitchen. Probably you are a creature of habit. Cleanliness is a priority and you are sharply aware of what is useful and what is not! Your sense of comfort comes from having order around you, which you have structured, and you have a 'feel' for what will or won't work. Health and fitness are important to you, and you have excellent taste. When you stop analysing and lose yourself in creating something tangible then you are at your finest – and your happiest!

Talents ★ You have excellent taste and discrimination.
★ You are creative and practical.
★ Order and common sense are your priorities.

Pitfalls ★ You tend to analyse life instead of living it to the full.
★ Your need for control can stand in the way of achievement and experience.
★ You have to be careful that you do not become obsessive over details.

Phases *New Moon in Virgo:* If your Moon is very new in Virgo, you probably have the Sun there too. Probably you are a great one for all the health fads and even alternative therapies and diets. Resourceful and practical, you may be a whiz in the garden and kitchen. You are a busy bee, always sorting, tidying, cleaning, either in a practical sense or with your accounts, your studies or even just in your head! Creating a sense of order may give you quite a buzz!

If you were born before the Moon caught up with the Sun then you are likely to be more analytical than active, needing to probe things very deeply. Chances are you know a thing or three and you may be just a bit of a cynic! Privacy is essential to you.

Waxing Moon in Virgo: If yours is an exact first quarter Moon, then your Sun will be in Gemini. Possibly you live on your nerves and often find you get the jitters. This may be through a system overload, where you are trying to process too many things at once. You need to try to limit your involvements because you aren't happy unless you do things perfectly. It may feel as if you have to prove you are right all the time by quoting chapter and verse, but really the only person you need to satisfy is you. You are a great organiser, but my, you get irritable about it sometimes! You are the tops when it comes to doing a job intelligently and with detailed precision, but you need to feel appreciated and there should be a limit to the responsibility you undertake. Try not to get sidetracked into trivia and remember that not all facts are useful or relevant – your well-being is the most important thing!

Full Moon in Virgo: If you have an exact Full Moon in Virgo, then your Sun will be in Pisces. You feel drawn to analyse everything because you fear that if you do not you will be overwhelmed in some way. Try to make sure that your analysis is constructive and that you are not demolishing what is essential to your life path. You are well-equipped to whittle down your dreams into something workable, but do not whittle them totally away. Build your dreams brick by brick, creating the most wonderful garden or the nicest home, and finding the most effective forms of diet and therapy for you. If you feel discouraged, you must realise that this is part of the process of learning what you can mould into shape and what needs to be discarded. You have a clear sight that will show what works and what doesn't, but never reason away your feelings.

Waning Moon in Virgo: If your last quarter Moon is in Virgo, then your Sun will be in Sagittarius. People may come to you for advice, which you love, but you may feel you have to be an expert on everything and may run yourself ragged by sifting information and trying to work out what it means. You have the talent to discriminate between philosophies that work and those that don't, and between facts that are 'going somewhere' and those that aren't. You may have a 'pragmatic spirituality' with a wealth of schemes and projects on the go, but you may take on too much, and often feel very torn between what you want to achieve and what you are comfortable with. You may like to keep a diary of your adventures. How good you feel about life depends on how meaningful your achievements are, so weigh things up before you go down blind alleys, rather than waiting until your back is up against the wall.

Mixing and Matching

You tend to hold back just a little. You like to protect your body space and so a little peck on the cheek may be preferable to a bear-hug. You like to know exactly who and what you are dealing with before you let anyone close, and so you keep your mouth shut and your eyes and ears open while you size people up. Your way of participating may be to hand round drinks and clear up – always in the kitchen at parties. This suits you in many ways, not least because it gives you more time to decide who is worth talking to – and probably the one that comes to help you will have your vote, as being a useful and practical type! You don't want anyone disturbing the order and control that you have in your life, or interfering with your clothes or possessions. But once you do decide that you like someone, then you can be very tactile – as long as you feel personal hygiene is in place! If you decide to enter into a relationship (and you do not take this risk lightly!), then you are faithful and very industrious about creating a home and making things work. You need to feel sure that your chosen mate will respect your sense of order and your need for privacy. Actually you are a sensitive soul and you need to be handled with care.

Moon in Virgo with Sun Signs

Aries Sun: If you find something's wrong you give 'em hell – who can blame you?

Taurus Sun: Well-stocked fridge, well-stocked cellar, well-swept floor!

Gemini Sun: You like to keep up with the gossip as well as the chores.

Cancer Sun: To you cleanliness really is next to godliness – or goddess-liness!

Leo Sun: Sometimes you do wish you didn't keep drawing attention to yourself.

Virgo Sun: You won't settle for less than one hundred per cent.

Libra Sun: Perfection isn't enough; it has to be exquisite, too.

Scorpio Sun: The trouble with getting to the bottom of things is that you can't always find your way back!

Sagittarius Sun: You want adventures but may get bogged down packing your case.

Capricorn Sun: Remember all work and no play makes Jack a dull boy – and a poorly one!

Aquarius Sun: You like a wide circle of friends but rarely get close to anyone.

Pisces Sun: You need 'hyacinths for the soul' – things that nourish the spirit – so grow them yourself!

Moon in Libra

Beauty and harmony are the very stuff of life to you. The first thing people may notice about you is that lovely smile. You have the gift of seeming to be able to lose yourself in the other person because you have a need to please. Your feelings must be kept in some sort of balance and this means that you may spend a lot of time thinking about them and analysing them. Strife is hateful to you and internal strife is the worst of all! When all around you is peaceful, then you feel secure. You have to restore calm wherever it is lacking and also to create surroundings that are attractive and pleasant. Take note of how internally balanced you feel because this is your intuition speaking and it will tell you much about a person, situation or thing. Ugliness and disharmony can truly make you ill – physically and mentally – and even though you love people, if there are arguments and upsets you prefer to be alone at least for a while. Wherever you find yourself, there you will create beauty, because without it you feel lost and forlorn. Even if your circumstances are straitened, temporary, or otherwise difficult, you will still create a tasteful environment and use colour combinations that invoke an atmosphere of serenity. For instance, if you have to be in a shabby waiting room you may spread a colourful scarf on your knees to cheer you up. If you can't do this, you may simply escape to an exquisite internal landscape. But peace at any price may not be what you want, and the milk and honey may dry up if someone is being treated unfairly. You can't help speaking up to redress the balance.

Talents ★ You are capable of creating beauty and harmony anywhere.
★ You are charming and gentle.
★ You can become totally absorbed in another person.

Pitfalls ★ Sometimes you spend too much time weighing up your feelings.
★ You may take the line of least resistance.
★ Often you can be indecisive about what you want and need.

Phases   *New Moon in Libra:* With your New Moon in Libra, the Sun will probably be in the same sign. You are dynamically creative and artistic. You tend to spend considerable time making your surroundings beautiful. In friendships and partnerships you are ready to take the initiative, albeit in a gentle fashion. But although you do indeed need company badly, the rapport you seek is mental rather than emotional and sometimes you back off when things get too heavy; for you that isn't closeness – it's being thrown off-balance and smothered. If the Moon hasn't yet reached the Sun, you will be particularly discriminating and you will choose to be alone rather than risk being wrong-footed by people who are not your sort.

Waxing Moon in Libra: If your first quarter Moon is exact, the Sun will be in Cancer. You need to find a unique way of expressing yourself that will not destroy the harmony that you seek. Every so often you may need to detach yourself to regain your equilibrium, so that you can come back to relating to others with renewed enthusiasm. Sometimes you would like to feel certain things but have to admit to yourself that if you are honest, you don't – if you work with this you can become very self-aware, uncomfortable though it may be. You need to be careful that you do not fall into the habit of acquiescing and tending to the needs of others, regardless of what you think, in order to avoid facing what is really going on inside you. True balance comes from being with your own truth.

Full Moon in Libra: If your Libra Full Moon is exact, the Sun will be in Aries. Only by developing a true sense of your inner needs can you form relationships with others that make you feel secure. You may have to face some strife, although this will be only temporary – it is a means to gauge what is really going on in a relationship, to give feelings an airing and eventually to create a deeper harmony. This will help you to grow as an individual. Sometimes you feel that you want to make other people do what you say, because you are sure you know the best way to create peace. But the trouble is that fighting for peace is something of a contradiction! You are clear-sighted and have very strong principles – you will speak out loud and strong about injustice. You may be especially good at tuning in to the viewpoints of others and fighting their corner, especially in the case of a partner or close friend.

Waning Moon in Libra: If your last quarter Moon is exact in Libra, then your Sun will be in Capricorn. It is probably important to you to communicate with groups of people and use what influence you can to make them understand certain principles and ideas. Your understanding and diplomatic attitude can help you rise in your profession or general standing, but you will find it hard to face some of the unpopularity that goes with this. Using your mind and remaining objective gives you a feeling of security, and this feels even better if you can bounce your ideas off other people and use their responses. You need practical achievement as well as the knowledge that you are liked.

Mixing and Matching

Yours is probably the most pleasant and well-liked of the Moon signs. In fact every party and public function should have its resident Libra Moon to keep things running smoothly! You are welcoming and responsive, never over-the-top but always tuning in to the needs and wishes of others. Your style and grace make people feel special, but your intention isn't to nurture and hold, but rather to create an atmosphere of calm civilisation. You may seem to yearn to get close, but what you want is mental rapport. You like to feel that the other party has ideas that sit well with your own but if there are too many emotional demands you may glide away – not that you'd wish to upset anyone by leaving, of course! You may be prepared to compromise some of your individuality in order to form a strong relationship with someone you judge suitable – in fact, with the right person, you express your individuality through bonding. You never feel quite complete until you are one half of a charming couple, although what really keeps you together will be the thoughts that you share.

Moon in Libra with Sun Signs

Aries Sun: Oh dear! You do wish you didn't keep smashing your bone china!

Taurus Sun: That old chair might be comfy, but you'll have to get it re-covered.

Gemini Sun: Do you *always* have the right thing to say at the tip of your tongue? Yes!

Cancer Sun: You are a good counsellor, as long as you avoid getting too involved.

Leo Sun: A real Charisma Cookie, aren't you! Shine on!

Virgo Sun: Refined and elegant, your standards are the highest.

Libra Sun: A soul-mate is what you need, and you're prepared to be a true partner.

Scorpio Sun: However suspicious you are, you give people the benefit of the doubt.

Sagittarius Sun: Forming a philosophy of life and debating with others is important to you.

Capricorn Sun: Your standards are very high and you think a thing worth doing is worth doing well.

Aquarius Sun: You'll charm anyone, but you're unlikely to let them get close to you.

Pisces Sun: You hate to say 'no' so you make polite excuses!

★ ✦ ★ *Moon in Scorpio*

For you, love and hate may be two sides of the same coin. Your emotions are unbelievably strong but you tend to keep them bottled up inside where they steam and seethe like a pressure-cooker. It can be a challenge to take the lid off! You may interpret your intuitions negatively in the light of your turbulent inner feelings but sometimes your internal promptings are compelling and you ignore them at your peril. Scorpio Moon is in its Fall because the sign is opposite Taurus which it rules (see page 37). Your emotions are hard to deal with because often it all just feels too raw and overwhelming. You need to be in control all the time but you aren't happy with the superficial, and this includes the emotions of others as well as your own. Often you feel drawn to dig and probe until you find the inevitable worm in the apple, because you know the human heart has its dark corners – none better! Jealousy and vengefulness are sometimes strong within you and while you yearn to satisfy these feelings you also want to cleanse yourself of them – you hate the thought that they might control you. Try not to blame other people for provoking these feelings within you, for whatever anyone may have done (and often they have not done anything as bad as you think), your feelings belong to you alone. It isn't nearly so important to find out the motives of others as it is to understand and face your own. On the plus side you have tremendous courage and endurance and you are capable of heroism – yours is a do-or-die attitude and your intensity means you not only succeed but you also command respect. Everyone wants to have you in their corner, and certainly when you love you do so with your whole soul. Remind yourself – ' To live well is the best revenge.'

Talents ★ You have tremendous intensity and sticking power.
★ You see deeply into anything and anyone.
★ You are capable of undying love.

Pitfalls ★ You can be vengeful.
★ Because you fear being overwhelmed, you may bottle up your feelings.
★ The Green Eyed-Monster gets you from time to time.

Phases   *New Moon in Scorpio:* If you were born with an exact New Moon in Scorpio, then the Sun will also be there. You are hungry for deep and challenging experiences and emotions fascinate you. Probably you are something of a sex-pot, and your sex appeal may be a used to gain power over people – you know what's hot and what's not! Although you value your privacy, you need to be able to come out of your shell when the mood takes you, on your own terms. You can be persistent because you want to get a strong response from people and you may keep on keeping on until you tease it out. Although you can be a little invasive, people find you exciting and challenging and forgive you because of your lust for life. Also you are willing to give uncompromising help to people who are prepared to be really open with you.

If the Moon hasn't yet reached the Sun, you could be a little obsessive on occasion and you could be a little morbid – cheer up! You can cope with anything and your courage and loyalty are second to none.

Waxing Moon in Scorpio: With an exact first quarter Moon in Scorpio, your Sun will be in Leo. Sometimes you are at odds with yourself because you want to be open, generous and very creative, but your internal censor stymies this with suspicion, resentment and a need to control. Don't be so serious! Yes, it is important for you to get to the bottom of things and that's fine, but try not to manipulate because then you won't think well of yourself. Use your deep perceptions to extend your influence, not to give rise to negative thinking. You may be very proud, and you have a strong spirit, but you will not get the response and the admiration that is rightfully yours if you allow yourself to be spiteful. Really you are above all of that. You have tremendous courage and determination and you have the guts to start something controversial, if it seems right, and then to see it through to the end.

Full Moon in Scorpio: If you have an exact Full Moon in Scorpio, you will have Sun in Taurus. Your issues concern ownership, to a great extent. Possibly you can see fairly clearly that you are laying depth charges for yourself! You may have occult gifts and a very strong intuition regarding the motives of others. You desperately want to be honest in relationships, especially who owns what and who feels what – and who owns whom! Your sexuality is strong and your emotions overwhelming. Try not to be so possessive – sometimes you even want to know what the other person is thinking – does it matter? The important thing is that you have ownership and understanding of your own thoughts and impulses. If you want to, you can use your own struggles and the understanding you have reached to make some very fundamental changes in your life – you know what's really best for yourself. And you have the strength to build something good and enduring.

Waning Moon in Scorpio: An exact last quarter Moon in Scorpio will have the Sun in Aquarius. You may be desperate to make sense of your internal turmoil so that you can explain it to others – sanitised and toned-down, of course! At the same time you find it quite hard to be truly honest about your feelings because you feel ashamed of them – especially ignoble things like jealousy. This is one of the most difficult phases, simply because you may try to hide your feelings even from yourself – and your feelings are so strong! However, if you really do not want to be controlled by your emotions, your best bet is to face up to them so they do not operate unconsciously. Resist the temptation to use your powers of analysis on other people in preference to yourself! You can be a brilliant psychologist with the skills to understand things that may be puzzling to others. But your best skills come from what you learn through facing yourself. Give yourself a pat on the back every time you face up to an 'unworthy' emotion. You are a real human being, and a wise one into the bargain!

Mixing and Matching

You tend to prefer to stand back a pace and stir things, if you can. You aren't all that keen on meeting new people but you get satisfaction from vetting newcomers and giving people the benefit of your shrewd insights. You don't miss much, from initial handshake to body language, and your penetrating gaze could make some people uneasy. It isn't easy for you to get close and you may only open out when the other party makes themselves emotionally vulnerable to you – but then you feel tempted to exploit this to your own advantage! But you really long to be close – in fact you feel almost obsessed by this need and you spend time wondering how you can maintain control in the relationship. When you give your heart it is complete, utter and not a little scary, most of all to you. You may feel that you want to manipulate your lover or even withhold from them so they need you more – don't do this! Show the positive sides of your passion and how much you are prepared to give, for this is how you will get what you need. It's worth the risk!

Moon in Scorpio with Sun Signs

Aries Sun: You're a loaded gun, so be careful where you point it and don't shoot yourself in the foot! Use that power well.

Taurus Sun: Possessive, jealous and stubborn – hang on only to what is worth the effort.

Gemini Sun: Give you time and you'll get to the bottom of anything.

Cancer Sun: Your feelings are strong and deep and you keep yourself to yourself.

Leo Sun: The pride and the passion – impress others but impress yourself most.

Virgo Sun: There isn't a worm in every apple – honest! Use your analytical talents positively.

Libra Sun: Keep up that pleasant exterior – they'll never guess what lies beneath!

Scorpio Sun: Intense, focused and determined, that's you!

Sagittarius Sun: Try to be *really* as cheerful as you appear.

Capricorn Sun: Control and stability are central to your life.

Aquarius Sun: You are detached and idealistic, but don't try to detach from your own needs.

Pisces Sun: Your dreams are powered by an internal dynamo – go for it!

Moon in Sagittarius

Your inner landscapes are vivid – you see life as something wildly interesting, full of meanings and ramifications. Unless of course it's a wet Monday and you feel dull, bored and chained to routine. Usually your feelings are extravagant and extreme and your emotions may seem overwhelming, but you feel the urge to find out what they mean in a general sense and where they fit into the vast scheme of things. Your intuitions may come as visions and inner revelations. While these may not feel very personal, there may be meaningful personal symbols to be decoded; however, sometimes they may be prophetic and general. You're quite a philosopher – you have an instinct to find 'God's eternal plan' and you like to see the funny side. After all, what's the point of sitting po-faced and miserable? What makes you feel secure is having a meaningful reason to be alive. If you find this, then you can cope with most things. You are very future-orientated – the things that other people find essential to life, like routines, predictability, a neat garden and locks on the windows, just make you irritable; you don't like trivia. Freedom is the stuff of life to you, but you may put up with being physically restricted as long as your mind is free to roam. Your 'home' is a spiritual one and you need to be playing with concepts, beliefs and philosophies. If you feel overwrought, motion may soothe you, such as a car drive. In your emotional life there are no half-measures and you can lose your temper big-style at times. But sometimes you try not to feel things like jealousy because you prefer to think such emotions are beneath you. Nonetheless, your irrepressibly frank nature means you usually tell the truth, even to yourself – in fact you may 'tell it like it is' a tad too much, because you can be tactless at times! That honest opinion just pops out. When your friends have problems you always feel there must be a way out, and your determination to find it can make you a pain, when you should simply be empathising. However, your greatest gift is your faith in life – spread it about!

Talents
★ You are positive, cheerful and encouraging.
★ You feel that anything is possible, you are resourceful and you seek enlightenment.
★ Spiritual things are important to you.

Pitfalls
★ You can be restless and hard to pin down.
★ You may spend too much time rationalising everything.
★ With your eyes always fixed on tomorrow you can miss the 'precious present'.

Phases
New Moon in Sagittarius: If your New Moon is in Sagittarius, your Sun will probably be there also. Your enthusiasm probably knows no bounds! You have bags of drive and energy – there is no such word as 'no' and you launch yourself into projects with a Tigger-like bounce. Your sense of humour is irrepressible and your tongue probably runs away with you at times. Life to you is a huge adventure and you respond swiftly and warmly.

If the Moon hasn't yet reached the Sun, the chances are that you are sometimes spaced-out and abstracted. You are always searching for meanings and you may seem to be in a world of your own.

Waxing Moon in Sagittarius: With an exact first quarter Moon in Sagittarius, your Sun will be in Virgo. Probably you are always trying to escape from self-imposed restrictions and routines. This may make you irritable and restless. It is likely that you will achieve much that is useful, and indeed excellent, but it is unlikely that you will ever be satisfied because you never meet your own high standards. You often feel uncomfortable at the way you get yourself tied down. Often you reason away what you feel, only to find that it suddenly gets the better of you as you are impulsively drawn to a course of action that worries the life out of you! You are an interesting person whose keen observations of life often manifest in wry humour and philosophical insight.

Full Moon in Sagittarius: An exact Full Moon in Sagittarius will have the Sun in Gemini. You may feel pulled between searching for facts and searching for meanings. You want to get both the Big Picture and the detailed information. You may alternate between being very rational and very passionate. You may want to 'justify the ways of God to men' and may strain yourself trying to find all the answers. Greedy for experience, you nonetheless feel that you are missing something when everything is buzzing around you. Your intuition can be excellent when it comes to seeing things from a wide perspective, but sometimes you miss what's under your nose. You may also fail to tune in to other people's feelings, although in matters of philosophy you may be very wise. Your task is to make your intuition work for you, without reasoning it away or being totally caught up in intangibles.

Waning Moon in Sagittarius: An exact last quarter Moon in Sagittarius will have the Sun in Pisces. You are probably passionate about everything and you want not only to express emotions but to arouse them. In life you tend to 'squander' yourself because you enter deeply and utterly into many things and you have vivid dreams and ideals. You may throw yourself into many forms of experience but also into the feelings of others, whose emotions you may feel for them! Sometimes you interfere because the boundaries between yourself and others may feel indistinct, and you may feel unable to bear their unhappiness. You have considerable wisdom but you need to develop the discrimination to use it wisely, for we all have to learn our own lessons. A spiritual path is vital to you.

Mixing and Matching

You have such enthusiasm that your mere presence is a boost – unless you have your eyes fixed on the horizon. On a good day you love to meet new people and you will do so with a grin from ear to ear. You love a good giggle, getting all the gossip and giving your opinion to anyone who will listen. You gravitate towards interesting people but, let's face it, you are quite capable of ignoring anyone you think is boring. You don't mean to be rude, but you just forget such people. People may think that you are really easy to get close to because your fiery nature means you seem very warm, and you may be quite physical, giving out hugs, kisses and pats very generously. But if there isn't enough response you simply go off and hunt elsewhere; you have the instincts of a seeker and you need meanings, beliefs and stimulation. You can run several close relationships concurrently, remaining loyal, after a fashion, to all. However, once someone lets you down, that's it – you will drop them like a hot potato. You hate dishonesty but you will stretch the truth where it suits you!

Closeness, to you, is not two people looking at each other but fixing their eyes on the same goal far ahead. You want a travelling companion you can trust.

***Moon in
Sagittarius
with Sun
Signs***

Aries Sun: Life is an adventure, but let your feet touch the ground sometimes.

Taurus Sun: You live life to the full and your extravagance worries you at times.

Gemini Sun: You want to know not only the 'whats' but also the 'whys'.

Cancer Sun: Sometimes the greatest inner security comes from letting go.

Leo Sun: Sunny, dramatic – and a bit over-the-top at times!

Virgo Sun: Don't worry, you have the inner resources to cope with anything – even yourself!

Libra Sun: You believe in fairness and openness, but be open about your true feelings as well.

Scorpio Sun: Sometimes you trust where you know you shouldn't, but this makes you all the more loveable.

Sagittarius Sun: You have wanderlust, even if you are only an armchair traveller.

Capricorn Sun: You eternally seek meaning in life's vicissitudes – don't forget to smile!

Aquarius Sun: Freedom of all kinds is vital to you and you are very fair-minded.

Pisces Sun: Dream those dreams, scheme those schemes – and make them happen!

★ ⁎ ★ *Moon in Capricorn*

No one knows how you feel – often not even you! The Moon is in its detriment in Capricorn because this sign is opposite Cancer, which the Moon rules (see page 44). This means you tend to keep yourself to yourself and your emotions are understated. Being quite down-to-earth, you may not set much store by your intuitions but often you know in your bones what's going to happen. If someone asks you how you feel you will probably tell them what you are going to do – that is, if you don't simply change the subject! Your ambition is to proceed from birth to death in systematic fashion. Control freak? Sometimes. Your sense of security comes from knowing where everything is in your environment and keeping an eye on the clock, so you know what to expect. People may die or walk out of your life and you may simply march on. It may seem as if your most meaningful relationship is with your work. However, this is certainly not because you do not have feelings but because you are afraid of your own vulnerability; it is better to attach yourself to something you can do something about, rather than be at the mercy of another person's whims and fantasies.

Being part of a useful organisation gives you your sense of well-being, and you also understand the value of money. You do not like to embark upon a relationship unless you have had time to test it out and even then you like to keep a part of yourself to yourself – it feels safer. Also you may avoid impractical relationships, especially ones that are likely to be expensive. Occasionally others may experience you as cold, but they also find you a tower of strength when things go wrong. It is very important for you to do the right thing – you feel very 'wobbly' when departing from your 'duty'. You have a sense of tradition and may be very attached to the 'old days' and your place and family of origin – in fact you can be surprisingly sentimental at times. Actually there is an old-fashioned charm about you that can be reassuring in this hectic world, so put on the kettle, get out the album and settle for a ramble down memory lane.

Talents ★ You are reliable and practical.
★ You prefer to look before you leap.
★ You do not expect other people to cater to your whims.

Pitfalls ★ Because you want to protect your vulnerability, you may seem cold, and this can be self-perpetuating, evoking the very rejection you fear.
★ You can be chained to routine.
★ You like to control everything so you are not faced with surprises.

Phases *New Moon in Capricorn:* With a New Moon in Capricorn, the Sun also will be there. You have certain childlike qualities that sit rather strangely with your general wish for control. Yes, you have common sense, but amid the attention to duty and routine you may have many whimsical schemes, dreams and cunning plans! You have an enthusiasm about life that even your fears cannot quench. However, your practical application may let you down for you could be stuck in a time-warp, seeing the world as it was 50 years ago. However, you can get a lot done if you take it in bite-sized pieces.

If the Moon has not yet caught up with the Sun, then you are more likely to be a bit negative, training yourself to accept the 'inevitable' when it may not be! But you are probably wise and patient and some would call you 'an old soul' – make sure, however, that you are not old before your time. Cheer up, it may never happen! And use that sense of realism to build something real.

Waxing Moon in Capricorn: With an exact first quarter Moon in Capricorn, the Sun will be in Libra. You know you want to get ahead, so why do you so often find yourself going backwards? You realise that the only real way to get results in life is by co-operation and you respect the idea of relationships. However, you so often find that you have to rely on your own resources and your motto may be 'If you want something done, do it yourself'. You may sometimes feel frustrated and let down, but actually you accomplish a great deal. Perhaps you expect too much from working partnerships? Remember, you can't make an omelette without breaking eggs and it isn't the end of the world if someone somewhere gets put out – that's life. You need to learn to be ruthless in the right places and accommodating in others – the problem is that you may find it easiest to be accommodating at work and harsh at home. If this is so, review it and think again – what are your real priorities and 'duties'?

Full Moon in Capricorn: With an exact Full Moon in Capricorn, you will have the Sun in Cancer. The issues here are likely to concern family and work and how you can blend these parts of your life to support each other rather than pull in opposite directions. You like to follow family traditions, although if your family was unsupportive in some way then you may prefer to make a clean break and establish something of your own. You may be fascinated by looking into your family tree. You want to know where you have come from so you can sort out where you are going – it feels like part of a process. Often you try to find ways of looking after people, institutions or objects in the best way possible. If you have children, their futures are very important to you, but you need to be careful of trying to fit them into your own mould. Try to be very aware of your feelings and don't confuse your own needs and preferences and view them as some kind of dogma. There is more than one way and what is right for you may be wrong for someone else. Try not to fear closeness – it is what you need to develop.

Waning Moon in Capricorn: Your Sun will be in Aries with a last quarter Moon in Capricorn. You have a continual urge to make your presence felt in life but inside you there is a Greek chorus intoning 'Be careful now… You never know – shit happens,' etc. This can be very hard for you, and frustrating into the bargain. But a good side to this is that what you do succeed in constructing is probably on so solid a foundation that an earthquake will not shake it. Be careful of those odd times when you get so impatient with yourself that you ignore your instincts because then you may go to the other extreme. Because of your experience you may be very helpful to others when it comes to making their ideas real. Probably you have leadership ability, courage and staying power – when the going gets tough, the tough get going. Just try to keep counting what you have achieved, not what you still have to do. You may be at your best when faced by obstacles, but try not to create your own.

Mixing and Matching

You aren't really keen on pressing the flesh – your own company is often the most pleasant. You like to organise get-togethers, but having done so, you may be strangely absent on the day! Or if you are there, you give yourself the task of putting out chairs and hanging up coats. When you decide to take part, your old-fashioned manners and consideration for the comfort of others win you friends. Generally, however, you avoid getting close because mostly you don't see any point in it. Who needs it? Sometimes you wonder what 'closeness' is and may even think you are close to someone when they regard you as an acquaintance – someone they can depend on and whom they would like to know better but who tends to keep them at a distance. Once you make a friend you keep them, but remember that for others to trust you with their feelings you need to trust your own. For you, the stuff of a live-in partnership is shared routines and responsibilities and you may show your love by filling the dishwasher. You expect to be valued for what you do, not what you say, and you may forget that others need words of love and 'hyacinths for the soul'. However, like good wine, your relating skills improve with age. But you are not a total stranger to romance – after all, red roses are traditional!

Moon in Capricorn with Sun Signs

Aries Sun: You want to get on, so why is something always pulling you back?

Taurus Sun: Security, tradition, routine – is there anything else?

Gemini Sun: Reflect on any changes – will you feel comfortable with them?

Cancer Sun: Home sweet home – you love that security blanket!

Leo Sun: Impressive, or repressive? Make plans, not obstacles.

Virgo Sun: Practical, restrained and well-organised – but a worrier nonetheless!

Libra Sun: Sometimes there's no alternative but to talk things through – trust yourself, it will be worth it.

Scorpio Sun: Privacy is paramount to you, but you need to take risks to achieve closeness.

Sagittarius Sun: You like to wander, but only in the sturdiest of boots!

Capricorn Sun: Don't erect your own barriers; you'll feel better if you get on with it.

Aquarius Sun: You accept life – you've seen it all. But don't be too hard on yourself.

Pisces Sun: Your help and sympathy are practically applied.

★ ✦ ★ *Moon in Aquarius*

With your Aquarian Moon you like to be calm, cool and reasonable. Strong emotions make you a tad uneasy, although you can be quite wise and accepting if you are not overwhelmed, and very helpful, too. You can be very intuitive, finding you just 'know things' although you may not have much of a clue what other people are feeling. You respect the freedom of others and it is essential to you to have your own rights respected. However, although you are a pleasant, low-key and sometimes abstracted individual, you do become upset by inequality and injustice. You may appear to be on someone's side, but there is always a part of you that remains detached. You feel secure and at ease in an environment that supports openness, honesty and justice. Because ordinary families, being what they are, rarely come up to these ideals, you prefer to remain pleasantly aloof. Things that make others feel cosy drive you crazy – you like windows and doors open, and minds that are open, too. A wide circle of friends and people you can team up with at a moment's notice is very important to you, and your friends may be your 'family'. You may have unusual tastes and mannerisms, and while for the most part you are quite predictable there are those times when you are anything but, and then you can be quite abrupt, needing to disappear at a moment's notice, and very impatient. You may like to make changes but no one else can change you. You can be moody at times and issues in the world at large may upset you, especially matters involving conservation, factory farming and even politics, where liberties are concerned. Meanwhile you may not notice that you have no clean clothes and a bare larder. Generally extremely polite, you can be a little distant at times.

Talents ★ You are friendly to everyone and very open-minded.
★ You value justice, honesty and a civilised approach.
★ You are capable of making radical and well-thought changes in your life.

Pitfalls ★ You can be a freedom-freak, refusing to be 'tied down'.
★ Sometimes you can be distant and spaced-out.
★ You may not want to face your own nastier feelings.

Phases *New Moon in Aquarius:* If your New Moon is in Aquarius, your Sun is likely to be there also. Probably your visions and ideals are very strong and you rarely compromise your principles. You have an impulse to make things new, and as far as you are concerned sacred cows were made to be slaughtered. It's no concern of yours whether something has ever been done before – if you think it will work and you want to do it, you will do it anyway. Although you never mean to be unkind – in fact you like to be politically correct – you may run roughshod over people's feelings simply because they seem so nonsensical to you. However, you may not notice your own 'funny little ways' and you can be wilful and erratic, always changing your mind but never letting anyone else persuade you. But you are a free spirit, born to make a difference.

If your Moon has not yet reached the Sun you could be quite eccentric, although you will enjoy being alone more and you may love playing with technology, such as computers and other gadgets.

Waxing Moon in Aquarius: Your Sun will be in Scorpio if yours is an exact first quarter Moon. You may feel very tense at times because you want to get away from your strong feelings and to feel free. You may experience a 'freedom-closeness dilemma' – you keep asserting your need for independence, but when you have it you feel you must draw close again. You express yourself through attachments and being connected to your roots. If you are not very self-aware you may be possessive but blame the other party for it, and refuse to commit in an open way. However, you can be very loyal and deep down you realise that it is through channelling your passions that you grow most as a person.

Full Moon in Aquarius: The Sun will be in Leo if this Full Moon is exact. On the one hand you need to be detached and impersonal to feel comfortable, but something tends to draw you into situations where you are in the spotlight. You may not always handle this well because you disclaim and detach and then feel vaguely dissatisfied. At other times you embarrass yourself by being too 'showy'. You need to strive for balance here by being up-front with yourself – you may not be comfortable with too much attention but your life path asks that you use this constructively. You can square it with yourself if you find a way to make this serve the common good. Also, you can involve your friends in a democratic manner and feel you have made everybody grow an inch or two. You have an instinctive ability to home in on what will turn people on and you can be quite charismatic. Use your creativity to make sensible changes.

Waning Moon in Aquarius: An exact last quarter Moon in Aquarius will have the Sun in Taurus. Your main pitfall is being convinced that you are 'right' in some rock-solid, universal fashion. You need to resist this if you are really going to make something of those visions – and you can! You have the common sense to create the durable. Don't tell yourself you have found something entirely new – if you are selling old goods re-packaged, then fair enough. It is said there is nothing new under the Sun. Probably you are very stubborn indeed but maybe you can be persuaded by logical and sensible arguments – try to be open-minded. Sometimes you surprise everyone by making swingeing and fundamental changes. You are challenged to convey your ideas to others in a down-to-earth manner, and you can make the radical workable.

Mixing and Matching

You make friends very readily but you like to think you can go away again – you don't like to feel too committed or tied down. Always polite and pleasant, you have a sense of occasion and you can be a very good host and party-organiser, although you tend to forget little details. You like to hear what others think and love to see everything going well. But every so often you get that dreamy look in your eye and soon you are missing – off to something more interesting. If people are honest and open with you and tell you what they think, you are more likely to respond to them. All the better if you feel your individual approach is accepted – then you may become almost intense about a relationship. However, you always keep just a little bit aloof, and even when you feel quite close to someone they may feel excluded from your deepest thoughts. You aren't into being joined at the hip – you can easily feel claustrophobic. In relationships you have very high standards and you like to know there is honesty, trust and a true mental understanding. If you think all this is settled then you see no reason why you or your partner shouldn't do what you like. You are noble and just a little bit innocent as far as this sad old world is concerned, but where would we be without you? Any form of betrayal is hurtful to you, but your ideals and beliefs see you through.

Moon in Aquarius with Sun Signs

Aries Sun: Enterprise and imagination, but you may have to work on the practicality.

Taurus Sun: Security and freedom – can you have both?

Gemini Sun: Communication and shared ideals are what you live for, but you may not speak about your feelings.

Cancer Sun: You care for people but you don't like to let them too close.

Leo Sun: You don't know whether you want to keep ahead of the Joneses or shock them!

Virgo Sun: You hone your skills, but you need more than attention to detail to fill your life.

Libra Sun: Kind and polite, one of the few things that ruffles your feathers is injustice.

Scorpio Sun: You know the 'under-stains' are there but you feel more comfortable if you can overlook them.

Sagittarius Sun: Broad-minded and liberal, you seek the truth – but you miss what's under your nose!

Capricorn Sun: You're a traditionalist on the surface and a rebel at heart.

Aquarius Sun: A free spirit – and just a little cranky at times!

Pisces Sun: Compassionate and intuitive, remember your own interests too.

Moon in Pisces

Your emotions are very strong but you may not be quite sure what you really need. You may be almost bombarded by things you intuit and this may get all mixed up with personal feelings. You may, in fact, get used to disregarding the intuitive realm because it is so confusing and dismiss it all as fantasy, which of course it is sometimes. Write down your intuitive feelings, see which come 'true' and learn to discriminate. Often you drift from one thing to another in search of something that feels like 'home' but nothing quite fits the bill. You dream of something enchanting, but Fairy Godmothers being somewhat rare, you often feel let down. 'Beam me up, Scottie,' you plead, when yet again you are faced with forms to fill in and trains to catch. Ugh! Ordinary life just doesn't give you what you need. The truth of the matter is that you really need a spiritual home and you need to feel that you are a meaningful part of something that is greater than you are. However, it is hard to satisfy this, or even to sort out how it may be important in the plain old round of everyday life and the seeking of comfort and security. Yes, you need to feel protected but, whatever you have around you, you can't feel truly safe because you need something intangible. Possibly you often feel discontented because you are searching for what you need in the material world and do not realise that this isn't where it's at – not totally. In an effort to find that little bit of magic you may get side-tracked into collecting possessions, lovers or academic achievement. The other side of the coin is that you may throw yourself into some cause, but unless you have chosen well you may be sacrificing yourself needlessly. When you find out how to use your imagination and creativity to bring some magic into your life then you are on the stairway to Heaven.

Talents ★ You have a wonderful imagination.
★ You are adaptable, responsive and caring.
★ Spirituality is your deepest goal.

Pitfalls ★ You can be unreliable and confused.
★ Often you just don't know what you want.
★ You may spend lots of time looking in the wrong places and being surprisingly materialistic.

Phases *New Moon in Pisces:* If you have New Moon in Pisces, the chances are that the Sun is also there. You are so emotional you are almost awash, but strangely at times you can just switch off. Mostly you have the 'urge to merge' and want to lose yourself in something or someone else. Sometimes your own identity may almost disappear as you take on the colour of what is around you, like a chameleon. Occasionally you can be manipulative, using your insight into human nature to serve your own ends. However, the opposite may be true and you may devote everything to something worthwhile and display a great deal of wisdom.

If the Moon hasn't yet reached the Sun there will be less enthusiasm and more reflection. You may be quite psychic and very intuitive although you need to be careful not to be too negative.

Waxing Moon in Pisces: With an exact first quarter Moon in Pisces, your Sun will be in Sagittarius. You have a tremendous hunger to experience new things on all levels. In extreme cases you could be tempted to use drugs to get you out of your head and into something transcendent. You don't need this, for your imagination is very creative and almost boundless – use it positively! Probably you are very restless – make sure you recognise what you seek when you find it! You may be something of a pioneer and/or feel strongly about charities or a spiritual path. You could even feel almost Messianic at times, but don't get carried away! Although you are not always practical, you are inspiring and if you don't leave things better than you found them it isn't for want of trying!

Full Moon in Pisces: If you have an exact Full Moon in Pisces, you will have the Sun in Virgo. Possibly you feel torn between the need to feel part of everything and the need to assess the parts of everything! That feeling of belonging that makes you feel safe may seem only to come at the price of compromising your common sense. You may feel very worried and a prey to fears and negative imagination. Take heart, it is possible for you to feel not only contented but fulfilled, if you find something suitable to 'serve'. This isn't about being servile, but about being a sensible part of something to which you belong, but in which you are not lost. This could be anything from a relationship or a business to a cause or a religion. You don't miss much, either in respect of the feelings of others or in your material surroundings, and sometimes the sheer volume of what you sense can make you feel overwrought – it seems that there is too much to take into account. So don't! Learn to discriminate between what is useful and what isn't. The ability to combine the useful with the inspiring is your special talent.

Waning Moon in Pisces: If you have an exact last quarter Moon in Pisces, you will have the Sun in Gemini. You are brilliant at putting feelings into words and may do this for others better than for yourself. You may also be quite poetic or good at creative writing. You may prefer to brush away your own feelings with bright-and-breezy logic. You need to work at being very self-aware to make the most of your abilities. Sometimes you can be almost hypnotic in the way you express yourself. You have plenty of wisdom and you need to make sure that your insights aren't side-tracked into trivia, as this will leave you feeling discontented and restless. Use your mind to make real your visions rather than to catalogue and dissect them.

Mixing and Matching

In the company of other people you may sometimes lose your boundaries and viewpoint, often feeling what they are feeling, or sometimes merely becoming a little confused and uncertain. You tune into people and put them at ease for the most part, but sometimes you seem spaced out and miss the cues. When you really want to be welcoming you create a wonderful atmosphere. Getting close to you is more like absorption – you may seem to drop your guard, let people in and even cling like a limpet at times. But just when they feel they really understand you and connect with you, they may wake up to find that you were never quite there and all they have been looking at is their own reflection. In a close relationship you may lose yourself entirely and expect the other person to do the same, but you need to remember that if you sacrifice your individuality you give the other person very little to attach themselves to. Look beyond the relationship for a sense of identity and meaning and then you will have even more to bring to it, and it will be richer and more meaningful.

Moon in Pisces with Sun Signs

Aries Sun: You need somewhere cool to escape away from all the heat you attract!

Taurus Sun: Simple pleasures can be enchanting to you.

Gemini Sun: Change your clothes, change your partners, change your mind…

Cancer Sun: You need a safe harbour in the shifting tides of life.

Leo Sun: Dramatic talent and creative imagination – make them work for you!

Virgo Sun: Don't tidy away your dreams; use them.

Libra Sun: You used to be indecisive but now you aren't so sure… Charming, though.

Scorpio Sun: Privacy is as essential to you as emotional response.

Sagittarius Sun: You're on a quest – but you'll start tomorrow!

Capricorn Sun: You want to feel safe, but it takes more than brick walls and insurance. Grow those hyacinths!

Aquarius Sun: Ideals for the mind, dreams for the soul, meaning to the life.

Pisces Sun: Your search for enchantment ends when you look within and see it has been there all along.

CHAPTER 3

COMFORTING
MOON

...The best
Thing we can do is to make wherever we're lost in
Look as much like home as we can
CHRISTOPHER FRY, *THE LADY'S NOT FOR BURNING*

Moon Sign Awareness

It is one thing to understand something about your Moon sign, but it is
another actually to apply the knowledge. Our Moons are very good at getting
their needs met up to a point. The internal Moon can be rather like a nagging,
whingeing, crying – or even screaming! – child, and so we give in to it, to some
extent. However, we may do this without always understanding why, and sometimes feeling annoyed with ourselves that we have 'taken the line of least resistance' yet again. We may feel that our inner needs are at odds with what we want
to achieve. This will be especially evident if our Moon is in square aspect to our
Sun or some other important chart point. But there is no getting away from
that Moon and we function better if we accept and nurture our lunar needs
rather than trying to suppress them. In many respects the Moon is our 'inner
child' – that part of us that is simple, instinctual, innocent and very creative.
When all is well with the inner child, we are at our most creative and healthy.
It is worth fostering. As we have seen, the Moon sign may be especially impor-

tant when we are young. If our Moons are catered to when we are small, nurtured but not over-indulged, we learn how to be comfortable with ourselves.

This chapter contains stress-busting tips for each of the Moon elements. Of course there are certain activities that everyone finds calming, such as music, massage, certain scents, etc. The activities suggested here, however, are ones that are especially apt for your Moon sign element.

In this chapter we shall be looking at some of the practical ways you can make your instinctual self, and that of others, feel good. Then from a sense of internal warmth and 'okay-ness' you will be in a better position to use your instincts well and also to succeed in meeting the demands of the world.

This chapter is divided according to Moon elements, because these have much in common. It is often easier to live with someone whose Moon is in the same element, because you do things around the home in a similar way, and even if you get on each other's nerves (which we all do!) you still know where the other person is coming from. As the French say *Tout comprendre, c'est tout pardonner* – to understand is to forgive!

★ ✦ ★ Fire Sign Moons

If your Moon is in a Fire sign (Aries, Leo or Sagittarius), then you may define 'comfort' in a way that is not generally recognised. In other words, you may not think about your physical well-being – at least not readily! This means two things; firstly, you do actually need things that are *not* physical, for your comfort – 'Man does not live by bread alone' – and this must be respected. Secondly, you may well overlook your physical needs, to your own detriment, and so you need to be aware of this.

As a Fire sign Moon, you will tend to retreat inside your head in many situations, although you are also warm, often extroverted, lively and enthusiastic. However, you tend to be 'up in the clouds' to the extent that you follow your own train of thought. You are full of possibilities, you may think about the future or the past instead of what's under your nose, and you often pick up on subtle energies. For instance, when you are with people you may be aware of their beliefs, spiritual essence and even what has happened or is going to happen to them. You will also be concerned with whether they 'spark you off' or bore you. But you might forget to offer them a cup of tea, especially if you are excited about something. Fire sign Moons are especially intuitive, but their intuitions can be quite far-flung, meaning they have to be careful how they voice them and be aware of the need to be gentle. Fire sign Moons are all too prone to think they can cheer anything and everyone up, that warmth and energy are always needed and that confrontation and courage are necessary everywhere! You do not like to 'sit with' things. Often it really does soothe you to find meanings in everything and you are usually better at facing things and sorting them than living with them.

Fire Sign Décor   Fire sign Moons are often creative when it comes to décor, but too impatient for much DIY – you prefer to get someone else in, although your energy and impatience may achieve much! You take in a room in a broad sweep, and having satisfied yourself that things are generally okay, you then follow whatever interests you, untrammelled by the unpleasant, distasteful or boringly earthy. Probably you need bold colours, evocative and inspiring pictures and plenty of light. Windows must open smoothly and a good view will work wonders. You need plenty of cupboards to get clutter out of sight – you can cope if you can't see it! The largest possible home will be the best, because you like space, although you can create an illusion of it as long as you are not too cramped. Pictures should be dramatic, interesting or symbolic.

Aries Moon   You will try anything in décor, and you like changes to be made quickly. Simplicity and sharp contrasts appeal. You may like metal and stone, reds and oranges, even black and white, but nothing fussy – little ornaments annoy you and you may well break them. You like to feel that what you have is durable, tough and low-maintenance – you like stocky furniture and strong fabrics like leather and hessian. You feel best if what you look at doesn't make you feel that anything is going to get in your way.

Leo Moon   You need an atmosphere of opulence. Of all the Fire signs Moons, you are the most comfort-orientated, but the least likely to take to DIY. You like deep colours, gold, plush fabrics, but nothing tacky. This means that mess must be kept out of the way. Pictures should be good quality and give you a feeling of joy and fulfilment, but they can be abstract or symbolic. Ornaments must be well-chosen and of excellent quality – no 'Souvenir from Bournemouth' on a cheap ashtray, thank you! You feel best if you can look around you and feel positive and successful, so if you have trophies, display them!

Sagittarius Moon   You want an inspiring atmosphere. An atmosphere of the exotic will appeal, so fabrics, rugs, hangings and pictures from other cultures may suit, especially if they have spiritual associations. For example, Indian or Chinese designs may remind you of the philosophies of these countries. Colours should be vibrant and deep – wine, purple, deep red. You will feel best if what you look at makes you feel you can 'take off' and that there is more to life than the 'plain old, same old' and you are particularly aware of the overall impression of a room. You will probably like to have your books near you.

Your Inner Child   With a Fire sign Moon, your inner child is ebullient and enthusiastic, but it may just as easily become crestfallen and distressed.

Aries   You need a challenge! Make sure there is something in your life that stretches you, such as sport, long walks or mental challenges. You respond best when life is a tad difficult and find inner resources to match. Competition fires you. Freedom and independence are essential, but as with all 'children', too much freedom can make you feel unloved and angry. A little danger in life will bring out the best in you – but try to come to terms with your dependence. All kids need someone!

Leo   You need to feel special. Make sure there is something in your life where you are the best – or one of them – such as drama, sport, being captain, creating something impressive from DIY, or arts and crafts. You like competition but may not be the best loser in the world! You are very playful and you need lots of special treats, but like all children you can be a bit spoilt and demanding! You need to seek out situations where you are treated with warmth and receive admiration, but need to make sure you aren't so demanding that you do just the opposite.

Sagittarius   You need to feel inspired. Make sure there is something in your life that connects you with the cosmos, or with God/dess, or with something that is greater than you. Sports may appeal, being in the open air, and you may like to be involved with something spiritual. You may be drawn towards Buddhism, Eastern religions and similar. You like a good laugh and like most children can get carried away with it at times. You need forms of healthy escape but must be careful that these are healthy – e.g. sci-fi and fantasy can take you away from the banal and stimulate your imagination, but too much wine will only give you a headache!

Fire Sign
Moon
Children

These children need loads of freedom. Cover the plugs, lock up anything sharp or poisonous and leave them free to explore. If they are upset, try to distract them. But you should not do this to the point where they get in the habit of covering up their feelings and running away when they are scared! Always be especially truthful, but don't labour the point – for instance, if they know they are to be left at playschool there is no point in prolonging the goodbyes if they are going to be upset by Mummy leaving. Distract them with an attractive toy. Aries likes to climb and have mock fights, Leo likes to be adored and Sagittarius is especially good at being Houdini! Fantasy is especially important. At a young age they need routine and will be awake at three in the morning if not encouraged into sensible habits. As they grow older, these children need a sense of where they are going in life, lots of social interaction and a 'why' for everything.

Fire Moon
Intuition

While you are very intuitive in that you see things as a totality to the point where you know what is round the corner, you may struggle with applying this. You may get vague, general impressions and find them hard to sort out. You may also get too excited about life and what you can do with it to be bothered to use your inner eye. To develop your intuition, you need to start respecting it. Make notes of your feelings, and remember intuition isn't necessarily about big events – although you may tune into these more readily and find you have dreams before some major world event. Try any of the following ideas.

★ Train in some symbolic system, such as astrology or tarot.
★ Re-affirm your connections with the natural world by taking walks, watching cloud formations, touching trees, etc.
★ Make notes about little things you intuit, for you may dismiss the trivial. For example, who do you think will win the football match? How often are you right?
★ Distinguish between fantasy and intuition – there is common ground but they are _not_ the same.
★ Centre down in your body and be aware of your impressions.
★ Don't always try to see the subtle worlds with your own two eyes – what can you see with that inner eye?

Fire Moon
Stressbusters

As a Fire Moon you are subject to overload. You take on too much, you expend energy quickly, and you want to be everywhere, doing everything, all the time. Try these stressbusters.

★ Watch or read something that is fantastical and/or inspiring.

★ Get in the car and drive – carefully!

★ Play loud music.

★ Change your type of activity – if you have been working hard mentally, get up and do something hard physically, or vice versa.

★ Have a laugh.

★ Think about whether this will matter a year from now. Chances are the answer is 'No'. Believe it!

★ Look into the distance.

★ Play a game with yourself or others – from cards to eye-spy.

Your Comfort Zone

Here are some specific sign-by-sign pointers.

Aries ★ Remember that just because you want something, it doesn't mean you need it. Take a deep breath and step back.

★ You love stimulation and challenge, but try to understand that these things may make others feel exposed. Ask yourself also whether these always meet your needs.

★ Nevertheless, your life should always contain a challenge – does it?

★ Don't deny your need for the ordinary and everyday.

★ Make contact with your body by consciously focusing on different parts of it (as in, 'How do my hands feel today?').

★ What makes life meaningful to you? It will also be a source of comfort.

★ Being nurtured doesn't mean being imprisoned – you can be held but also free.

★ Your 'comfort zone' extends as far as the eye can see – spread out into it with confidence!

Leo ★ Find something at which you shine and do it in front of people.

★ You may need things that make other people – and even you! – uncomfortable sometimes, such as being noticed.

★ Try not to allow being afraid of looking foolish stop you from doing anything.

★ You need to have the best of everything, not because you are snobbish or greedy but because it feels right for you. Find ways to buy high quality as cheaply as possible, e.g. buying wines in bulk.

★ If your house is less than palatial, then invest in something to be proud of to have in it.

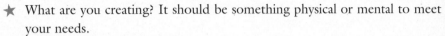
★ What are you creating? It should be something physical or mental to meet your needs.

★ Make time for play.

★ Put that big grin on your face – and see it reflected!

Sagittarius ★ Space is essential to you, inside you and without, although you may only realise this when you are cramped.

★ Seek situations where your openness and honesty are appreciated.

★ Always find something positive you can do about things.

★ Seek respect – you only feel good where those around you respect your views and understand them – which is not necessarily the same as agreeing.

★ You must have a quest in life – what's over the next hill?

★ There must also be a sense of adventure.

★ You need something to look forward to at all times – future comfort may be better than comfort here and now.

★ You need a 'why' to live, and this will probably be spiritual in essence.

Air Sign Moons

With your Air sign Moon, your comfort is in ideas and you may be quite sensitive to thoughts that are 'around' in a family situation. Usually it will be much more important to you to be civilised than to be comfortable in the usual way. For instance you could never feel comfortable if you thought you were being rude. In fact being polite may be the first thing you do to make yourself comfortable and you would rather stand in the cold than hog the best chair by the fire. You could not enjoy this at someone else's expense, not because you are super-attuned to other people's feelings as such, but because your 'comfort zone' is that of civilisation.

As an Air sign Moon, you may actually lose touch with your feelings – which is an odd concept, because the Moon is *about* feelings! So you need to strike a balance between realising that you do have a very real need to be pleasant and nice, but you do have basic creature-needs, too. You may find that you disappear into your own thoughts, talking and arguing with yourself, settling down into a nest of concepts which you compulsively try to sort out. You may find ideas repeat and repeat in your head, and that you feel the need to justify what you feel before you allow yourself to feel it. You may get involved in arguments that are pointless. For instance, an Air sign Moon may be heard saying, 'It's my turn for the shower and I've just played football, and you went first yesterday…' etc, while other Moon elements would just go and grab what they could first! (Especially true of Fire, and Taurus, Capricorn and Scorpio Moons.)

You may be so eager to talk to people that you forget to register their real feelings. Usually you are very sensitive to the views and opinions of other people and you like to seek consensus on this. You may feel you can reason anything away, or at least make it more comfortable by a bit of rationalisation. You feel best if you can think things through in advance and make sense of them. You will be most comfortable if you are articulate, but having your Moon in an Air sign does not mean that you will be adept with words (although it helps!). If you struggle with the spoken or written word (and this may be indicated by other chart factors), then you owe it to yourself to work on this. It will make you feel much more at ease to be able to put your thoughts into words. It is also important to you to know how things – and people! – tick.

Air Sign Décor

With your Moon in an Air sign, you need things to be light, airy and often quite cultural. You prefer contemporary design and technology is likely to be especially important to you, for you like to communicate. So you will need proper access to the Internet and plenty of phones. Also you will need to have air circulating – literally. There needs to be fresh air and windows that readily open. When you look at a room you like to feel that it will serve your need to be intrigued – it needs to be interesting. Colours will probably be pastel and designs clean. Pictures are likely to be modern, but not over-powering, and they may be chosen as part of the total design rather than for their own content. You like to have space to sort and catalogue your possessions. You probably do not like getting your hands dirty, so kitchen gadgets are favoured.

Gemini Moon

You need surroundings that are fresh and delicate. This Moon is incurably curious, so you will need space for magazines, newspapers, books and a telephone in every room. Pale yellow and apricot, light blue, stainless steel, mirrors and glass – all these make Gemini Moon feel free and uplifted. There should also be ample opportunity to move the furniture round repeatedly, so make sure that the locations of plugs and aerial sockets allow for adaptability and that shelves are movable. Ornaments should be interesting, preferably conversation-pieces, as should pictures. You may like pictures that are slightly diagrammatic, stylised or full of content that you can examine.

Libra Moon You need surroundings that are nothing less than beautiful. Untidiness can be tolerated (because clearing up is such an effort), but ugliness, never! You will need to have pictures and artefacts that you find beautiful. This is more important than souvenirs or something your kids have painted. Colours may be soft blues, greens and rose, and you have an eye for fabric design and what goes with what. Quality is less important than the attractive impression you can create and you are probably adept at interior design. Flowers will make you feel especially good. Every Moon in Libra home should have something that has been bought without any regard to expense or utility – just because it is breathtakingly lovely. Interior décor is usually of paramount importance to Libra Moon but very occasionally a Libra Moon will be concerned with concepts and ideals and may scorn interior design as trivial – but this is unusual.

Aquarius Moon You need something that is unusual. State-of-the-art technology will fascinate you. You may like quite stark contrasts such as black and white, and you may feel at ease with combinations and layouts that others find disturbing. Geometrical prints may appeal. Of all the Air sign Moons, fresh air is most essential to you. You are prepared to consider the very modern and avant-garde even if it is quite ugly. You may take the trouble to install, or have installed, the latest electrical gadgets such as a remote-controlled garage door, or you may simply be out too often to care that much! You may like bright colours such as electric blue or orange, or you may prefer an almost minimalist décor. Pictures may be futuristic, inventive, or just plain strange! If a person comes through your door and does not find something to surprise and intrigue them, then you are probably not living in your Aquarian ideal.

Your Inner Child Yours is an enquiring, eternally-curious inner child and its favourite question is 'Why?'

Gemini You need to be eternally finding things out. Make sure there is plenty in your life that is mentally stimulating, that you have puzzles to solve and ideas to explore. You need to be communicating – this frees something within you – so ensure there are plenty of opportunities in your life for chatter, but keep an eye on where this is going so you don't descend into trivia in order to escape emotional pain. Your hunger for knowledge must be fed so that you can be inventive and productive. You need variety and stimulation – try social clubs, anything that gets you moving from place to place, the Internet, chat-rooms, plenty of periodicals – but always ask yourself where this is leading you. Ditch what isn't really satisfying, however varied it may be.

Libra You need to be making things beautiful and creating harmony. Make sure there is plenty in your life that satisfies your thirst for art. Even if you are not particularly artistic, you will need to create harmony. This 'inner child' needs to be able to play the diplomat or make something look nice. Don't talk yourself out of doing pleasant things because you feel you have no talent. You need to be relating to people in all sorts of ways and playing with the nuances in a light and cultured way. You need also to play with being 'devil's advocate' because you like to see all sides of things. You may need to experiment with different forms of partnership and the varying ways in which people can inter-relate. You need company to be at your most creative but you need to remember that however much you compromise, you won't be satisfied if you compromise yourself.

Aquarius You need to be an individual. Make sure there is plenty in your life that gives you the opportunity to find out what it means to be different, because in this way you will be stimulated to be inventive and resourceful. You feel good if you can find new ways of doing things and you do this best in a friendly, accepting environment where your talent for putting the cat amongst the pigeons brings surprise and stimulation to others rather than consternation and condemnation. You need to feel that you are making a meaningful contribution to society and this will get your creativity going. What would you like to join? Resist the temptation to be a rebel without a cause – you aren't going to feel good if you do, or make the difference that you want to make. Work at accepting your slightly perverse but charming inner child and balance independence with good company, because you need both.

Air Sign Moon Children These children are even more full of questions than most and they shouldn't ever be fobbed off. If you don't know the answer, say so, and sort out a time when you can find out together. They are quite argumentative, but this isn't intended to be a challenge and they should not be told 'Don't argue'. Rather they should be encouraged to discuss and debate where possible. They also need to be encouraged to admit their feelings – if they feel jealous of their little sister they may feel especially unacceptable because of it and need to realise that 'nasty' feelings don't mean they are a nasty person. These children benefit from being able to talk early and if this is held up for some reason they may feel especially frustrated – every attempt should be made to communicate with them.

They need lots of books and interactive toys to stimulate the mind. They need to be out and about and will love to mix with as many friends as they can. They will benefit from being included in adult conversation as early as possible, thus developing good manners and social skills.

Air Moon Intuition   These Moons are in contact with the ether and may pick up on lots of things. However, being prone to intellectualise, they may regard this as irrelevant, or dissect it. Also it is hard for them to distinguish what is important in all the 'white noise' there may be inside their heads. If you have an Airy Moon you may be especially good at telepathy and find you just know what people are thinking. Try some of the following ideas to develop your intuitive side.

★ Practise telepathy by sitting opposite a friend and trying to 'send' them a colour or shape, such as a star or circle. You can do this over the phone, or at pre-arranged times when you are apart from someone close to you.

★ Try automatic writing – what 'writes itself' when you hold the pen in the hand you do not normally use for writing and close your eyes?

★ How often do you know what someone is going to say before they say it? Make a note of this.

★ How often do you guess who is on the phone when it rings? Learn to exercise this and trust it.

★ Consider learning a divinatory system such as numerology or graphology.

Air Moon Stressbusters   Airy Moons may be subject to overload of information or of contact with other people, and they can become overwrought. When you are stressed, your head may feel very full, and yet empty of anything that matters. You need to re-establish constructive flow of ideas.

★ Fresh air is especially therapeutic to you as it will clear your head.

★ Talk to an understanding friend who you know will calm you.

★ Have an interesting discussion on a subject other than what is distressing you.

★ Say a special mantra, chant or poem.

★ Occupy your mind with a puzzle, or distract yourself with a good book.

★ Like the Fire Moons, you may find motion soothing.

★ Find something beautiful to gaze at or be with.

★ Turn on the TV or radio for a while.

Your Comfort Zone

Gemini ★ Make sure your work and social commitments give you a feeling of freedom.

★ Always ensure that you have plenty of sources of information around you, such as the media, books and magazines.

★ You will need a telephone at all times, but should ensure that this doesn't result in you feeling bombarded.

★ Whatever you are doing, you need to be able to come and go as you please or you may become ill.

★ Travelling may soothe you.

★ You hate it if everything stays the same, so make sure your life has plenty of variety.

★ Life is about satisfying your curiosity – so go on, poke your nose in!

Libra ★ It's beauty – or it's cruelty! Surround yourself with the lovely!

★ Avoid strife – it will make you feel ill. Create peace of all kinds whenever and wherever you can.

★ Make sure you always have something attractive to look at – such as a vase of flowers – wherever you sit.

★ Look for people to charm – it does wonders for you – and them!

★ Remember you do not have to be alone to be an individual – company is natural to you!

★ Take care of your grooming – do not let yourself be hurried out of this. You will feel ill-at-ease if you do.

★ Smile – everyone else will smile too, and it will be reflected back at you. Bliss!

Aquarius ★ Arrange your surroundings in the way you like, however unorthodox. Who says you can't have a picture on the ceiling?

★ Unusual routines may suit you, for instance eating at one in the morning. But be careful to ensure this is really good for you, not just being different for the sake of it.

★ Make sure you have emotional and physical room to breathe, but don't distance yourself because you fear intimacy – you too need contact.

★ Atmospheres of tension and conflict will make you very uneasy because you feel at ease where things are civilised – so keep to them where possible.

★ A wide circle of friends is essential to you.

★ You feel good if you have a cause or wider purpose outside yourself, so look for this.

★ ✶ *Water Sign Moons*

Water sign Moons are the most emotional. However, while the Sun in a Water sign often makes for someone who is very conscious of the emotional realm, if you have a Water Moon you are more likely to get immersed in your own feelings, although you can be very nurturing and caring. Your comfort is in being needed and family bonds or their equivalent may be where it's at for you. You need to feel 'held' and contained. At times your feelings are overwhelming, and while you are not as subject to tantrums and passions as the Fire signs, you may find it almost impossible to stand back and get a perspective on your emotions.

It is very important that you meet your needs in a healthy way. This means that you should acknowledge they are needs, of a child-like and intense kind, and that is fine. Unlike the Air signs, you tend less to rationalise your feelings but you may fall into manipulative habit-patterns to get what you need, rather than being up-front. You are capable of creating an atmosphere of gentleness, calm and acceptance, and you may be content with the wordless – you just 'know' what is in the air and you don't need to express it or have it expressed. You pick up on atmospheres and the things other people are feeling and you may respond to this almost without realising that you are doing so. Generally you are looking for ways to get close, to blend in and attach. You probably do not feel comfortable in impersonal situations – you like the cosy and the familiar and you can feel 'okay' with someone, whatever their views and aims in life, as long as they will make you a cuppa, give you a cuddle and be nice to you. Yours is a very sensitive Moon and you can be very deeply hurt. Also you have a very long memory! It may be especially hard to leave behind hurtful things that have happened in the past and if your childhood was unhappy you will carry this emotional baggage with you. Of course, the good side to this is that you are less apt to rationalise experience like the Fire and Air signs, or go for substitutes like money, like the Earth signs. However, you may be very chained to ways of feeling and relating that are not necessarily in your best interests. You are at your best in situations where you can be deeply sympathetic and empathic, and also where your dreams can flourish. You can be very intuitive about those close to you, especially in regard to their emotional and physical welfare.

Water Moon Décor The important thing for you is that the place should be cosy, welcoming and private. You will want your home to accommodate close friends and family and will give a picture, photograph or ornament pride of place because of family associations. Gentle colour schemes please you and you may find blues and greens very soothing. Probably you favour furniture of a homely type, and a familiar old chair will have charm because you can remember Granny sitting in it, even if the stuffing is coming through! Tidiness may not be very important to you – or at least not important enough for you to overcome your hoarding instincts! You may love plants and flowers, and pictures of familiar scenes, although some dreamy, fantasy prints or prints on mirrors may appeal. You like lots of family photos around you.

Cancer You are the most homely of all, and your nest will need a family feel, even if you live on your own. A rambling old place may suit you best because you need plenty of places to put all the things you collect! Pictures that appeal to you may be seascapes or even moonlit scenes, but you will also like to have plenty of family photos. You like flowing lines – no sharp corners or handles. Draped covers, soft rugs and big cushions are your style and the colours you choose are likely to be gentle silvers, greens, blues and coral pink for warmth. Generally you are green-fingered, and your house plants will be luxuriant, bringing the natural world into your living-room. Ornaments may be memorabilia and things the children have made. You like to walk into a room and feel embraced.

Scorpio This is the most minimalist of the Water signs and you may pare things down so you feel less exposed – for having a multitude of possessions to care for makes you feel vulnerable. You need privacy, so you may favour thick curtains and dark colours, such as dark greens, browns, wine red and possibly black. You like unusual artefacts that appeal to you because they are emotionally evocative, although they may make others feel uneasy. When you look at a room you like to feel it will protect you completely. Like Cancer Moon, you love to have family photos and heirlooms although if your family has upset you, you will expunge all of this. Some of you scorn comfort as if to prove you can do without it, but others relish the luxury of sinking into an armchair that conceals you. Leather fabrics may appeal and pictures may be very simple and ordinary, as you may not wish to expose your tastes by hanging them on the walls!

Pisces This is the most fantastical of the Water signs! You may want your home to be very special, but it may be quite hard for you to choose décor because so many effects seem enticing. You would like to reside in a faerie castle if possible! When you go into a room you like to feel enchanted and uplifted. As with Cancer Moon, blues and greens may appeal, also purple and silver. Pictures may be whimsical, or family portraits. You may choose something like a water-feature or a fish-tank to give a bit of shimmer and magic. However, feeling safe and private is also very important to you and you can become anxious about locks and alarms. Like Cancer Moon, you often choose ornaments that remind you of good times and nice people and you hate to get rid of something familiar. And like Cancer Moon, your plants love you. Keep as much opportunity for change in the home as possible, for although you like the familiar, you also like something different. You may want to move furniture around, and change curtains and covers.

Your Inner Child Inside you there is a very sensitive little person indeed who needs caring for at all times if you are to function at your best.

Cancer You are capable of being a real infant! You need plenty of healthy support so you don't fall into self-pity. Make sure you have your self-nurture structure well in place at all times, so that it is there when you need it. You need someone to turn to when times are rough or you stop being able to do what you do so well – care for other people. You need a secure home, so make this a priority. Insurance will help, too. Counselling is something that will support you, and you should choose something constructive with a sympathetic counsellor rather than deep forms of therapy which will take you on endless inner swamp-trips. Your inner child needs care, so always attend to your creature needs, your stores of food, your heating, your bed. Always make sure that you put the needs of your inner child first, because this will (a) keep you from manipulating, and (b) set up a positive cycle where you feel good enough to nurture others. This in turn makes you feel nurtured, which makes you feel able to care for others more, and so on.

Scorpio You may be a difficult child! In the first place your needs are intense and in the second place you aren't about to admit to them! Coax your inner child by giving yourself a little of what you need in the way of closeness, and once you feel comfortable with this, you can have a bit more. Explain to other people that you are protecting yourself and holding back, for this is a positive statement and won't expose you like saying 'I'm scared and so needy'! Look below the surface, let that inner child pry and probe – the more you know, the more you are likely to feel able to reach out for what you need. Whodunnits and mysteries will appeal. This can be a turbulent, sulky and desirous little person who needs lots of patience before you feel safe to give and receive love – but that's the goal!

Pisces   Yours is a whimsical and unpredictable inner child. This 'child' needs some fairy stories in life and you need to give it some enchantment so that it can feel this world is an attractive enough place to settle into and to be creative within. There isn't any point going about the old nine-to-five routine and then wondering why that inner Pisces Moon feels all out of sorts and miserable. You need time to dream and drift, in order to make contact with the inspiration within. Not meeting the escapist needs of this inner child can result in unhealthy 'escape' through drink and drugs. Seek supportive relationships that are not symbiotic – this child will 'lose' itself willingly in order to be wanted, but then cannot find the creative satisfaction of really bringing something special into life. Explore arts and crafts and things like film and photography, drama and dressing up.

Water Sign   These may be sweet and loveable, but can also be moody and impossible to
Moon   console or reach at times. If your Water Moon child does not like a person or
Children   place, respect this, for with their powerful instincts they may be sensing something very important. Security and love, which are essential of course for all children, need to be especially strong with this one. They will pick up on every emotional undercurrent in the family and will learn to manipulate sooner rather than later. They may also feel disturbed and have bad dreams. Always be open about your feelings so that they can understand them, and be open about their own. In this way they will feel able to get their needs met openly. Never scorn their dreams and fantasies – encourage them to build on them. Let them know you understand their fears. However, encourage them to find their own ways of coping with scary situations – not by leaving them to fight their own battles, but by encouraging them to explore how they can best deal with things, in a way that will work for them. A Water sign Moon who has learnt self-protection is one who will always be secure, and make others feel the same.

Water Moon   The intuition of Water Moons is in the realm of feeling. You may know what
Intuition   other people are feeling (different from what they are thinking and often very different from what they are saying!), but you may react to this almost without realising you have picked up the intangible. There is also a danger that you may confuse what you feel with what you intuit. If you have a Water Moon then it is in the feeling realm that you need to start.

★ Take special note of your own feelings, needs and desires first, then you are best placed to separate these from intuition.

- ★ Ask yourself what other things you feel, that do not belong to you. Do you really feel sad at the moment, or is it your friend who is down?
- ★ Your dreams will be especially revealing so you should get into the habit of noting these down.
- ★ If you feel you have a particular psychic gift, you may like to train as a medium, for re-uniting people with their loved ones who have passed on will satisfy you greatly.
- ★ Skills such as palmistry may appeal, where you can touch the other person when you are practising.
- ★ Try scrying with a bowl of water and a silver coin or piece of jewellery in the bottom (see Chapter 5).

Water Moon Stressbusters   You Water Moons get most stressed by other people and their demands and feelings. You need a place of safety to which you can retreat.

- ★ Carry with you a piece of crystal into which you can gaze and enter the world within. Take this out and look into it occasionally.
- ★ Grab a few moments on your own.
- ★ Imagine you are beside a flowing stream that is taking all the tension and emotion away.
- ★ Take a drink of water, and/or dab some on your face and neck.
- ★ Give or get a big hug from someone.
- ★ Have a cuppa with a friend.
- ★ Take out a photo of a special person or place and look at it for a moment.
- ★ Overwhelmed by negative feelings? Light a candle and look at the dancing flame.

Your Comfort Zone

Cancer
- ★ Your may hang on to that 'zone' for dear life, but is this real comfort or 'for auld lang syne'?
- ★ Remember that your true needs may not be met by people being dependent on you, or vice versa.
- ★ Make sure you have the best and safest home you can procure.
- ★ Make sure you have plenty of good food, but avoid comfort-eating.
- ★ Caring for something or someone makes you feel good, but make sure it is healthy and reciprocal. Try to avoid being over-possessive because you can never own someone else's feelings.

★ Look for people and situations that support the adult in you, too.

★ Be your own best friend and carer – only you can understand your needs.

Scorpio ★ Privacy is a must so make sure you can get it whenever the need strikes.

★ Avoid debt – you will hate the lack of control.

★ The only way to get sexual and emotional needs met is to be up-front – sorry, but that's life! Other methods may seem to work for a while, but….

★ Trust that intuition – it will tell you who is safe to let close (but don't confuse intuition with suspicion).

★ Because you can be a little obsessive, cope with this by putting your energies into something very worthwhile.

★ You need intensity – settle on the price you are going to pay for it and make sure it is a fair one.

★ Don't bother over much with people who can't give you the deep interaction and the understanding you need.

Pisces ★ Remember that what gives you the greatest feeling of being protected is being part of something more meaningful than the ego – i.e. the spiritual. However, this should support your identity, not dissolve it.

★ Explore different forms of spirituality – this does not have to be of the conventional kind – for it will give your life meaning.

★ Your imagination will always provide you with an internal home.

★ If decisions are difficult, take time alone to listen to that inner voice.

★ Somewhere in your life there needs to be a touch of magic, where you can go and feel close to the Otherworld, listen to music and dream.

★ Don't be afraid of what is 'different' because the day-to-day may never satisfy you.

★ ⭒ ★ Earth Sign Moons

Yours is the most tactile and grounded of the Moon elements. To you, comfort is what you feel with your body. This means that you may be very good at looking after yourself physically. However, it also means that it can be hard for you to look beyond the material for your comfort and you may become hidebound, unimaginative and prone to erect your own barriers.

It is important to you to feel 'okay' on the physical plane and your main need is to feel secure. Money and sex are likely to be very important to you, and you need to have control over these aspects of life. You are less likely than the other elements to become a prey to fears and fantasies – although Virgo Moon may fuss over health issues. However, matters of physical comfort loom very large to the point where your whole life can be ruined by an uncomfortable bed! The plus side to this is that you can quite easily go out and get a new bed, whereas meanings to life and new partners are harder to come by! In general you are a simple individual and very basic things make you feel good – or bad! Routine is a favourite with you and you need to be especially careful that any routine is a good one as you will not readily change it once it is established. Rather like the Fire sign Moons, you feel good when you are engaged in some sort of action, but yours is likely to be of a much more basic and constructive sort – none of that rushing around and getting all fired up! You like to feel that your feet are planted on solid earth and you tend to instinctively check out people, places and situations for their reliability and their usefulness. This does not mean that you have no feelings, for you are very aware of the physical comfort of other people. However, you feel there is no point emoting over things that are going nowhere or getting involved in what is not going to produce anything in your life. You readily pick up on the body language of other people and may know when they are in pain, feeling full, hungry or unwell, or full of life. Yours may be a healing touch because you have a strong connection with the Earth. The intangible may make you a bit uneasy – what has that got to do with feeling at home? However, your intuition may be very sound because it is focused and very simple.

Earth Moon Décor

Now we're talking sensible, serviceable and – of course – comfortable. You prioritise the useful and may have little patience for anything that is purely ornamental, although you have a great sense of colour, form and texture, and will want those senses to be satisfied. Durable fabrics, sturdy wood, comfortable chairs and a bed that nurtures your spine are essentials! It is more important to you to make sure the drains are working properly than to choose the right colour carpet, but still you have a respect for beauty and will usually combine colours attractively, but rarely imaginatively. You like pictures of natural landscapes. Colours that appeal are likely to be natural shades such as beige, cream and brown. Your home should be a place of comfort, security and shelter. You like to have all the things you find useful readily to hand and you like to be organised, although tidiness itself may not bother you, as long as you can go about what you want to do untrammelled. You like to welcome guests with some real creature comforts and yours is the best cuppa, the fruitiest cake – and the finest wine!

Taurus Taurus is the most grounded of all, but also the most appreciative of beauty. Taurus decor may show a touch of the sumptuous because you like rich fabrics and the comfort of deep upholstery. You are the most tactile of the Moon signs, very aware of the 'feel' of carpet pile or chair covers. You may like rich blues, turquoise and rose pinks as well as natural colours and you may have an eye for art, choosing lovely paintings. You like to walk into a room and feel supremely comfortable. You will not choose anything purely for its appearance for you like things to last – your tastes rarely alter and you like the familiar. Like Cancer Moon, you may hang on to that old chair but only if it is kind to your limbs. Ornaments may be chosen with an eye for their artistic quality, but you will not like to be cluttered.

Virgo Yours is the tidiest of the Moon signs! To please you a room needs to be well-organised so you can walk into it and feel that the world is a manageable place after all! You are aware of the therapeutic qualities of a room, so you will not want to have sun in your eyes (because of headaches) or to feel the atmosphere is stagnant. Upholstery should be to orthopaedic standard. You may prefer pine to deep-stained wood and you are good with smaller plants such as herbs, which you tend painstakingly. You like everything to 'feel nice' and while you don't luxuriate quite like Taurus you detest anything scratchy that catches on things, so no unfinished wood or frayed curtains – ugh! You may favour greens and browns, and you like your lay-out to be sensible, with a place to put your coffee-mug. You like a change every so often, mostly because you are searching for the perfect way to set things out and never feel you have found it! For you, pictures are best small and detailed studies, perhaps of plants. You prefer ornaments you can use, so lovely china may appeal.

Capricorn This is the most utilitarian of the Moon signs. Your tastes are traditional, you insist on the durable and what things look like is often secondary to whether they 'do the job'. What is the point of that carved hall-stand if it isn't big enough for your coats? You aren't too bothered by clutter as long as you know where to find the things you need. You may favour browns and creams and you also insist on comfortable chairs, although you will be best pleased if they have been in the family for generations. Pictures that please you are likely to be homely landscapes, and like Cancer Moon you find it hard to throw out Mum's old chipped pot – but unlike Cancer Moon you may have to justify yourself by finding a use for it. You like to walk into a room and know that it is going to serve your needs and enable you to do what you need to do. You may well want space at home for stuff from work. Once you have chosen something you aren't bothered with changing it, unless it proves unserviceable. Ornaments please you if they have associations with the past and, like Virgo Moon, you prefer to be able to use them.

Your Inner Child
Within you there is a very pragmatic little person, very aware of bodily needs, but who may get bogged down in them.

Taurus
You need three things – security, security and security! You need first and foremost to know there is money in the bank, food in the cupboard and a sensible routine in place. You also need warmth, a cosy home and nice things to look at, to feel and to listen to. It's all very simple indeed. If, and only if, these requirements are met, your inner child can show you the way to being very creative. This can be an artistic placement, liking to get 'hands on' experience of something. You need contact with the Earth, and also to feel safe enough to let yourself take some risks. This inner child can be greedy and lazy, it has to be said, and food and creature comforts can be a substitute for living a fuller life. Admitting there are things you need that are not completely material or controllable (like the love of another person, or an ideal in life) and realising that you can't hold on to everything for ever, can enable you to plug into the deeper parts of yourself. Try any form of art or craft, gardening, music and also dance.

Virgo
You need to be self-sufficient and uncontaminated. This inner child holds back, wanting to be in control, and can be quite nervous and picky. This is the most analytical of the Earth sign Moons and you need to feel you understand before you can go forward. Nurture this inner child by finding out the whys and wherefores, only going as far as is useful and not becoming preoccupied with pulling things apart and destroying them to see how they work! All your feelings are valuable because they are part of the unique tapestry that is 'you' – they do not have to be worthwhile in any other sense, or even comprehensible. Get involved in practical, organisational things that make you feel productive, such as DIY, charity or communal work, organising events, etc. But be aware that less is more and that you may be able to keep tabs better on modest concerns. Nourish yourself with the healthy things you know you love and realise that imperfection is perfection, because it makes you human!

Capricorn
This inner child doesn't want to be a child at all, but an old person! Capricorn Moon wants to be able to cope with anything and will have got the message

that big boys and girls don't cry, however sympathetic a family they have come from. This inner child needs structure, routine and a timetable – give yourself enough of this but not so much that you believe it is the only thing that counts, because it isn't. Work may be all-important and you may measure your worth by your productivity, but be careful whose standards you use here. If this inner child feels sufficiently secure, you should be able to create your own meaning-ful standards. This inner child very readily feels judged and locks up their feel-ings in case they are unacceptable to others and so make them feel vulnerable. Stop trying so hard. Remember that you will be stronger if you face your feel-ings rather than denying them. Get yourself a plan of action and take small steps on your path each day – apart from that, let the inner child out to play.

Earth Sign Moon Children

These are very aware of their physical senses. There is no point in trying to dis-tract them when they are thirsty, hungry or uncomfortable and it is best to plan ahead to ensure that you can easily meet their physical needs. They are very tac-tile and may be reassured by cuddles and touching. It is very important to them to be able to touch things – but we keep telling children not to touch! Earth sign Moon children feel reassured by knowing how things feel. All children put things readily to their mouths but for children with Earth sign Moons it may be very important to taste everything, even the furniture and the cat! It is especially important to lock up anything poisonous, although they are rarely as quick and impulsive as Fire sign Moons. They are also very aware of their own bodies and may like to touch and explore themselves and other children. Taurus Moon chil-dren may be keen to experiment with sex as soon as they reach puberty. The worst thing one can do for an Earth sign Moon is to make them feel guilty about any-thing physical. Food needs to be kept in balance and not used as a reward. Needless to say, no child should be made to eat everything on their plate but for Earth sign Moons this may be especially bad, because it disrupts their own strong instincts for what their bodies need. This child will guide you as to how they should be nurtured physically, because they are aware of their bodies. However, they may need encouragement to use their imaginations and experiment with life.

Earth Moon Intuition

You may regard intuition as not very important, or conversely you may be aware of its sound benefits. You are intensely aware and 'present' in the moment and the place where you are and this means you may quite readily pick up on things that are on the borderline of the physical. While the Fire sign Moons are speculating and preoccupied, it may well be the Earth sign Moon that actually sees the ghost of Uncle Bertie on the stairs. Also you have a way of knowing things in your bones. Sometimes you will know something because you feel physically ill or well.

★ Take special note of your body. How does it feel? Is there a reason for it to feel like this or are you 'picking up' something?

★ Understand that intuition is valuable and useful and can give you information about life that can make you more comfortable.

★ You may feel a special affinity with plants – touch the plant. How do you feel? How do you think the plant feels?

★ Exploring something Earth-based like dowsing may appeal, especially if it helps you to find things you have lost!

★ You may find it fun to experiment with traditional folk divinations like tea-leaf reading.

★ A hands-on skill like psychometry, where you try to pick up impressions from objects, may appeal to you.

Earth Moon Stressbusters   Earth Moons get stressed by material concerns, especially money and security issues. Try any of the following ideas.

★ Have a massage – tactile things soothe you. If you can't get someone else to do this, then massage your own feet with peppermint lotion.

★ Use scent as a soother – e.g. lavender oil heated in a burner.

★ Have a nice meal but not if your stomach is churning. Have nourishing food – not a whole box of chocolates!

★ Sex will take your mind off all that stuff (although Virgo and sometimes Capricorn may be too preoccupied with their jobs).

★ Going about your routines will reassure you.

★ A steady walk with your feet making solid contact with the Earth will be therapeutic for you.

★ Gardening and contact with plants is a great unwinder.

★ Put some music on and tidy up.

Your Comfort Zone

Taurus ★ Don't confuse comfort with indulgence, because that can actually make you very uncomfortable.

★ Concentrate on your true needs and take steps to satisfy them. Avoid laziness and overeating as compensation.

★ Make your boundaries clear – if you are too placid it will be worse later on.

★ Let other people make you comfortable – you don't have to do it all yourself.

★ Consider changing your routines sometimes. 'The way it's always been done' may no longer be the best for you.

★ Never feel guilty about sensual enjoyment – you need it!

Virgo ★ Your zone may be quite narrow – define it with care and ensure your possessions are safe and tidy.

★ Explain gently and carefully to others what you need. Show you also respect their comforts.

★ Try tidying up as a form of therapy – there's no need to talk yourself out of it.

★ You love being clean, so treat yourself to baths and showers with high quality lotions containing natural ingredients.

★ Look after other people and get them sorted – this makes you feel worthwhile.

★ Develop some practical skills such as gardening or home remedies – this will make you feel satisfied.

Capricorn ★ Be careful not to spend too long organising your environment for there is a limit to how far this is useful, or possible.

★ Reduce your needs to the bare minimum to feel the most secure. Control will then be easier, but be realistic about what you can control and what you cannot.

★ Think about your real needs; there may be more to them than work and money!

★ Create your own standards as distinct from those of your family, friends or work.

★ Finding out how to free that inner child is a serious business – study hard!

★ ⋅ ★ *Bringing the Moon into your Home*

You may have been inspired by the Moon sign information on décor to revamp your living space. If so and you would like to make the Moon more of a general presence in your home, you can try the following ideas:

- ★ A fish tank, especially if filled with silver fish
- ★ An indoor fountain
- ★ Silver plates and ornaments
- ★ The use of pale blues, creamy whites, deep blues, sea greens, violet and purple in your décor and soft-furnishings (these could include black tones in cushions and ornaments)
- ★ Lots of flowing shapes and designs, avoiding sharp corners where possible
- ★ Paintings and prints that include the Moon, the sea or Moon-ruled items and plants such as willow trees (*The Weary Moon* by Edward Robert Hughes is an example of a true lunar painting)
- ★ Crystals and Moon-ruled stones such as chalcedony and moonstone – the larger the better
- ★ Crystal and silver bowls
- ★ Ornaments shaped like the Moon or with a lunar design
- ★ Goddess figures
- ★ Flowering white plants
- ★ Lunar designs on mugs and plates
- ★ White and/or silver candles on display
- ★ Gardenia, eucalyptus, lemon balm, jasmine, sandalwood or myrrh fragrances in an oil burner
- ★ Dreamy music, perhaps including the sounds of whales and dolphins and the sea
- ★ Soft, sensuous fabrics, squashy cushions, deep-pile carpets.

When you are considering your home comforts, please bear in mind that we are working here with a lot more than décor! If you create a lunar haven, you will be making a space that has a potent effect on you. Bedrooms are good places for some lunar energies, but a room where you need to think clearly or entertain guests in a vibrant way will be 'deadened' by too much Moon. Also be aware of your needs in life. Are you a driven person, caught up in the rat race, who needs to learn to relax at home? Then you need more of the Moon's influence. If you lack vitality, then the reverse may be the case. This is quite a complex matter, because, for instance, if you *are* very tense you won't be able to switch off straight away, and lots of Moon influences around you could make you irritable and moody. Make any changes gradually and monitor their effect on you and those you live with.

★ ∴ ★ *Live-in Moons*

It is when we live with a person that we become most conscious of their Moons, because these show in their habits and reactions. Because the Moon sign is a matter of instinct, it is more difficult to observe Moon sign than Sun sign preferences. However, it is always possible to find common ground!

Aries/Aries You are going to compete and fight but there will be much that you share. This won't stop you getting annoyed, however.

Do ★ Have a good fight and laugh about it.
★ Have shared interests and quests.
★ Find something you can fight together, on the same side!

Don't ★ Get violent – ever!
★ Pretend you don't need each other.
★ Compete about freedoms and individuality.

Aries/ Taurus Taurus will wind Aries up just by being there because they can be so immobile! However, these signs can complement each other.

Do ★ Find something you can construct together.
★ Separate out the domestic duties for your preferences will differ.
★ Make love, not war!

Don't ★ Settle for completely separate lives.
★ Refuse to talk about things.
★ Be mutually locked into your stubborn selfishness.

Aries/ Gemini This can be a pretty good combination, although Gemini may find Aries rather terse.

Do ★ Say what you mean at every opportunity.
★ Seek mental stimulation together.
★ Keep on the move in some fashion.

Don't ★ Keep snapping at each other – that isn't communication.
★ Refuse ever to wait for the other.

★ Be too impulsive about shared matters.

Aries/Cancer This is a toughie because Cancer is so sensitive and Aries is very blunt!

Do ★ Be warm and demonstrative with each other.
★ Respect each other's attributes and apportion the relationship.
★ Make sure you each have ways of taking care of each other.

Don't ★ Get the sulks – it's a killer!
★ Lie about your needs.
★ Be too selfish.

Aries/Leo These two Fire signs may get on well, but you need to respect each other.

Do ★ Have a demanding hobby you both share.
★ Respect each other's sense of importance and independence.
★ Compete in healthy ways.

Don't ★ Become abusive – you'll never forgive each other.
★ Ignore each other.
★ Put each other down in public.

Aries/Virgo You can wind each other up something dreadful yet you have so much to offer each other.

Do ★ Find something you can both complain about that isn't each other!
★ Have a constructive plan in life.
★ Negotiate fairness in the domestic sphere.

Don't ★ Argue all the time.
★ Pretend you don't need each other.
★ Try to be in control.

Aries/Libra You complement each other so well, but strain may be evident!

Do ★ Keep talking.
★ Have a shared ideal or goal.
★ Have shared friends.

Don't ★ Lead parallel lives.

★ Wince at each other's habits.

★ Destroy what matters to the other.

Aries/ You are both intense folk and can meet each other's needs if you will let your-
Scorpio selves!

Do ★ Be passionate with each other.

★ Face tantrums and make up afterwards.

★ Be open about your needs.

Don't ★ Sulk and withhold.

★ Try to control the relationship.

★ Plan to get your own back.

Aries/ You are great comrades, and you both have loads of enthusiasm for life.
Sagittarius

Do ★ Have shared adventures and challenges.

★ Plan your futures together.

★ Play together.

Don't ★ Lose your tempers too often.

★ Try to direct each other.

★ Deny your emotional needs.

Aries/ Here there is bound to be some struggle but if you pull together you'll
Capricorn achieve lots.

Do ★ Make a plan, but keep it flexible.

★ Make sure you are building something together.

★ Work hard, play hard.

Don't ★ Boss each other around.

★ Try to achieve separate things in the same space.

★ Ignore your real needs.

Aries/ You both need similar things but go about getting them in different ways.
Aquarius

Do ★ Give each other plenty of freedom.

★ Look for shared stimulation.

★ Have the same group of friends.

Don't ★ Have an 'open' relationship.

★ Be perverse for the sake of it.

★ Insist you are 'right'.

Aries/Pisces This is quite a challenge, but there are ways to make it work!

Do ★ Have shared dreams and wishes.

★ Look after each other in your different ways.

★ Be prepared to trust and share your feelings.

Don't ★ Play the martyr.

★ Be unrealistic about what you can achieve.

★ Make stupid demands on each other.

Taurus/ Taurus Two immovable objects – but at least you know where you both stand!

Do ★ Enjoy sensual pleasures together.

★ Make sure the sex is right.

★ Make sure the money is sorted.

Don't ★ Stop communicating altogether.

★ Get too set in your ways.

★ Refuse ever to compromise.

Taurus/ Gemini A difficult one this, but you each have what the other lacks.

Do ★ Keep the dialogue going.

★ Keep variety alive without disruption.

★ Have confidence in each other.

Don't ★ Become contemptuous of each other.

★ Evade real issues.

★ Try to be totally independent.

Taurus/
Cancer

This is a pleasant combination, but you are both a bit limpet-like!

Do ★ Find nice ways of looking after each other.

★ Plan your comforts together.

★ Build a lovely home.

Don't ★ Get moody and sulky.

★ Manipulate each other.

★ Be self-indulgent at the other's expense.

Taurus/Leo

Mutual stubbornness and some very different needs make this a challenge!

Do ★ Plan special things to do together.

★ Be very loving and attentive to each other.

★ Indulge each other.

Don't ★ Make demands and give ultimatums.

★ Spend each other's money.

★ Dig in your heels!

Taurus/
Virgo

You are both tactile and practical but you can still annoy each other!

Do ★ Create a comfortable and neat environment.

★ Organise your life.

★ Give each other massages.

Don't ★ Insist on routines that are separate.

★ Be so immersed in the practical that you forget each other.

★ Find yourselves with nothing to do.

Taurus/
Libra

You both love beauty, but in very different ways.

Do ★ Find forms of art and music you both enjoy.

★ Build a peaceful environment.

★ Compromise.

Don't ★ Both insist on your right to do nothing!

★ Indulge yourselves but not the other.

★ Keep taking the line of least resistance.

Taurus/
Scorpio

You are both so possessive – who owns whom?

Do ★ Try to meet each other's needs.

★ Tell each other where you are going and when you'll be back.

★ Make sure your sex-life is terrific!

Don't ★ Sulk and withhold.

★ Go looking through handbags and pockets.

★ Expect to control each other or the relationship.

Taurus/
Sagittarius

This is such a contrast, but actually there are common denominators.

Do ★ Find luxuries you both enjoy.

★ Join each other on a search for sensation.

★ Laugh a lot together.

Don't ★ Become contemptuous of each other's viewpoint.

★ Stop communicating.

★ Procrastinate.

Taurus/
Capricorn

You have lots in common, but it could get boring – so watch it!

Do ★ Work out the money together.

★ Have joint plans, especially practical ones.

★ Organise the household.

Don't ★ Withhold from each other.

★ Try to control the relationship.

★ Keep on with 'same old, same old'.

Taurus/
Aquarius

You each need the other's perspective but it might not be easy to see it!

Do ★ Find ways you can be socially useful together.

★ Respect each other.

★ Say what you feel – not physically, but emotionally.

Don't ★ Get stubborn and sulky.

★ Fly into a tantrum and throw everything away without thought.

★ Expect the other to conform.

Taurus/ Pisces Taurus can give form to Piscean dreams, but may also trample them.

Do ★ Sympathise with each other.

★ Create privacy together.

★ Get comfy-cosy as often as you can.

Don't ★ Decide you have nothing in common.

★ Have arguments about money.

★ Bring out the negative and dependent sides of each other.

Gemini/ Gemini There is plenty of talk, but are you saying what matters?

Do ★ Have time to listen as well as talk.

★ Read the same magazines and papers.

★ Go out to interesting places together, and meet interesting people.

Don't ★ Refuse to commit to each other.

★ Take delight in catching the other off guard.

★ Spar intellectually instead of having emotional contact.

Gemini/ Cancer You have very different needs, but there are ways to come to terms with this.

Do ★ Talk about feelings and work at different definitions.

★ Have change in your surroundings.

★ Be childishly playful together.

Don't ★ Give up trying to communicate.

★ Worry all the time.

★ Say, 'My feelings don't matter.'

Gemini/Leo You are both bright and breezy individuals, but Gemini may not give Leo enough commitment.

Do ★ Seek out entertainment you both enjoy.

★ Laugh together.

★ Discuss your opinions together.

Don't ★ Fail to respect each other's viewpoint.

★ Withhold affection.

★ Try to be too serious.

Gemini/
Virgo
You could run each other ragged, so step back every so often.

Do ★ Discuss and analyse everything.

★ Find shared intellectual or friendly pursuits.

★ Have pets.

Don't ★ Find fault with each other.

★ Reason away your need for each other.

★ Lose your integrity.

Gemini/
Libra
There are lots of similarities, but can you find depth in your relationship?

Do ★ Share a circle of friends.

★ Have lots of debate and discussion.

★ Co-operate.

Don't ★ Compare your relationship to other people's.

★ Always insist the other one decides.

★ Eternally compromise your real feelings to avoid strife.

Gemini/
Scorpio
This is one of the more difficult combinations so you will need to work at it.

Do ★ Find puzzles to solve together.

★ Explore life and experience.

★ See how your different skills dovetail.

Don't ★ Psycho-analyse each other.

★ Pretend you know everything about the other person.

★ Pry into each other's affairs.

Gemini/
Sagittarius
You are a great duo, although you will find each other tiring!

Do ★ Share a circle of friends.

★ Talk about your views and philosophies.

★ Give each other plenty of freedom.

Don't ★ Fall into the habit of contacting each other by notes on the fridge.

★ Rationalise everything.

★ Fail to speak of your real feelings.

Gemini/
Capricorn
You can form a good partnership or be a strain on each other.

Do ★ Make plans together.

★ Share work interests if possible.

★ Organise your lives in co-operation.

Don't ★ Worry each other.

★ Conceal your real needs.

★ Demand perfection.

Gemini/
Aquarius
You have loads in common, but how much do you really care?

Do ★ Keep open house for shared friends.

★ Formulate ideas and philosophies of life together.

★ Be inventive and open to change.

Don't ★ Try to be 'above it all' all the time.

★ Insist on being both 'free spirits'.

★ Make abrupt and unilateral changes.

Gemini/
Pisces
Change is the order of the day, but the 'changes' may be on different levels.

Do ★ Keep talking even if you seem at cross-purposes.

★ Share fantasy and whimsical ideas.

★ Keep your shared life full of variety and intrigue.

Don't ★ Try to pin each other down.

★ Make each other fret.

★ Refuse to face material circumstances.

Cancer/
Cancer
You are joined at the hip, but is it really that comfy?

Do
★ Cuddle each other lots.
★ Sympathise with each other's feelings.
★ Share family concerns.

Don't
★ Take on all the feelings of the other as if they were your own.
★ Depress each other.
★ Become a gruesome twosome by manipulating each other.

Cancer/Leo
This is not such a difficult mix as you might think.

Do
★ Be prepared to be kids together.
★ Protect each other in your differing ways.
★ Show each other lots of love and affection.

Don't
★ Vie for attention with each other.
★ Over-dramatise your feelings.
★ Pretend you don't need each other.

Cancer/
Virgo
You make a smooth duo although there can be drawbacks.

Do
★ Enjoy making your home as neat and clean as possible.
★ Find something you can take care of together.
★ Get into a productive routine.

Don't
★ Make each other anxious.
★ Fall into being petty.
★ Demand attention for your own aches and pains continually.

Cancer/
Libra
You both need to be in a partnership, but you define it rather differently.

Do
★ Be prepared to say 'I need you'.
★ Co-operate with and support each other.
★ Keep talking about your relationship.

Don't ★ Pretend that you don't need the other person.

★ Become too dependent on each other.

★ Say 'peace at any price'.

Cancer/ There is lots of shared understanding here, but is that going to make it easy?
Scorpio

Do ★ Create a private and comfortable home.

★ Commit to each other.

★ Be very close and cuddly.

Don't ★ Manipulate each other.

★ Sulk and give 'the silent treatment'.

★ Punish each other.

Cancer/ This is a difficult one, but there are always ways round problems.
Sagittarius

Do ★ Stimulate each other's imagination.

★ Be generous with each other.

★ Give each other encouragement.

Don't ★ Avoid issues.

★ Mislead each other.

★ Indulge in unhealthy escapism.

Cancer/ There is lots of mutual support available, but you may also get each other
Capricorn down.

Do ★ Build a solid and comforting home together.

★ Have good routines in the home.

★ Make each other feel emotionally safe.

Don't ★ Withhold from each other.

★ Pretend you don't need each other.

★ Judge each other by what you do rather than what you are.

Cancer/ You are poles apart in many ways, so willingness to co-operate is essential.
Aquarius

Do ★ Be consistent in how you deal with each other.

★ Develop a shared social life.

★ Be prepared to learn from each other.

Don't ★ Pretend not to need each other.

★ Refuse to engage in proper meaningful discussion.

★ Seek too much gratification separately, outside the relationship.

Cancer/ Pisces This is a mix made in Heaven, but the trick is to keep it there.

Do ★ Share your dreams and hopes.

★ Look for magic in life.

★ Sympathise with each other.

Don't ★ Try to out-manoeuvre and manipulate.

★ Tell lies.

★ Depress each other.

Leo/Leo These are two stars together, so who will shine the brightest?

Do ★ Show you appreciate and admire each other.

★ Play together.

★ Be warm and loving.

Don't ★ Put each other down – ever.

★ Try to beat your partner at their own game.

★ Insist on being boss.

Leo/Virgo You are very different people but you can complement each other.

Do ★ Make a plan in your joint life.

★ Aim for 'the best'.

★ Praise each other and be positive.

Don't ★ Criticise each other.

★ Try for one-upmanship.

★ Try to control the relationship.

Leo/Libra   You are two 'beautiful people' – will you have a ball together?

Do   ★ Enjoy art, beauty and theatre together.
     ★ Admire each other.
     ★ Find harmonious ways of asserting yourselves.

Don't ★ Overspend – or the coffers will be drained!
     ★ Have separate friends.
     ★ Insist on everything being wonderful all the time.

Leo/Scorpio   Here is pride and passion, so it needs effort to make it work.

Do   ★ Show your respect for each other.
     ★ Be passionate and full of feeling.
     ★ Have a great sex life.

Don't ★ Insist on controlling the relationship.
     ★ Have battles of will.
     ★ Sulk and withhold.

Leo/ Sagittarius   This is a cheerful combination of big-hearted enthusiasts.

Do   ★ Share lots of laughs.
     ★ Have adventures of all sorts together.
     ★ Find shared meanings in life.

Don't ★ Compete for superiority.
     ★ Insist on freedom.
     ★ Refuse to see the negative side.

Leo/ Capricorn   Both of you like a measure of status, but you need to work on other aspects.

Do   ★ Agree on shared goals.
     ★ Make sure your work patterns dovetail.
     ★ Find things to take pride in together.

Don't ★ Refuse to be vulnerable.
     ★ Find substitutes for expressing affection.

★ Have different standards.

Leo/ Aquarius There could be some troubles as you have a different take on what you need for comfort.

Do ★ Find ideals and causes you can both support.
★ Respect each other's individuality.
★ Be original together.

Don't ★ Be too proud to communicate.
★ Refuse to admit you need the other.
★ Insist on taking the lead.

Leo/Pisces This could be hard at times, but also enchanting.

Do ★ Find shared interests in drama and fantasy.
★ Talk about your dreams and wishes.
★ Share a sense of values and spirituality.

Don't ★ Become self-obsessed.
★ Over-idealise each other or the relationship.
★ Over-dramatise everything.

Virgo/Virgo This could either be a perfect match, or double trouble here!

Do ★ Create an environment that is orderly in a way that pleases you both.
★ Encourage each other.
★ Work together in some form.

Don't ★ Ever criticise each other.
★ Compete to see who can be ill the most frequently.
★ Nag and fuss.

Virgo/Libra Both of you long for perfection of a different sort.

Do ★ Find shared ideals and goals.
★ Share standards.
★ Enjoy excellence where you find it.

Don't ★ Spend time endlessly analysing your relationship.
       ★ Find faults.
       ★ Shift responsibility for decision-making onto the other party.

Virgo/ You can be comfortable together if you can find ways to relax.
Scorpio
   Do ★ Find mind-games and puzzles to do together.
       ★ Find shared tasks and challenges.
       ★ Analyse constructively.

Don't ★ Poke and probe too much at each other.
       ★ Try to organise and tie down the other party.
       ★ Be pessimistic.

Virgo/ These can find common ground but it is all too often shifting sand!
Sagittarius
   Do ★ Have lively debates.
       ★ Realise that you each have something to give the other.
       ★ Share tasks sensibly.

Don't ★ Procrastinate and dodge issues.
       ★ Go on the defensive.
       ★ Get edgy and impatient.

Virgo/ Standards are shared and there is plenty in common, but this relationship may
Capricorn not be warm unless you try to make it so.

   Do ★ Make a point of expressing affection.
       ★ Try to share work, or tasks.
       ★ Get organised with your lives.

Don't ★ Carp and criticise.
       ★ Be negative and erect obstacles.
       ★ Try to control everything and each other.

Virgo/ You both like to analyse life, but your priorities are very different.
Aquarius
   Do ★ Have shared schemes and plans.

★ Give each other space and independence.
★ Share scientific and exploring interests.

Don't ★ Get farther and farther apart.
★ Fail to see the need for deep emotion.
★ Stop having sex.

Virgo/Pisces Be kind to each other for you are both very sensitive in different ways.

Do ★ Keep your life as adaptable as possible.
★ Care for things together, such as pets.
★ Help and encourage each other.

Don't ★ Wind each other up.
★ Feed each other's worries and fears.
★ Escape into being ill.

Libra/Libra This could be a charm contest, but it isn't all love and peace.

Do ★ Find artistic and cultural things you both enjoy.
★ Surround yourselves with all the beauty you can afford (but not more!).
★ Share a wide circle of friends.

Don't ★ Keep trying to force the other to decide.
★ Avoid everything unpleasant.
★ Be relentlessly joined at the hip.

Libra/ Scorpio You were made to upset each other, but something has brought you together.

Do ★ Make love a lot.
★ Do something creative together.
★ Try to be honest about your needs and feelings.

Don't ★ Be afraid of each other.
★ Insist on fairness before affection.
★ Use sex as a substitute for closeness.

Libra/ Sagittarius   You are two cheery souls, made to live it up – but how much does it all mean?

Do
- ★ Share views and philosophies.
- ★ Celebrate together.
- ★ Seek out forms of entertainment you both enjoy.

Don't
- ★ Avoid important issues.
- ★ Intellectualise everything.
- ★ Be hypocritical.

Libra/ Capricorn   You both like to make a good impression, but there are few other similarities.

Do
- ★ Share standards of excellence.
- ★ Recognise each other's talents.
- ★ Make plans and structure your lives.

Don't
- ★ Refuse to show vulnerability.
- ★ Stop talking about anything that matters.
- ★ Compete for who can be most perfect.

Libra/ Aquarius   You are great mates and have lots in common, but feelings might be a bit cool.

Do
- ★ Have a wide shared circle of friends.
- ★ Have debates and discussions.
- ★ Share ideals.

Don't
- ★ Keep avoiding darker feelings at all costs.
- ★ Insist on meaningless politeness.
- ★ Ever betray the trust of the other party.

Libra/Pisces   This relationship could be a bit wishy-washy, but pleasant and peaceful.

Do
- ★ Have lots of shared dreams.
- ★ Sympathise with each other.
- ★ Keep each other good company.

Don't ★ Procrastinate and avoid major – and minor – decisions.

★ Be perpetually discontented that it isn't all utterly wonderful.

★ Be impractical and airy-fairy.

Scorpio/
Scorpio   Although you are very similar, this relationship could become a battle-ground if you aren't careful.

Do ★ Try very hard to express your feelings.

★ Work at making sure the sex is good.

★ Trust each other.

Don't ★ Withhold and manipulate.

★ Invade the other's privacy and secrets.

★ Try to be one jump ahead.

Scorpio/   You can complete each other's lives or make a complete disaster of them.
Sagittarius

Do ★ Take on challenges together.

★ Talk about your needs and try to understand each other.

★ Share spiritual ideals.

Don't ★ Insist on your own way.

★ Let each other down.

★ Try to outwit each other.

Scorpio/   You may be a pessimistic pair, but you have much in common.
Capricorn

Do ★ Have a solid structure to your lives.

★ Protect your privacy as a couple.

★ Face challenges together.

Don't ★ Keep looking on the black side.

★ Try to control each other.

★ Clam up and withhold.

Scorpio/
Aquarius   The differences between you are quite radical, but you can both be determined and focused.

    Do ★ Make a commitment to each other.
       ★ Look for original and inventive ways to do things.
       ★ Be honest about your needs.

  Don't ★ Avoid intimacy.
       ★ Get preoccupied with empty stimulation.
       ★ Deny each other the different freedoms you seek.

Scorpio/
Pisces   There is plenty in common here, although Scorpio can be a bit heavy for Pisces.
    Do ★ Have lots of cuddles.
       ★ Protect each other as much as you can.
       ★ Cherish those private times alone.

  Don't ★ Get suspicious.
       ★ Wallow in negative thoughts and emotions.
       ★ Make each other feel guilty.

Sagittarius/
Sagittarius   You are two explorers and philosophers together, but are you on the same journey?

    Do ★ Have plenty of debate about your beliefs.
       ★ Go on adventures together.
       ★ Cheer each other up and giggle.

  Don't ★ Encourage each other to go over the top.
       ★ Avoid commitment.
       ★ Focus on the future at the expense of the present.

Sagittarius/
Capricorn   This relationship will be a test for both of you, but you can pass it.
    Do ★ Allow yourselves to complement each other by taking care of separate areas.
       ★ Have joint aims and objectives.
       ★ Take a pride in each other's achievements.

Don't ★ Drift further and further apart.

★ Frustrate each other.

★ Despise each other's standards.

Sagittarius/
Aquarius
There is lots of common ground and mutual inspiration here, but you could be friends more than lovers.

Do ★ Find things that excite and motivate you both.

★ Support the same causes and projects.

★ Guard each other's independence.

Don't ★ Intellectualise the relationship.

★ Refuse to admit you need each other.

★ Avoid committing.

Sagittarius/
Pisces
This can work out well or it can be a disaster.

Do ★ Find shared dreams and beliefs.

★ Escape together in whatever ways you like.

★ Stimulate each other's imagination.

Don't ★ Drive each other to excesses, or take risks.

★ Lose contact with reality.

★ Lie to each other.

Capricorn/
Capricorn
You can get each other down big-style or help and support each other.

Do ★ Be constructive together.

★ Work out a timetable that suits you both and involves fun times.

★ Share your working lives if possible.

Don't ★ Repress and deny your needs.

★ Fear letting the other person close.

★ Tell yourselves it is just a 'marriage of convenience'.

Capricorn/
Aquarius You share many things, and differ on many also.

    Do ★ Respect each other's personal space.

       ★ Invent things together.

       ★ Find shared values and standards.

   Don't ★ Completely deny you have vulnerabilities and feelings.

       ★ Make changes without consulting the other person.

       ★ Pretend to be self-sufficient.

Capricorn/
Pisces Capricorn can make Pisces feel safe, yet alone at the same time.

    Do ★ Make a commitment to each other.

       ★ Be prepared to learn what the other needs.

       ★ Protect what is precious to you both.

   Don't ★ Play martyr.

       ★ See who can worry the most.

       ★ Depress and frighten each other.

Aquarius/
Aquarius You're such free spirits, it's a wonder you ever got together at all!

    Do ★ Share your idealism and visions for life and the world.

       ★ Be best mates.

       ★ Respect each other's independence without separating too far.

   Don't ★ Rationalise everything you feel.

       ★ Pretend you don't need each other.

       ★ Always insist on making any changes you feel necessary at any time.

Aquarius/
Pisces You have some things in common, but deep within you are on different planets.

    Do ★ Find something you both believe in, e.g. a charity.

       ★ Share friends and interesting pursuits.

       ★ Have a varied lifestyle.

Don't ★ Threaten each other's wellbeing and make each other feel unsafe.

★ Refuse to empathise.

★ Treat the other like an alien.

Pisces/Pisces Oh, if only things could be as wonderful as you both imagine! With two of you at it, they might!

Do ★ Share imaginative and magical things.

★ Make each other laugh.

★ Find healthy forms of escape.

Don't ★ Lie and evade issues.

★ Refuse to make decisions.

★ Cry all the time.

CHAPTER 4

MYTHS & MOONSHINE, DEITIES & DEMONS

Look for me by moonlight;
Watch for me by moonlight;
I'll come to thee by moonlight, though hell should bar the way
ALFRED NOYES, 'THE HIGHWAYMAN'

The Moon –
Goddess
or God?
You will have noticed that I have chosen to refer to the Moon as 'she' in this book, for reasons that will be come clear as we unpack the bundle of lunar lore. However, the fact of the matter is that in most ancient cultures, such as those of the Celts and the Egyptians, the Moon was seen as 'he'.

✶⋰✶ *Male Moon*

Although we can readily associate the Moon with the subconscious and the instincts – traditionally viewed as 'feminine' qualities – the Moon is also a very precise time-keeper. To early hunter-gatherer tribes, time-keeping may not have been essential, but with the advent of a more structured society and developments in agriculture, these properties of the Moon became valuable. Using the Moon to measure time involved the application of the intellect to something abstract, i.e. the phases of the Moon and matching them to the passage of time. Solar cycles are longer and less clearly definable (the Solstice, for instance, is hard to pinpoint within less than a week without some measuring equipment), but it was easy to see differences between the aspects of the Moon from night to night. This more 'logical' association of the Moon became more readily linked to Moon Gods than to Goddesses.

Many tribes once regarded the time-keeping male Moon as being the 'other husband' of women, responsible for making them pregnant. In these cultures the glorious Sun was, by contrast, the life-giving, all-powerful Goddess. Native Americans, the Australian Aborigines and the Japanese all had a God of the Moon, who was the husband of the Sun Goddess in more ancient times. The Japanese Moon God was called Tsukiyomi, husband of Amaterasu, the Sun, while the Aboriginal Moon God was Bahloo, husband of the Sun Goddess Yhi. The Persian Mah was a Moon God, as was the Inuit Igaluk.

Moon Gods

Thoth Thoth was a powerful and influential God in Ancient Egypt and the most clearly defined Moon God. He was depicted as an ibis, an ibis-headed man or as a baboon. He had powers of creation, for as an ibis he was said to have hatched the World Egg, from which all of life was born. By the sound of his voice he created four Gods in the guise of frogs and four Goddesses in the shape of serpents. This echoes the biblical 'In the beginning was the Word...' and reminds us that all of existence is, in fact, vibration. The eight deities continued the work of creating the world, by singing.

Some say Thoth rose out of primordial chaos at the beginning of time; others that he was the brother of Osiris. His wife was Ma'at, Goddess of truth and cosmic order, to which her husband gave manifestation. He was a God of measurement, and a Moon God. As the knowledge and understanding of humans grew, so did the attributes of Thoth, who became associated with wisdom, science, mathematics and architecture. He was the inventor of writing, scribe to the Gods and arbitrator of disputes. A story tells how Thoth found a way to bring together the Earth God Geb and the Sky Goddess Nut. (It is interesting that, to the Egyptians, the earth was male and the sky female.) These were brother and sister and their father, Ra, tried to separate them using the God of Air, Shu. He decreed that Nut should bear no children in any month of the year. Thoth felt sorry for the couple and so he played draughts with the Moon, winning a portion of her light. This he converted to five intercalary days. These were added to the 12 approximate lunar months of 30 days each, to make a total of 365. Nut could then bear children on five days of the year. This tale is, in fact, a dramatisation of the difficulties of fitting the lunar calendar into the solar one.

Although Thoth remained master of the Moon, he left it with a caretaker-Goddess 'Woman-light of the Shadows' and she looked after him whenever he visited. Thoth was the magical partner of Isis and was loyal to her and Osiris against the evil Set. He helped to judge the souls of the dead by presiding over the process of weighing against the feather of Ma'at, to see how truthful they were. Thoth was always peaceful and fair – a just and wise ruler. Thoth can be invoked for wisdom, magic, knowledge, justice and the ability to manipulate forces at our disposal.

Chandra Chandra was the Indian Moon God born in the time-before-time when the ocean churned. He was husband to the cow Goddess, Rohini (cows are associated with the Moon through their giving of milk), and his magical weapons were the bow and arrow.

Mah Mah was the Persian Moon-God and a ruler of Time.

Sin Sin was the Babylonian God of the Moon. He was a wisdom God and also a measurer of time, for the Babylonian calendar was lunar. He was known as the God with the deep heart that none could penetrate. As each month came to a close all the Gods came to him for a consultation and he would make decisions for them. He was the enemy of evil for his light illuminated the night, when people are most likely to be up to no good. Call on Sin for justice and equilibrium. He is seen as an old man with a beard the colour of lapis lazuli.

★ ⁚ ★ *Mother Moon*

In latter years, the Moon has been 'feminised'. 'She' is looked upon as seductive, mysterious and capricious. Called the 'Lesser Light' by the old astrologers, she has been seen as the 'weaker' feminine to the masculine of the Sun, reflecting his light and presiding over the less active night time and the functions of instinct and feeling. Modern astrologers also relate the Moon to our habits and reactions, our behaviour in the domestic sphere and our emotions. Not surprisingly, some feminists object to the 'weaker' Moon being regarded as female!

However, for most of us today it feels right to think of the Moon as feminine. In fact the word for 'Moon' is a feminine noun in Russian, Latin, French and Spanish. She echoes women's rhythms and fluctuating moods, in contrast to men's more linear approach. And there is really nothing 'inferior' about instinct, feeling, nurture and intuition! In fact this is just as necessary to a full life – and indeed survival – as the logical consciousness represented by the Sun. Women now are largely on the way to 'equality' in the developed countries and they can compete with men in a man's world. But largely it is just that – a *man's* world, based on the competitive tendencies of the male of the species. Women's wisdom and often more gentle perspective, their rhythms and needs, and their obligations as mothers and carers are still largely ignored. Women can be as successful as men but they do not always have their femininity respected, or even receive the recognition that it is important.

True femininity and the meanings and associations of the Moon are what we need to redeem. Daytime, with all its demands, its schedules, organisation and objectivity, is not superior to night, the time of instincts and dreams when we can more readily contact our inner nature. The Moon, ruling our inward tides, is not inferior to the Sun, ruling our dynamic nature – they are equally necessary and complementary. It is good to remember that a candle flame is scarcely visible in bright sunlight, but in moonlight it is bright and clear. Some things to which we may ordinarily be blind are revealed to our lunar, intuitive selves. At this point in history, it seems fitting to me that the Moon should be linked to femininity, and both given due respect!

The Greek Moon

The Greeks took much of their mythology from the Babylonians but they switched the genders of Sun and Moon, and their thinking has come down in part to us. The Moon was regarded by the Greeks as the crudest part of the Heavens, the last base of the soul before coming down to Earth to be reborn. The poor Moon was even seen as being linked to the processes of decay, for she waned and disappeared each month. The 'sub-lunary sphere' was the lowest place, far from the rarefied upper Heavens. So the Moon is a gateway to the soul. But the door swings both ways – we can contemplate the Moon and be uplifted and expanded in so many ways.

The Triple Goddess   The Moon is strongly linked to a very ancient concept of the Divine Feminine immortalised in artwork as far back as the Paleolithic Era in, for example, the cave paintings found at Cogul in North-Eastern Spain. This understanding of the Divine Feminine is also expressed in the form of the Triple Goddess. The Triple Goddess is Maiden, Mother and Crone, and in her all the phases of womanhood are honoured. The phases of the Moon, Waxing, Full and Waning, are obviously linked to Maiden, Mother and Crone, and Goddesses that personify each of these may be linked to the phase in question.

Here the Moon teaches us about the different aspects of the Feminine and that all are honourable and valuable. In Celtic mind-set, darkness comes before light, day begins at sunset, the year begins at the start of winter and the Crone comes before the Maiden. She is the heart of all wisdom and experience. She leads the way into the Mystery, from which the Maiden is reborn. But sadly, in our times the Crone receives scant honour. Older women are marginalised and are not respected for their wisdom and experience. In this we are cutting ourselves off from something that is intensely valuable and enriching, something that could give balance to our society.

In some traditions there is a fourth aspect to the Goddess, which is the Mystery itself. The Crone leads the way to this dark and ineffable Goddess who may be fearsome but who incubates life. She corresponds to the Dark-of-the-Moon.

These days, we don't really want to know about anything that isn't light or bright, but pretending that it doesn't exist just makes us more scared of it. It also means that whole areas of knowledge and awareness can be closed to us. Sometimes Paganism is criticised for the honour it pays to darker things. People say, 'There are enough bad things in life.' But giving them attention and their own place, really *looking* at them as opposed to running away, seeing the valuable and the sacred in them, helps us not only to deal with them but also to make the transformative passage from these 'darker' things into the new and the bright things to which they are the precursor. Without death there can be no rebirth. In her dark aspect, the Moon teaches us to honour darkness and even loss sometimes. She also teaches us that it does not go on forever!

Whilst ancient cultures may not have worked consciously with the Triple Goddess, she nevertheless appears to have been an instinctual concept, as many Goddesses had (or have) an explicit three-fold nature. For instance, the Greek Goddess Hera, wife to the Olympian monarch Zeus, is thought of primarily as a 'mother' Goddess, but at Stymphalus in Greece there were three temples for her worship: one to the child-Goddess, another to the wife-Goddess, and a third to the widow-Goddess. Another example of a tri-fold Goddess comes from the Hindu pantheon in the guise of Bhavani, who has three aspects. Similarly, the Chinese have a Buddhist triad called the Triple Pussa, which has links with Kuan Yin, the benevolent bodhisattva. In Voodoo, Erzulie is teamed as *La Maitresse* with *La Sirene*, or the Maid, and Gran Erzulie as the Crone.

The concept of the Triple Goddess can be discerned in many other cultures and religions, although often hidden – even in Islam there are three daughters of Allah, although the Koran describes them as 'empty names'.

As well as having three aspects that connect with Maid, Mother and Crone, Goddesses sometimes appear in groups of three, as seen the example of Hecate, Demeter and Persephone. In Norse myth there are the three Norns, in Greek tales the three Graces and even a three-times-three grouping in the nine Muses. The Celtic Goddess Brigit/Breed is often regarded as 'triple' in nature and the Celts, who tended her Sacred Flame for centuries in Ireland, are certainly believed to have worked with her three distinct aspects.

Moon Goddesses

Here is a selection of Moon Goddesses to inspire you.

Artemis This mighty maiden is often shown roaming the forests with her hounds. A Greek Goddess, she was wild, free and savage, setting her dogs onto any man who dared to spy on her nakedness and tearing him to pieces. But Artemis has other guises, and we see her also as the many-breasted Goddess of Ephesus, who personifies the fertility of the natural world in its awesome power. She was also the war Goddess of the Amazons.

Artemis really embodies all of the powers and energies of the Feminine, as she journeys through life. She contains many contradictions – a maiden who promotes promiscuity, an animal protector who is also a huntress. She was seen as a bear, a tree and the Moon herself. She was 'Lady of the Beasts' – embodiment of the primal force within the Greenwood. Hunters who pursued pregnant beasts feared her wrath, for she would slay them with her merciless arrows. Women in childbirth called upon her for protection. On nights of the Full Moon, her ecstatic followers would gather beneath the trees for an orgy of revelry and mating. Truly she represents natural law and the inexorable life within Nature. She gives us a link between bears and the Moon, for her name means 'bear' – these are instinctual and wise animals who know how to seek out herbs that will make them well. Dogs also are 'lunar animals' baying at the Moon, following their noses on the paths of instinct. Artemis is a Moon Goddess who helps us connect with nature at its primal core, to revel in it and to 'walk on the wild side'!

Diana Diana was the Roman counterpart of Artemis but is a tad more refined! This may be more apparent than real, for men fought for the privilege of being her priest, knowing they would eventually die at the hands of another contender. So Diana is also associated with that implacable dark Goddess wisdom that knows what must die, and when. Diana had her own Italian mythology in earlier times and may have been Goddess of the Sun as well as the Moon, for her name comes from the word for 'light'. She was the sky Goddess, always worshipped outdoors, and she ruled the earth too, as a giver of sovereignty and fertility. Because of this she is called Diana Trivia, 'three-fold Diana'. She was very much a woman's Goddess, called upon for help in all matters feminine. Diana is the Moon Goddess who can help us to contact the sky-queen within and feel a part of all of life and experience its feminine power.

Hecate This sinister Greek Goddess walked the roads at night, at the dark of the Moon, bearing a torch and accompanied by her dogs. Her followers left offerings for her wherever three roads met. Some said she could look three ways at once and even that she had three heads, that of a serpent, a horse and a dog. Sorcerers met and worshipped her behind closed doors and learnt the secrets of magic through her revelations. Some say she is linked with the Earth mother Goddess Demeter and her daughter Persephone, the maiden. So she is the Crone aspect of the triple Goddess. Hecate was queen of the night, ruling the spirits of the dead and the magical powers of transformation and rebirth. She was called upon to keep the dark forces, which she ruled, at bay. She was the bitch Goddess and the snake Goddess. Sacrifices were made in her honour, usually of black lambs, black dogs and honey. In the worship of Hecate we see something that is sadly absent from our lives – honouring the dark side. For death is a part of life, and without endings there can be no beginnings. Herein lies the wisdom of transformation that is the basis of magic. Like the fearsome Hindu Goddess, Kali, she brings us the gift of facing our fears and finding the freedom and release that this brings, and so she is a kindly Goddess.

Call on Hecate when you need to face the unmentionable in yourself and others, and when you seek the deep wisdom that leads to radical and positive change and the bestowal of magical powers.

Ishtar Babylonian Ishtar was a later and more multi-faceted form of the Sumerian Goddess Inanna. She embodied all three aspects of the Triple Goddess – bright Maiden, fecund Mother and wise Crone. Ishtar, the proud and queenly Moon Goddess, pounded on the gates of Hell to reclaim her sacrificed lover, Tammuz. Her sister, Ereshkigal, queen of Hell, made her strip off her garments, one by one, at each of the seven gates, and some versions of the story say she even hung her on a meat-hook to rot. The life of Tammuz, the vegetation God, was given back, and Ishtar was released. She surged through the seven gates, reclaiming her shining raiment as she went and reappeared glowing, as the Moon does in the sky. This is a story of the cycles of life, for Tammuz, as the God of vegetation, must continually die and be reborn, as the Moon disappears and again comes back to the sky.

Call on Ishtar for the courage to face life's confrontations and transformations, to 'walk through the valley of death' and to emerge re-born, shining brighter than ever.

Isis It is hard to cover the story of Egyptian Isis in a small passage because legends about her are complex. She and her husband Osiris were benevolent rulers over humankind, teaching them the civilised arts, until Osiris was murdered and dismembered by his treacherous brother, Set. Great was her sorrow, and she journeyed over many lands, looking for the precious corpse, which was found beneath a tamarisk tree. Isis carried the corpse of her husband back to Egypt to be buried, but Set stole it and dismembered it. But Isis still did not give up. She began searching again and found a dozen pieces of the body, which she put back together again. The body was complete except for the phallus, for which Isis substituted one made of gold. She then invented the rites of embalming, which she later taught to the people. Osiris rose up, reborn, and Isis conceived a child by him, Horus, the Sun God. Osiris himself took up his new place as king of the Dead. Isis was a witch, who had power over all the Gods, and she was a sorrowing widow, a faithful wife and a loving mother. She it was who taught culture and brought health. She is depicted with a throne upon her head to signify that she is Sovereignty, the essence of the land by whose grace the king rules. Isis was the Moon, the mother of the Sun, Lady of Ten Thousand names, known also as Hathor, Meri and many others.

Call upon the lady Isis when you need a real miracle, for she has power over Fate itself. She also bestows the eternal life that comes from being aware of the cosmic web, and feeling a part of it.

Ix Chel This is a Moon Goddess of the Maya, and also a Goddess of snakes, water, childbirth and weaving. She took the Sun to her bed, but her enraged grandfather killed her with a bolt of lightning. Dragonflies sang over her corpse for 13 days, after which she revived and followed the Sun to his fiery home. For a while they lived happily, but the Sun grew suspicious and jealous and threw Ix Chel from heaven. He found he could not bear to be without her so he persuaded her to come back, only to mistreat her again. Poor Ix Chel tired of being abused and she left the Sun to wander the night landscapes on her own, making herself invisible whenever her old husband drew near.

Call on Ix Chel with help for any problems that are connected with abuse of the Feminine, from wife-battering to unfair pay at work. Call on her also when you need understanding and concealment, and she will provide a haven.

Hina This great Polynesian Goddess has many myths and associations, some of them contradictory. In Tahiti she was the mighty Goddess for whose sexual pleasure the first man was fashioned. Some say she reached the Moon in a canoe, which she loved to sail in. Finding the Moon an even better boat, she stayed there to guide earthly travellers on the waters. Another legend says that she was thrown there by her brother who became angry at the noise she made beating tapa cloth. Because this process was believed to be similar to human death, Hina was also a death Goddess. Another story tells how she lived on Earth as a mortal woman for a spell and took an eel as her lover. She met the eel while bathing in a quiet pool, but her people were afraid and killed the eel. However, Hina had, in fact, been having intercourse with a God. Sorrowing, Hina cut off the head of the eel and buried it. Five nights later the first coconut tree grew where the head had been interred and became a staple food for the followers of the Goddess.

Call on Hina for sexual pleasure, the delights of sensual love and the bounty of nature.

Chia Chia was worshipped by the Chibcha people of Columbia. She was a wild woman, a Goddess of drunkenness and joy, rollicking along behind her straight-laced husband, Bochica. Bochica taught puritanical values and useful crafts, and Chia then appeared to wreck things with her reckless ways and infectious joy in life. Chia was the owl-woman, Goddess of magic. She raised a flood by her arts, and her husband grew angry with her, throwing her up into the sky, where she became the Moon.

Call on Chia when you need to have the cheek to set the cat among the pigeons!

Demeter and Persephone

These Goddesses are not specifically 'lunar' but their story is about the cycles of Nature. They are often teamed up with Hecate to form a trio in the Triple Goddess mould, Persephone being the Maiden/Waxing Moon, Demeter the Mother/Full Moon and Hecate the Crone/Dark Moon.

Demeter was the Greek Goddess of nature and she had a beloved daughter, Persephone. One day while out playing with her friends Persephone spotted a huge and luxuriant bloom, growing just out of reach. Although her friends begged her to leave it, Persephone could not bear to. She reached for it and tugged and tugged but it would not come free. A rumble started beneath the ground and her companions fled, but Persephone stubbornly clung to the stem. The ground opened beneath the flower and out rode Pluto, Lord of the Underworld, who abducted Persephone to be his queen. Demeter mourned, searched and tore at her hair and garments, so great was her loss, but Persephone was nowhere to be found. Meanwhile the Earth grew barren and perpetual winter held the land in its grip of steel. People and animals died in their multitudes. Eventually Zeus, the king of the Gods, decreed that Persephone should return to her mother if she had not eaten anything in the Underworld. But Persephone had chewed a pomegranate, and so she was only permitted to return for part of the year. The myths vary considering the exact number of months she was to spend above or below ground – some say three, some say six, and I suppose that depends on how long winter endures in a country. During the time Persephone spent with her mother, Demeter brought summer and fruitfulness, and while she was away everything decayed and died.

This is a story of many meanings, for Persephone is the maiden who subconsciously wishes to lose her innocence. Even the suffering and loss of Demeter are part of the natural cycle. The pomegranate is a symbol of fertility and Hecate was an Underworld Goddess, hinting that as well as going to be with Pluto, Persephone was also in the realm of her grandmother. These complex strands convey the importance of cycle, how one aspect shades into another. The story shows that change is fertile, and that birth and death are linked.

You may like to think about the various aspects of this story during the lunar cycle, for as the Moon wanes and goes to dark, then you may think of Persephone's hidden journey, and when the Moon is full, of the joyful aspects of the tale. Which aspect do you most identify with? This may tell you where you are in your life at present, and what your next step may be. Are you currently tugging at the flower? And what, do you think, will be the outcome? Are you Demeter, sorrowing or rejoicing? Or are you Hecate, waiting in the darkness, to give of your wisdom?

Selene   Selene was a Greek Moon Goddess. She was daughter of Thea, Goddess of light, and spouse of the Sun. Crowned with a crescent, her white wings behind her, she drove the lunar chariot across the sky each night. This shining chariot was drawn by two white horses. When Selene disappeared, at the dark of the Moon, she was said to be visiting her human lover, Endymion, for whom she had bought eternal life and youth.

Selene fell in love with the handsome hunter Endymion, who was said to be one of the most beautiful men who ever walked. One night, tired from his labours, he fell asleep on a moonlit hillside and that is when Selene spotted him. She was entranced! Her silver light rippled over his muscled limbs and she longed for her fingers to do the same. She could not resist him and so the radiant Goddess came down from the sky and kissed him and caressed him so that he fell into an enchanted sleep from which he could never awaken. In this way Selene ensured that no mortal woman would ever possess her lover and that he would never die. But sadly he could never awaken to return the passionate kisses of the Goddess. Night after night Selene returns to make love to him but she finds no joy – only sighs and longing.

This melancholy tale has psychological meanings, as is the case with most classical stories. Poor Selene is an example of some of the worst characteristics of our lunar selves, when we feel the need to hang on, to possess and to be secure in the love of our dear one, or what is familiar. This may be seen in mother love, where the mother does not really want the child to grow up and leave her. Despite all her care, she may keep him in a kind of 'sleep' where all his creature needs are met and he is prevented from facing life's challenges because they are 'dangerous'. If such a mother succeeds, she binds her child to her but there can be no real fulfilment for either party – for the true urge of motherhood is to raise another human that can take an effectual place in the world – or the mothering is not complete. We may see a similar dynamic in some relationships where one party 'smothers' the other in the name of caring, preventing them experiencing a full life and thus not really being able to be a full adult partner.

Other stories tell us that Endymion did not sleep forever but awaited his beautiful lover in Asia Minor, when she disappeared from Greek skies. All sleepers must awaken in the end, and after all, Selene was a Goddess!

★∴★ *Moon Myths*

The Man in the Moon We were all brought up to look for the face of the man in the Moon – but how did he get there?

Many stories tell a tale of punishment. For instance, one folk tale describes how a man who gathered sticks on the Sabbath was banished to the Moon. The woodcutter met a strange man in his Sunday best as he was leaving the wood, bearing his bundles on his back. 'Do you not know this is Sunday, day of rest, when all must go to church?' asked the handsome stranger.

The woodcutter laughed. 'What does it matter to me?' he asked. 'Sunday, Monday – it's all the same.'

'Then let it be Moonday forever for you, as you carry your bundles into eternity,' said the man. 'You shall be a warning to all those who would break the Sabbath.'

And so the man was transported up into the Moon where he has stood ever since.

In other stories the man is a thief of some sort, or is incestuous. Sometimes he is Judas, Isaac or Jacob. A Malaysian tale says the man is a hunchback who wants to fish everything up from the Earth, but is stopped by a rat eating his line. In Germany he is a giant, who scoops up the tidal waters. In the best stories he is a merry soul, who likes his quaff of wine but doesn't like to be pointed at – so beware!

It could be that negative associations with the Man in the Moon have arisen from a fearful, paranoid and dogmatic religious attitude, with 'bad things' more readily associated with the Moon – which is, after all, connected to instincts and natural rhythms.

The Woman in the Moon Many tales are told of a Woman in the Moon. The Maori believe she is an old woman who grumbled because the Moon went behind a cloud when she went to get water. When the Moon reappeared it pulled her up to it along with her bucket, basket and a tree that she tried to hang on to. To the Iroquois Indians she is also a complaining woman. But on the island of Mangaia there is a more charming tale of the Moon-woman who makes white clouds into cloth for a sail. Her husband was a mortal man and they lived together happily for many years, but when he grew very old she sent him back to Earth on a rainbow, so that the Moon should not be sullied by death.

The Chippewa tell a story of a beautiful maiden called Lone Bird who was sought after by many braves. But her heart was cold and she could not find it within her to love any of them. Still, Lone Bird was sad and isolated. One night she went out to collect the sap from maple trees. It was springtime and the birds and animals were all finding mates. 'It is not right to be so alone,' she said, and sat beside the moonlit lake, feeling unhappy and bereft. She looked up at the shining Moon and thought that it was the most beautiful thing she had ever seen. 'Ah,' she said. 'If only you would love me I should never be alone again!' The Moon, seeing her lovely face and her tears, reached down and lifted her up to him. When Lone Bird did not come home her father went to look for her, but he could find her nowhere. Tired and despairing, he came to the lake, sat down and looked up at the Moon. There he saw his daughter looking down at him, smiling, held in the Moon's arms.

In Europe there are fewer stories about a Woman in the Moon but in one version she is Mary Magdalene.

Dead Moon – a Folk Tale Long, long ago, in the North of England, there were many dangerous bogs. On Moonless nights evil and ghastly things stalked the marshes and it was dangerous to be out. Many were the poor men and women who had been attacked by ghouls or demons, dragged down below and never seen again. People stayed close to their firesides during the dark of the Moon, and shuddered.

The Moon learnt of their plight and decided to find out what was going on when her back was turned. She wrapped herself in a black cloak, from the top of her shining head to the tip of her bright feet, and went down to the boglands. Lightly she tripped from tuft to tuft, as dead people rose up from the marshes and fixed her with their baleful eyes, will-o-the-wisps darted round her and goblins peered from behind stones and tussocks. The Moon had never seen so fearsome a collection of vile creatures. Distracted, she lost her footing. Feeling cold hands grasping her feet, she struggled and struggled. Then she heard the sound of screaming and shouting. Her mind taken off her own dire predicament, the Moon raised her head and saw a man running in desperation from the ghouls that clutched at him.

The kindly Moon became angry and struggled harder so that her hood fell back and light streamed from her brilliant face. The man was overjoyed – now he could see the way and thankfully he escaped from the bog as the creatures of darkness scuttled into the shadows. But the Moon was exhausted by her struggles and couldn't fight any more. The demons and bogies were exultant on realising who they had caught. Now their enemy was at their mercy. They tied her up and tried to make up their minds how best to kill her. Daylight came and still they had not decided, so they pushed her under the mire and placed a stone over her.

Night after night passed by and the Moon did not appear in the sky. The people grew more and more fearful. The vile things from the marsh were creeping closer and closer to their homes every night and folk were afraid to put out their lanterns, or even to sleep. They went to the old wise woman in the village but her crystal ball told her nothing. She gave them charms and special herbs to keep their homes safe. Then the man who had been lost in the bog recalled what had happened the night the ghouls had been chasing him. Again they went to the wise woman, and again she looked into her crystal ball. This time she saw a stone shaped like a coffin within the marshlands, and she knew that was where the Moon lay.

Furnished with charms and chants to repeat as they went into deadly danger, the villagers set off in the direction given by the wise woman. Quaking with terror and waving their lanterns in arcs around them to keep away the dead things, they at length found the stone, just as described. While several of them wielded the lanterns, four of the strongest heaved the stone away, and there shone the Moon, her light bathing glory all around. All the demons fled, and the Moon rose slowly into the sky, lighting the passage home for her rescuers.

And that is why the Moon is at her most radiant over the marshlands. She knows about the foul things that creep within them and she wants to reward the brave people who saved her.

And the moral of this tale? It means that our dark times, our fearful and miserable times, are the ones that make us stronger and wiser, and, in the end, more radiant, for we come out of them re-born.

Fireflies Long ago in old Japan, a man and his wife lived at the foot of a snow-capped mountain. Although they had everything they could wish for, they had never been blessed with children. One night, as the snows on the mountain gleamed under the Full Moon, the wife went out and held her arms to the heavens, begging the mountain and the Moon for her own little one to hold in her arms.

She watched with awe and amazement as a tiny star appeared on the mountain and bobbed down, lower and lower, until it lodged in the branches of a bamboo tree nearby. Slowly the woman approached it and saw that it was a tiny child, sent by the Lady of the Moon. She and her husband rejoiced.

The child grew into a beautiful girl, adored by all who knew her for her lovely face and sweet ways. The Emperor heard about her and came to seek her hand in marriage, but the Moon girl refused, for she had been told by her real mother, the Moon, to come back to her when she reached the age of 20.

The night came for her to leave and her parents and suitor were overcome with sorrow. A silver beam came down from the Lady in the Moon and the girl glided upwards as smoothly as she had descended, 20 years earlier. As she rose she cried silver tears, in grief at the parting. Her tears turned into fireflies, and can still be seen when the Moon shines – the tears of the Moon princess as she looks for her earthly dear ones.

Why are so many tales of the Moon melancholy? Because the Moon is about dreams, and we can never hold on to them. But we are so lucky to have them at all!

The Chinese Myth of Yi and Chang E

Yi was a magical archer who, in the time-before-time, saved the world. In those distant days there were ten Suns, sons of the Creator God Di Jun and his wife, Xi He. Di Jun and Xi He had forbidden their Suns to travel the sky all together but one day they disobeyed. Instead of taking it in turns, they all went to play across the heavens at once and the Earth was dried and burnt up. So Yi the Archer was called, and one by one he shot the Suns out of the sky. They fell to their death, leaving only one Sun behind, and that is the Sun that shines on us today.

The people owed a great debt to their saviour Yi, the archer, and the Emperor gave him his heartfelt thanks. But Di Jun was distraught. 'Woe is me,' he said. 'Nine of my children are slain. It is true, Yi, that you did as I asked. But my dear ones are dead and I can no longer bear to look upon you. You and your wife Chang E must leave Heaven, leave my presence forever.'

Chang E was bitterly disappointed to have to leave Heaven and make her home upon the Earth. She felt that her husband was keeping things from her, for he was always away performing heroic deeds. Yi also wished to regain his place in Heaven and had been to work for the Queen Mother of the West, the great Grandmother Goddess. He had built her a gorgeous palace of the finest jade and fragrant timbers, and in return she had given him a gift of the Gods, a Pill of Immortality, to give him eternal life. Proper purification of the body was necessary before taking the Pill, which was meant for two persons, not one alone. Carefully Yi took the pill and concealed it in the rafters of his home, wrapped in finest silk. During one of his many absences Chang E noticed a magical glow coming from the roof and she climbed up to investigate. There, nestling in a corner between two beams, she found the wonderful pill. Discarding the wrapping she held the pill in her palm. Its enchantment drew her and she put out her tongue to lick it, but just then she heard Yi come home and, in her haste, she swallowed the pill whole.

Immediately the pill took effect and Chang E began to float upwards. Yi tried to grab at her but it was too late. Already she was leaving the ground far behind. She floated out through an open window, high in the wall. She grasped desperately at the roof-top and the branches of a tree but the magic was too strong and nothing could keep her down. Up and up she floated, crying helplessly, until she came to the Moon itself. There she alighted and there she has remained ever since, with a hare to keep her company.

Left on the ground, Yi despaired at the loss both of his beloved wife and his chance for immortality. But the Gods took pity on him. He was allowed to build himself a shining palace on the Sun, and so he could at least be near his wife in the sky. At Full Moon, when the Moon shines its brightest, Yi is visiting his wife Chang E.

This myth really reminds us about Yin and Yang and the search for balance. Yi is a very 'Yang' figure in his over-zealous aggression (for the full myth tells how he would have shot all ten Suns out of the sky had he not been prevented by the Emperor). Chang E is the more passive, reflective Yin force, drawn by instinct. At the end of the story these two are in balance and the Full Moon as a time for flowing emotions is symbolised by the meeting of Yi and Chang E.

The urge to see human shapes in nature, in such things as trees, animals and of course the Moon, is not merely a naïve wish to see these things in our terms. It stems from a very real perception of the natural world as sentient, having a wisdom and personality of its own. It is a way of seeing Gods and Goddesses everywhere, and as we know 'God is Man writ large' – presumably Goddess is Woman writ large, too! This is more than silly egoism – it stems from a realisation that there is intelligence and power all around us. After all, last century, the scientist James Jeans observed that the Universe was beginning to look more like a great thought than a great machine. Perhaps we have known this all along.

✦ ✦ *Creatures of the Moon*

The Hare in the Moon
The story of Chang E is one of many stories, mostly arising in the East, which mention a 'hare in the Moon'. In India Chandra, God of the Moon, is believed to carry a hare. A Buddhist tale tells how the Buddha was wandering hungry in the forest when a hare approached him and offered itself as food. He told the Buddha to light a fire and when the flames were burning it leapt within them,

so that it might be cooked! But the Buddha saved it and placed it in the Moon as an example of self-sacrifice.

In the light of the Moon in springtime, hares are often seen boxing. This may be one of the reasons that they are seen as animals of the Otherworld, sacred to the Goddess. Witches were believed to take the shape of hares as they escaped to their eerie gatherings on moorland or in the heart of a forest.

When an object or animal regularly turns up in stories it is worthwhile looking for the symbolic theme behind it. Everything in life has a chain of associations – this is part of the cosmic web. This symbol can have relevance on many levels, for the development of a culture, for urges within the human personality, and, of course, in magic. The hare is a symbol of sacrifice. However, in Goddess-wisdom, sacrifice isn't about putting oneself through suffering in order to show how little regard one has for oneself! It is about having the courage to let go of certain things in order to change and to transform. It is a putting aside of the little everyday self for the sake of the evolution of the larger Self, which can then go forward to its own advantage and that of the collective. Something has to die in order to be reborn. It is fitting that images of transformation, death and rebirth should be linked to the Moon, with her monthly demise and reappearance, shiny and new. This is a promise of renewal, and one of the lunar gifts.

The hare has other interesting meanings that are linked. It is a common symbol for the trickster, which really is a part of the personality that, in defiance of logic, likes to throw the 'cat amongst the pigeons' and so bring change into our lives – transformation again. The hare in the Moon is a reminder of our lunar themes of natural cycles and changes. Because of the movements and habits of the hare, it has long been seen as a rather magical creature – a 'shape-shifter' like the Moon. People used to believe that hares could change their sex when they wished. This hare is actually quite a far-reaching and subtle symbol, because its unpredictability combined with its apparent powers represents a stage in the creation of civilised culture and also in the formation of an individual ego. It symbolises the beginning of social behaviour, where we realise our place in relation to others and to the Universe, moving away from simple instinct. When creatures and symbols play on our minds in ways we cannot fully understand, there is often a very deep meaning attached. However, hares love to play in the moonlight – perhaps that's all we need to know!

Frogs and Toads Here we have witchy animals indeed, both of them 'seen' on the face of the Moon. The Salish people of the Northwest Pacific tell how a wolf once fell madly in love with a toad. As he was running after her, he beseeched the Moon to shine brightly so that he might catch his love and possess her. The Moon, friend of lovers, did as he asked, but presumably she also felt sorry for the little toad! For just as the toad was about to be caught, she made a desperate leap and landed on the Moon, where she has been ever since! Here the Moon shows us that she can see both sides – but still be tricky, as the wolf discovered!

Toads are similar to frogs, and witches were believed to keep them as 'familiars'. In fact it is possible to extract hallucinogenic substances from toads, and these may have been used to induce trance. Frogs and toads are associated with water, and this naturally links them to the Moon. Certain versions of Chinese legend says there is also a toad on the Moon.

Vampires

Vampires have many symbolic meanings, and some of these may be connected with taboos concerning menstrual blood. For further discussion of this, please see my book *Vampires, A Beginner's Guide*, listed in Further Reading. Because of this, and because they come out at night, vampires are 'lunar' creatures of the more sinister kind! There are vampire tales of the most gruesome kind all over the world and a few of them are fairly well documented. The vampire is generally a re-animated corpse, although sometimes it is a spirit or a shapeshifter. Again we have the theme of transformation and rebirth – although in this case it is more 'un-death'! Vampires are fearful, yet compelling. Maybe the Moon shows us a side of ourselves and of life and death that we would rather not contemplate.

Werewolves

Since ancient times there have been deranged people who have believed that they turn into wolves when the Moon is full – this condition is known as 'lycanthropy'. In Medieval times people were subjected to the horrific death of being burnt alive for the offence of being a 'werewolf' and committing bestial and unmentionable crimes when in their animal state. Legends state that the unfortunate werewolf – usually a man, but occasionally a woman – is born under a curse that condemns them to turn into a beast in this way. In some stories the werewolf is a magician who purposely transforms himself for nefarious reasons. The form adopted is not always that of a wolf – many other dangerous animals appear, from tigers and leopards to sharks, crocodiles, eagles and snakes.

What are we to make of this? Our theme of transformation persists, along with the power of the Moon to put us in touch with our instinctual, animal side. Films have depicted this Full Moon shape-shift, as the writhing man sprouts facial fur and falls on all fours before going on a grisly forage for victims, usually among gravestones, for added atmosphere. (This old legend re-appears with

Harry Potter in J K Rowling's third book *Harry Potter and the Prisoner of Azkaban*.) Hunted in his animal state, the werewolf receives a wound that remains when he again becomes human, and so he is found out and usually killed. Perhaps it is the 'animal' instinctual part of us that is wounded? Perhaps if we listen to this at Full Moon it may stop us being savage and give us its wisdom? This essentially Pagan wisdom has been demonised by our culture and so that may be why the werewolf is seen as a monster. Even in horror films the Moon has something to teach us!

Faeries Do you believe in faeries? Whatever your daytime answer, the one you might give out in the woods at midnight when the Moon is riding high is probably different! Faeries are the spirits of nature itself and they come in many guises, some of which are quite scary. Faeries are usually depicted as creatures in human form, some delicately beautiful, some hideous and threatening. Many Pagans do believe that there are different spirits in the natural world, tending plants and stretches of ground. Some of these might understandably be shy of humans and even antagonistic!

There are many legends of people who disappeared into the land of Faerie and were not seen for a hundred years, and believing they had only been gone a few hours when they returned. Rip van Winkle is the best known of these. This leads us to conclude that faeries are from another dimension and their time moves at a different rate to ours. Some people have equated them with UFOs and 'little green men' and it is possible that they do share a common source. Faeries are said to inhabit barrow-mounds, places where the faerie triad of trees grows (oak, ash and thorn), and any magical and special place. Why not the bottom of your own garden, indeed?

There are several times of day favourable to faeries, but the Full Moon is always their special time, as you might expect, and when the ivory glow bathes the hills and fields you may see the faery host on the move, skipping from tussock to tussock as they pipe their strange, hypnotic music. The first night of the New Moon and the last night of the Old Moon are special times too, as these are crossover points when the veils between the worlds may be thin.

In her charming book *Fairy Spells* (see Further Reading), Clare Nahmad gives this spell to obtain a faerie gift, which you can try at Full Moon near Midsummer. It involves offering a gift to the faeries with a true heart, and so winning their trust. First bake a little cake with honey and wine, or offer a poem that you have made up, or a tune or dance that you have composed. As you do this say, 'This is for the faeries.' Say this again when you are out of doors, in a quiet and lonely place where you deliver your gift. After this the faeries will give you a gift that may come in any guise. Look out for this in quite ordinary ways and places over the next few days. It might come in the form of silver coins, or a beautiful object from Nature. It may be something as small as a pebble, but this may be a 'toadstone', believed to come from the head of a toad, having many delicate and beautiful colours in its markings. Sleep with this under your pillow for it is very lucky.

When you do Moon magic, be especially careful to leave out a small gift for the faeries – the Irish call them 'the people of the Sidhe' (pronounced 'shee'). This 'gift' may just be a piece of cake or some wine. Ancient lore tells us that while the faeries do not consume the physical food, they draw out its essence. Whatever you do or do not believe, putting out an offering is a simple way of honouring the natural world and showing that as you take, so you are prepared to give back.

For more information on faeries you may like to start with my book *Faeries and Nature Spirits – A Beginner's Guide*, listed in Further Reading.

Your Lunar Altar

In Chapter 1 we touched on the idea of an altar to the Moon to connect you with natural cycles. Using knowledge about deities and lunar stones, herbs and spells (see Chapter 5), you can make your altar more complex, if you wish, choosing to honour upon it any deities whose help you feel you need. You can embellish it with herbs, stones, flowers, figures of animals and birds, incense, and any object you feel adequately evokes what you desire. This isn't a mental exercise; it is an intuitive one, about what you prefer and what feels right for you. There is no formula, no colour of candle or herb that you *must* have. Just use what ideas feel right to you and deck your altar as you wish. For instance, if you wish to draw wisdom into your life, especially as an ongoing process, or if you are studying, then you might like to purchase a figure of Thoth, place sprigs of lavender on your altar (lavender is ruled by Mercury and produces peace and mental clarity) or burn an essential oil or joss stick of that fragrance. To represent Thoth you could roll up a sheet of A4 to represent parchment, place a quill pen there, or simply a large feather, etc. Let your imagination guide you. You can still observe the phases by changing the card and candles, as suggested in Chapter 1, and you might choose to move things around on the altar to reflect your fluctuating processes during the phases.

To honour Ishtar/Inanna, you might have a small Goddess figure adorned with veils and jewellery, that you take off as the Moon wanes. You might cover her with black cloth to represent her sojourn in Hell, and adorn her again as the Moon waxes. To give yourself courage to face a situation, you might like to place a small token before your Ishtar figure as the Moon waxes – perhaps a silver bracelet. Bring the Goddess fresh flowers each day, and on the day of the Full Moon put the bracelet on your own arm. Give thanks, make an offering (e.g. incense, a promise of a gift to charity or whatever) – and go off with confidence.

To bring sensuality into your life, you might acquire a picture of a Polynesian woman that you think fits Hina – or find a statue. Bring the Goddess roses, place before her a piece of consecrated rose quartz, burn ylang ylang oil, or even dance naked in her honour. Place around her something that represents the eel/serpent – even a plastic snake might do. Tend your altar and ask Hina to show you how to express your sensuality and find gratification and love.

To invoke the protective qualities of Ix Chel, any female statue that you like can represent the Goddess. Place before her some black cord, and ask for her powers of protection and concealment. Leave this there as the Moon wanes and place it about your wrist at Dark Moon. Burn patchouli in your oil-burner.

It is fairly easy to acquire an Isis figure, and you may choose to make this great Goddess central to your altar. Bring her fresh flowers, burn incense or oils of frankincense for its majesty, and pray to the Goddess for your heart's desire. Sapphires, crystals, willow, lilies, owls, lions and cedarwood are among the vast array of correspondences for this Goddess. Silver is also associated with her, and you may wish to wear this in her honour, dedicating a silver ankh to her and placing it on a chain around your neck. The ankh, a looped cross, is an Ancient Egyptian symbol that symbolises life, but is also said by some to be the menstrual napkin of the Goddess.

These are just a few examples. Please do not feel you must restrict yourself to deities from these pages. The point is that you should call on your own powers of imagination and play with your own ideas. This is all part of the process of awakening and activating your lunar abilities. You can also note the comments about toads, bears and other animals and use these as lunar totems, if you so wish. You may want to mark your own menstrual cycle and call on different Goddesses in connection with this. The choice is yours.

*⁚★ *A Deity for Your Moon Sign*

You can invoke and bond with any deity that feels right for you, but here are some associations for each of the signs of the Zodiac.

Aries – the courage and enterprise of Ishtar are very Arien.

Taurus – sensual Hina is appropriate for this earthy sign.

Gemini – the wisdom of Thoth is the finest expression of Gemini.

Cancer – domestic, moody Chang E is Cancerian, along with Selene.

Leo – Isis is Leonine, although she is everybody's Goddess.

Virgo – the virgin Artemis is very Virgoan.

Libra – again we are irresistibly drawn to Thoth, who used scales to weigh souls.

Scorpio – mysterious Hecate is appropriate for Scorpio, as is fearless Ishtar.

Sagittarius – Diana, the sky-queen and huntress is Sagittarian, as is Chandra.

Capricorn – Lone Bird is a rather Capricornian figure.

Aquarius – The Babylonian Sin is an Aquarian figure.

Pisces – The Mayan Ix Chel, who escaped her cruel husband, is a Piscean figure, and so is dreamy Selene.

All the associations and hints that I give cannot take the place of your own explorations. It is only right to honour your own special Goddess or God at whatever phase of the Moon you feel appropriate, even if they have no lunar associations that you know of. They have one now – and that is you!

CHAPTER 5

MAGICAL RITUALS AND SPELLS

Swiftly walk o'er the western wave,
Spirit of Night...
I ask of thee, beloved Night –
Swift be thine approaching flight,
Come soon, soon!
SHELLEY, 'TO NIGHT'

The Moon is Witch-Queen, highest of High Priestesses. With her pale fingers, she points the ways along the shadowed paths of magic, twitching the veils between this world and the Otherworld, but never opening them wide. From her we learn the wisdom of concealment. In her soft light we open wide our inner eyes and understand the mysteries of ritual.

Throughout the ages the Moon has been linked to the occult, to ghosts and enchanters, dreams and premonitions. A hidden part of us, ancient yet youthful, primitive as a reptile, innocent as a child and full of mischief as an elf, is awakened by the Moon. In fact, at night time, certain hormones are active that heighten subtle awareness. People who regularly practise magic prefer the hours of darkness, not just for concealment, but also for effectiveness. And they know that the phases of the Moon rule the subtle tides that flow around us.

Full Moon is considered the most 'magical' time. Certainly any working related to creativity and fulfilment is favoured at this time. A Waxing Moon is good for spells concerning growth and increase and a Waning Moon for anything that needs to be shrunk or got rid of, such as a wart. When the Moon is dark it is better not to attempt magic, as this is a time of stillness, when it is best to meditate and go within. Just after New Moon the energies may be somewhat unpredictable as the Moon is only just separating from her conjunction with the Sun. The time for magic again unfolds as the silver sickle climbs in the evening sky.

Magic is performed by witches, but sadly the word 'witch' remains very much misunderstood. True witchcraft is nature worship, and many people are, in a sense, witches without ever realising it! Witches – including those known as Wiccans – are very spiritual people to whom worship of the Goddess is vital. Because they see all of existence as energy, and as connected, they also work magic. What we are looking at in this chapter is truly 'wise craft' – the use of gentle magic to give the powers around us a nudge in the direction we would prefer them to flow.

Before performing spells and rites, it is a good idea to meditate about what one is trying to achieve and how. The phase of the Moon is something on which to reflect. Things can always be adapted – for instance a healing spell with a Waning Moon could concentrate on banishing the illness, whereas with a Waxing Moon it would be better to visualise increasing wellbeing. If you really have to, or very much want to do your ritual at the Dark of the Moon, be aware that this may be a time of lower energy, or even slightly unreliable.

Magic is wrought on the understanding that the mind is engaging with the forces of nature. There is no split between matter and spirit, just a variation on the rate of vibration, along a spectrum. Observing the Moon is one of the ways we tune in to the here-and-now and the surrounding cosmos, learning first to 'go with the flow' and then to direct our course.

Seasonal Festivals

Most present-day witches and Pagans have eight seasonal festivals, celebrating the cycles of nature and the process of growth, decay and rebirth of which we are a part. Naturally certain festivals lend themselves to being marked with a Full, Waxing or Waning Moon.

The eight festivals are as follows.

★ Yule (Midwinter) around 22 December – this is a joyful time of rebirth when the Sun stops retreating, 'stands still' (the meaning of 'solstice') and begins to return.

★ Imbolg, 2 February – this is when the first signs of spring growth are seen and the lambs are born. 'Imbolg' means 'in the belly' and deep in the 'belly' of the Earth life is stirring.

★ Spring Equinox, around 21 March – this is a festival of plant fertility and marks the time when day and night are equal in length.

★ Beltane, 30 April – now human fertility is celebrated, with the Sacred Marriage of the Earth Goddess and the Sun God.

★ Midsummer, around 22 June – this is the climax of the seasonal cycle, when the hours of daylight are longest.

★ Lammas, 31 July – now the first part of the harvest is cut. Abundance is celebrated, but this is also a wake for the Corn Spirit.

★ Autumn Equinox, around 21 September – this is when mists are rising and the veil between the worlds is at its thinnest.

★ Samhain, pronounced 'saw-ain' (Hallowe'en), 31 October – now we mark the darkest time of the year, the death and decay we know must be gone through for new growth to arise.

These festivals are naturally surrounded by mythology, tradition and customs, which may vary from person to person, or from place to place.

The Equinoxes and Solstices are astronomical dates linked to the position of the Sun – because these vary from year to year I have only given approximate dates. However, the other 'cross quarter' festivals are believed by some people to be older, and dependent upon the rhythms of plants and animals. In fact these dates may have varied even more, according to whether the season was early or late. In the present day the festivals may be celebrated at the nearest convenient weekend.

It is not hard to see that different phases of the Moon may be linked to different festivals. In fact the yearly cycle of the Sun is echoed by the monthly cycle of the Moon. Yule, for instance, is associated with New Moon and might be most appropriately celebrated at this time, while at Imbolg we imagine that virginal sliver in the evening. Spring Equinox is associated with the first quarter, Beltane with pre-Full Moon, Midsummer with Full Moon and so into the waning cycle until Samhain at the approach of Dark Moon. As you note the phases of the Moon and their effects, you may also tune in to the different times of year. The wan, shrinking Moon haunting the small hours at Hallowe'en may look all the more melancholy because of the late autumn, while a Full Moon around Beltane may seem even more juicy and luxuriant! In older times the festivals were probably celebrated at the nearest New or Full Moon. However, there is something special about Full Moon at all times. Note the different characteristics of Full Moon, sharp and glacial by winter, veiled in autumn, resplendent in summer, and vibrant in the spring.

Each of the eight festivals is called a 'sabbat' but witches traditionally have other festivals, called 'esbats', and these may focus on the Moon. You may compose your own lunar esbat, but first it is helpful to know about the magic circle.

The Circle of Power, and the Power of the Circle

Occultists perform their rites inside a magic circle. This circle is made of your own subtle energies. It is a good idea to start by imagining a protective egg-shape around yourself whenever you have a spare moment. Imagine this is made of blue or golden light, and is all around you in a sphere. You can put it in place whenever you have to face something or someone that you find somewhat threatening. Remember to dismantle your circle when you no longer need it, or it could make you feel isolated when you do not want to be.

This 'practice circle' is a first stage to making your magic circle. The magic circle performs several functions. It holds in the power you raise by chanting, dancing or just 'willing', until it is ready for release. It protects you from distractions, or from any spirits who may be attracted to the ritual, and it acts as a half-way house on the way to the Otherworld.

To make your magic circle to do your lunar spells you will need:

★ A silver knife (this should be blunt) – solid silver or crystal is best, or you could purchase a crystal wand that would do the job beautifully. However, you may have to make do with a simple knife from your kitchen drawer! Cleanse it in salt and water first, to prepare it for the ritual.
★ Water, in a large cup.
★ Salt, in a pot.
★ Candles.
★ Incense or joss stick.
★ A white stone.
★ Some cake and a glass of wine or fruit juice.

It will also be handy to have a box or small table that you can use as an altar. Cover this with a cloth of an appropriate colour. For lunar workings, the best choices are black and silver, or possibly white, violet or dark blue. You may also like to have Goddess, and/or God figures associated with the Moon, and various other bits and pieces that you need for your particular rite or spell. Witches also have a pentacle (a disc with a five-point star engraved upon it), chalice, cauldron, besom and wand. All these have symbolic meanings and are fully explained in other books, notably *Spellbound!*, *Witchcraft, a Beginner's Guide* and *Witchcraft, A Complete Guide* – see Further Reading. For now, the above articles will suffice for your lunar workings, but if you find visualisation difficult, a circular rug will help you to imagine your working space. Carefully chosen recorded music can also greatly help the working.

Casting your Circle

Many of the spells suggested in this chapter may be performed impromptu. You may wish to surround yourself by your 'quickie' circle while you do them, nonetheless, for it is always a good idea to signal to the unconscious mind when ritual consciousness is due to begin and end. However, making a full circle gives a peaceful and transcendent sensation and is always a good idea.

Start by having a bath or shower with lavender essence or shower gel. Make sure you will be left in peace by family and pets. Allow yourself to slip into a dreamy state. Meditate about your rite – do you feel good about it? Maybe at this stage you will want to revise your plans. Get your things ready peacefully, enjoying the feel and appearance of them. (One of the reasons why it is best to have beautiful artefacts is that they make you feel good.) If the Moon is up, open the curtains to her (if this is possible without compromising your privacy).

Think firstly about where you want your 'altar'. It is usual to position this roughly in the North of your working space, although South would be better in the Southern Hemisphere. Put on your music, if you so wish, light your candles and joss stick, and stand, knife in hand, facing your altar. Thus you are facing the 'blind' side of the sky in which Sun and Moon never roam, home of the mysteries. Witches traditionally pay special honour to this quarter. However, if the light of the Full Moon is shining in upon you, you may be better advised to have your altar in the opposite quarter, so you can face the Moon.

Standing facing your altar, begin moving clockwise (anti-clockwise, in the Southern Hemisphere) and make a circle around you with your knife, about three metres in diameter, so you have room to move. Visualise a blue light streaming from the tip of your knife – you are using it to 'cut' reality-as-we-know-it and to generate your circle of power. When you feel your circle is in place, cleanse it by imagining any negativity as grey clouds that you are chasing away by movements of your hands. See these being sucked out of your circle, the perimeter acting like a membrane, just as the skin on the human body will let sweat out but prevent moisture from coming back into the body. This task is accomplished by witches using a besom – by all means use one, if you have one handy.

Take up your bowl of salt and say, 'Great Mother, bless this salt, to purify and preserve me and my endeavours.' Then take up your water and say, 'From water comes all of life. May this water be blessed, to sweeten and to cleanse my sacred space.' Sprinkle the salt into the water and say, 'As the salt sea girdles the Earth and rises to the rhythms of the Moon, so I sprinkle salt water about my circle, to dedicate it to the Old Ones and the Powers of Nature.' Sprinkle the salt water around your circle, moving clockwise (or anti-clockwise, in the Southern Hemisphere, to mirror the movements of Moon and Sun as they are seen from Earth). Your circle of power is now ready to invite the presence of the Guardians.

Summoning the Guardians

Four potent Guardians, corresponding to each of the four cardinal points of the compass, can now be summoned to watch over your circle and to give you extra voltage. These also correspond to the four elements of Earth, Fire, Air and Water. (If you wish to explore these further, please consult the books listed under Further Reading, as suggested above.) North is linked to Earth and to grounding, practicality, building, making real and protecting; East to Air and to communication, swift thought, movement, inspiration, analysis and the creative function of the mind; South relates to Fire and to visions, drive, imagination, resourcefulness, courage, spirituality and revelation; while West is allied to Water and to healing, emotional bonds, feelings, compassion, empathy, love, cleansing and evolution. Again there is a variation for the Southern Hemisphere, where the circle of associations should be moved to South for Earth and North for Fire, because Sun and Moon are seen in the North of the sky.

These associations are deeply ingrained into witches, but if this is new to you, you may need some practice with this, and some reminders. If you wish you can place a bowl of earth or a stone in the Earth section of your circle, a bowl of water in the Water section, a red candle in the Fire section and a joss stick or perhaps a feather or windblown seed in the Air section.

There is also a link between the phases of the Moon and these four quarters. The North (South in the Southern Hemisphere) and Earth are linked to Dark Moon, East/Air to Waxing Moon, South (North in the Southern Hemisphere) and Fire to Full Moon and West/Water to Waning Moon.

The powers that guard these four quarters can be imagined in a variety of ways, as a God and Goddess with their attendants, as a multitude of spirits or merely as the 'feel' of the element in question. Your next task is to summon them, ask them to be with you and guard and support you, for you will need all their attributes at different times, in different workings. Sometimes these may be called upon directly (for example, in a healing spell you may emphasise Water), but it is good to have them there even if you are not going to 'target' any one specially. These Guardians make your circle complete. Witches invoke them by forming a pentagram (see Figure 6), or five-pointed star, in the air, with a blunted ritual knife known as an 'athame' (pronounced 'athaymee'). The pentagram can also be formed with the finger tip.

Figure 6: The Pentagram

As this is a lunar working, your words to call the Guardians should reflect this. Start with the Earth element. Face North, raise your arms and say:

> *Lady and Lord of the darkness, the depths and the Mystery, come to me from your ancient caverns and bless my circle with your wisdom and protection.*

Visualise the opening of a cave and the Lord and Lady appearing in it, clad in dark colours and bringing with them the sweet scent of the Earth.
Now turn to the East and say:

> *Lady and Lord of the silver crescent, of swiftness, dawning and new beginnings, come to me born on the breeze and bless my circle with your freshness and inspiration.*

Visualise a mountaintop, the air sparkling and clear, and the Lord and Lady wearing robes of gleaming white and silver as the breezes play around them and a silver sickle sparkles in the sky above.
Now turn to the South and say:

Lady and Lord of the Full Moon in all her glory, powers of vision, revelation, dreams and desires, come to me in the heat of your splendour and bless my circle with your energy and creativity.

Visualise bank upon bank of candles surrounding the Lord and Lady clad in robes of crimson or gold, as warmth, welcome and encouragement flow towards you and you see fireworks cascading into the air behind their crowned heads, where a golden Harvest Moon presides.

Now turn West and say:

Lady and Lord of the waning crescent, of peace, tranquillity, deep feeling and intuition, come to me on the swell of the tide and bless my circle with your insight, your gentleness, your healing presence and your love.

Visualise the Lord and Lady standing within a grotto beside the ocean as the waters flow around them. They are dressed in robes of blue and green and with them come the tang of the ocean and the rhythmic song of the waves. Behind them is the waning crescent.

Your circle is now in place for your lunar ritual or spell.

At the End of the Rite Conclude your rite by raising your plate of cake and glass of wine up to the Moon and giving thanks to the powers of life for their bounty. Then the cakes and wine can be enjoyed, in consciousness that they are a blessing.

When you have finished your ritual, make sure that you thank each of the Guardians in turn for being present and mentally close the opening to their worlds by visualising a door being shut between you and them as you bid farewell. You may simply say:

Lady and Lord of Earth/Fire/Air/Water, thank you for being present at my rites and as you depart to your own magical realms I bid you Hail and Farewell.

Mentally re-absorb the energy of your circle, snuff out your candles, pat your body all over to ground yourself and eat and drink something. Make a note of your experiences in a special ritual book, so that important realisations do not fade. It is surprising what may be revealed to you in the circle that can then be lost when you re-enter ordinary consciousness.

Leave a small offering out for the faeries, if you can – perhaps crumbs from your cake, or drops of wine. This is a sign of respect for the Earth, who gives life.

★ ⁂ ★ *A Simple Consecration Ritual*

To put a magical 'stamp' on your tools, it is best to consecrate them before using them in rituals. This applies to the tools you are going to use regularly such as your ritual knife, the stone you have on your altar, any crystal you use for scrying (see below), your salt pot and your water cup. 'Consecration' means 'making sacred' and what you are doing by this ritual is:

★ cleansing the tool of any subtle influences that may linger on it, for instance from other people who have touched or used it, which may affect your workings

★ dedicating the tool to the purpose for which it is intended. This is a special task, for these articles are helping to connect you to the divine realms. Besides, any ritual you do has an effect on your subconscious mind, enabling you to 'see' the tool as special and thus more readily change your consciousness.

Cleanse the article initially by soaking it in salt water overnight. For more delicate items you may prefer to wipe them with a little lavender oil, diluted in water. You can also do this mentally by imagining the object being held beneath a glistening waterfall; if your powers of concentration are good, this will do the job well enough. But a little ritual always helps!

For lunar workings, it is especially good to leave the tool out overnight in the light of the Full Moon if possible.

When the object is psychically clean, cast your circle and dedicate the tool to each of the four quarters in turn, passing it through incense smoke for Air, holding it over the candle flame for Fire, dipping it in water and touching it upon the stone for Earth. Lay it on your altar before your Goddess or God figure (if you have one) and say:

> *I dedicate this [name the item] in honour of the Triple Goddess, Maiden, Mother and Crone. May it serve me well in my rites, so the Goddess may work through my hands. Blessed Be.*

Should you wish to consecrate a statue or representation of a God or Goddess not lending themselves to the 'triple' concept, then use the words 'in honour of the bright and changing Moon' instead.

Naturally you will have to work your first circle with unconsecrated tools. However, it is possible to cast your circle with your finger-tip, and work from there. Or you can simply use cleansed tools and consecrate them in their first using. It doesn't matter. Consecration of candles and incense is less important because these substances change as they are burnt, but it is always helpful to consecrate anything you use in your rituals.

General Hints

When doing any form of magic there are a few points that it is important to remember. Magic tweaks at the cosmic web, and that is no small matter. However, most things we do, even riding a bike, need some care. So this is not to say you need to agonise about everything – spells should be fun! But you do need to be responsible.

The first rule is to harm no one. Never break this – it isn't worth it. Magic used to get your own back will harm you and it is a gross misuse of a beautiful tool. Never seek to influence another person directly, except possibly in a healing spell, unless they have asked you to do so. Usually it is much better to help them to do a spell than to do it for them, for then they can bring their own will and desire to bear on the matter – and it is likely to be stronger than yours for it is their concern. If you are doing a love spell, be general! In other words, do the spell for the sort of love you want, not to gain the love of a special person. Sorry to be a spoilsport!

Some other useful pointers are:

★ Get out there and make it happen! That love, money and luck can't find you if you hide under the duvet!
★ Don't worry about asking for things for yourself. There's no need to be greedy, of course, but fill your well so you can give to others!
★ Usually spells are best in the full magic circle because then you will be in the right state of mind. The true purpose of ritual, in the end, is to link us with the divine and the Goddess and God within – and it's a great feeling!

A Safety Note Essential oils are often used in magical work, and several suggestions for their use are made in this chapter. However, it is very important to note that these are not necessarily harmless substances. There are contra-indications to almost every oil and none should be used during pregnancy without first checking with a qualified aromatherapist. Oils should always be tested for allergic reaction 24 hours before the ritual.

Lavender oil is the only oil generally believed to be safe, and is the only one that may safely be placed undiluted on the skin. Because lavender oil is cheap, easily available and gentle, it may be used as a substitute wherever necessary – it is as adaptable as its planetary ruler, Mercury!

★ ⁂ ★ Moon Sign Magic

Your Moon sign will give you particular magical talents that you can work with when you are doing your spells.

Aries Moon The particular talents you bring to magical work are your vehemence, the strength of your desires and your inner urgency and energy. Regardless of your Moon phase at birth, you may feel most at home when the Moon is a waxing crescent. When you do your lunar spells, be especially conscious of gathering your fiery energies and throwing them into the work. When you are in your circle, meditate in the Fire/South quarter, burning a red candle to enhance your emotional strength. Ask Earth to keep you safe, Air to give you a measure of detachment and Water to help you understand the feelings and needs of others.

Taurus Moon The particular talents you bring to your lunar spells are your consciousness of your own true needs, your patience and sound instincts. You may feel most serene when the Moon is waxing or full. When you do your lunar magic, be especially conscious of your ability to draw power up from Mother Earth as if you had roots within her – which you do! In your circle you may like to light a dark green candle and meditate facing the Earth/North quarter asking for your practicality to be blessed. Ask Air for the ability to change when necessary, Fire for some get-up-and-go, and Water to enhance your imagination.

Gemini Moon The special talents that you bring to your lunar spells are your inventiveness and resourcefulness, especially with words. When you do magic, be especially conscious of all the many vibrational levels around you and tune in to what will work best. You may feel most lively with a waxing Moon. Burn a yellow candle and meditate in the Air/East quarter to ask for your awareness and understanding to be enhanced. Ask Fire for passion, Earth for common sense and Water for the ability to accept others rather than continually question them.

Cancer Moon Your Cancer Moon gives you the magical talents of really tuning in to the lunar tides and the meanings of your dreams. You may feel most intuitive when the

Moon is full. When doing your lunar magic, be especially aware of your dreams and intuitions and let them guide you. Burn a silver candle and face the West/Water asking for your intuition to be strengthened. Ask Earth to make you feel safe, Air to give you a measure of detachment from your insecurities, and Fire to make you bold and positive.

Leo Moon With your Leo Moon, the special talent you bring to your lunar magic is your power and conviction. Visualise a steady flame burning within you. Full Moon may energise you most. Light a gold candle and meditate in the Fire/South quarter asking for your courage and generosity of soul to be enhanced. Ask the Earth to keep you humble, Air to enable you to think clearly and Water to help you to take human nature into account, including your own.

Virgo Moon The special talent that you bring to your lunar spells may be a sensitivity to herbs and oils and their meanings. When you do magic, be especially aware of your bodily sensations. You may feel best when the Moon starts to wane. Light a light green candle in the Earth/North quarter and ask that your special abilities to discriminate and understand be increased. Ask Water for healing for your worries, Fire for courage and conviction and Air for clear-headedness.

Libra Moon The special talent that you bring to your lunar magic is your sense of beauty, for the world is beautiful and magic is a thing of beauty. The loveliness of the Full Moon may move you most. When you do magic, use your sense of balance to ensure everything is in place and looking good. Light a rose candle in the East/Air quarter and ask for your aesthetic senses to be enhanced. Ask Water for depth, Fire for energy and conviction and Earth for decisiveness.

Scorpio Moon The special talents you bring to your lunar magic are your depth and your utter dedication. You may feel most at ease at Dark Moon. When you do magic, put all of your emotional energy and conviction behind the spell. Light a black candle and meditate in the West/Water quarter asking for the ability to use your emotions in a healthy way and to feel sure you are loved. Ask Earth for protection, Air for a measure of detachment and Fire for good cheer and the fulfilment of passion.

Sagittarius Moon The special talents you bring to your lunar magic are your faith and intuitive flashes. You may feel at your best with a New Moon in the sky. When doing your lunar magic, follow your impulses and use your visionary abilities. Light a wine-coloured candle in the South/Fire quarter and ask for your sense of adventure and wide possibilities to be enhanced. Ask Earth to keep your feet on the ground, Water to connect you to the past as well as the future and heal any lack of belonging you may feel and Air to keep you abreast of the facts as well as the theory.

Capricorn Moon   The special talents you bring to your lunar magic are a special affinity with the earth and stones. You may feel most contented when the Moon is waning and appears in the small hours. When doing your lunar magic, centre yourself and be very 'in' your body, feeling your connection with the Earth and your ability to contain the power until the right time. Light a brown candle (if you can get one – if not, a dark green or black candle will do) in the North/Earth quarter and ask for your constructive abilities to be increased and well-applied. Ask Fire to give you a positive attitude, Water to help you open out when appropriate and Air for wider perspectives.

Aquarius Moon   The special talent that you bring to your lunar spells is your belief that anything goes and your willingness to experiment. A Waning Moon in the dawn sky may suit your quixotic temperament. When you do spells, be aware of the electric energy within your body and direct it into your work. Light a bright blue candle in the East/Air quarter and ask for your idealism and future vision to be enhanced. Ask Water to keep you connected to your own feelings and those of others, Fire to enable you to stay with your own desires where necessary instead of concentrating on group concerns, and Earth to keep you within sensible bounds.

Pisces Moon   The special talent you bring to your lunar magic is your ability to *believe* in it and to use your imagination and ability to create enchantment. Full and Dark Moon both have their appeal for you. When doing your lunar magic, be aware of any other spirit entities and nature spirits/faeries that may be close and be especially careful to include them by leaving out an offering after the spell, of wine, cake crumbs or similar. Light a purple candle in the West/Water quarter and ask for your wisdom and insight to be enhanced. Ask Air for analytical ability, Fire for energy and courage and North for protection and focus.

A Lunar Cycle of Rites, Spells and Celebrations

A Rite for the Full Moon

When the Full Moon rides high, we feel the Otherworld is close and the desire for magic courses in our veins. A rite at this time can be designed to heighten creativity and awareness, to open the inner eyes so that we may walk in the ways of the Mighty Ones. Witchcraft is about opening ourselves to the God or Goddess within ourselves, and touching the transcendent. Here is a simple ritual that you can perform, to honour the Full Moon.

In addition to the requirements for casting the circle, given above, you will also need a large bowl or cauldron filled with water, some wine, a silver dish laden with white or light-coloured fruit such as green grapes, bananas, green apples, or similar. You may also feast on white cakes or biscuits, and white cheese. Some flowers for your altar will set the scene. Although the Full Moon shines with a white light, she is often linked to the colour red, colour of the blood that flows at birth, so this can be reflected in your choice of wine and flowers. Incense of jasmine, sandalwood or lemon will help the atmosphere. You will also need some sandalwood oil (diluted at the ratio of two drops per teaspoon in a carrier oil such as grapeseed) to anoint yourself, a silver circlet or necklace, and a soft white cloth.

Play appropriate music and dance around your circle, weaving your arms in and out of the moonlight and the incense smoke. If you wish you can dress yourself in layers of white and silver scarves, which you take off one by one until you stand naked in the light of the Moon. If the night is cloudy or if you must keep your curtains closed for privacy, use the largest silver candle you can find, instead, to represent the Moon. Now you are as the Great Mother made you, in her love and wisdom, and you stand bathed in the ethereal glow.

Face your altar and anoint yourself with your oil on the forehead, lips, heart, belly and feet, saying:

> *Queen of the Night, Queen of the heart,*
> *Mistress of Magic, Bringer of bliss and inspiration*
> *White lady that walks the ways of beauty and truth,*
> *Bless me and come to me, let thy ways be mine.*

Now stand with the bowl of water between your feet, or hold it up so that the Moon (or the light of your silver candle) is reflected in its surface. Now say these words, or similar:

Bright Goddess, my soul is open to you.
Enter me, your priest/ess,
Light my being with your inspiration.
Let your wisdom dwell within me, let your power flow through me.
May I shine with your blessed light.
Guide my footsteps down the ancient paths
That lead to that mysterious centre
So I may know that which I seek is deep within me
And find the peace and fulfilment of true knowledge.
Great Goddess, Aradia, Diana, Isis, Astarte,
Be with me now.
Blessed be.

You may feel the lunar energy rush towards you and fill you. Take a deep breath, steady yourself and allow that transcendent feeling to permeate you. Stand for as long as you wish, feeling the beauty of the moment, breathing in the incense and drifting, your mind journeying over the white fields, rising into a star-filled Heaven.

You might like to use one of the lunar meditations given in Chapter 6. Choose the one for the sign the Moon is in at the time – remember that this will be the one opposite the Sun, as explained in Chapter 1. Or if you prefer, you could do the meditation for your own Moon sign (see page 183).

Drop your necklace or circlet into the water where the Moon's reflection (or that of your candle) is caught. Slowly take it out, watching the glistening drops fall from it, back into the bowl. Dry it carefully on the white cloth and place it about your head and neck. You are girdling yourself with the power of the Moon.

Now celebrate by feasting. Offer your wine and food to the Moon, with the simple words, 'I dedicate this to Lady Moon and eat and drink in her honour.'

Close your circle when ready.

Drawing Down the Moon

The ritual given above is a simplified form of a special time-honoured Wiccan ceremony called 'Drawing Down the Moon'. Wiccans are witches who work in covens and have specific rituals, many of which were created, or adapted from older material, in the 1950s. No one is quite sure how much of the rituals is truly ancient and how much was 'made up', but there is little doubt that the spirit of the rites goes back into the mists of antiquity, and the words can be very beautiful. The Great Mother Charge, written by the priestess and witch

Doreen Valiente, who died in 1999, is recited during the ritual for 'Drawing Down the Moon' and the words are especially lovely. The High Priestess begins by reciting:

> Whenever ye have need of anything, once in the month, and better it be when the Moon is Full, then shall ye gather together in some secret place and adore the spirit of me who am Queen of all Wytches. There shall ye assemble, ye who would fain learn all sorcery yet have not yet won its deepest secrets. To thee will I teach things that are yet unknown. And ye shall be free from slavery, and as a sign that ye be really free ye shall be naked in your rites. And ye shall dance, sing, feast, make music and love all in my praise, for mine is the ecstasy of the spirit and mine also is joy on earth, for my law is love unto all beings. Keep pure your highest ideal, strive ever towards it, let naught stop you or turn you aside. For mine is the secret door that opens upon the land of youth, and mine is the cup of the wine of life and the cauldron of Cerridwen, which is the Holy Grail of immortality. I am the gracious Goddess who gives the gift of joy unto the heart of wo/man. Upon earth I give knowledge of the spirit eternal, and beyond death I give peace, freedom and reunion with those who have gone before. Nor do I demand sacrifice for Behold! I am the mother of all living and my love is poured out upon the earth.

The High Priest now says:

> *Hear ye the words of the Star Goddess, she in the dust of whose feet are the hosts of heaven, and whose body encircles the Universe.*

The High Priestess continues:

> I, who am the bounty of the green earth, and the white Moon among the stars and the mystery of the waters and the desire of the heart of man, call unto thy soul. Arise and come unto me for I am the soul of Nature, who gives life to the Universe. From me all things proceed and unto me all things return; and before my face, beloved of gods and men, let thine innermost divine self be enfolded in the rapture of the infinite. Let my worship be within the heart that rejoiceth; for behold, all acts of love and pleasure are my rituals. And therefore let there be beauty and strength, power and compassion, honour and humility, mirth and reverence within

you. And thou who thinkest to seek for me, know thy seeking and yearning shall avail thee not unless thou knowest the mystery; that if that which thou seekest thou findest not within thee, thou wilt never find it without thee. For behold, I have been with thee from the beginning and I am that which is attained at the end of desire.

This completes this very moving and splendid section of the ritual. Often the High Priestess will find she alters the words, not because she doesn't remember them (although, understandably, that sometimes happens!), but because she is in a transcendent state and the words somehow alter themselves, often to a form more in keeping with the specific time or occasion, for whatever reason.

This Great Mother Charge is surprisingly easy to memorise, however, and it surely forms the definitive Goddess litany of our time. Parts of it are often quoted, for there are so many kernels of wisdom in it. You may like to write it out and stick it up on a wall somewhere, where you can remind yourself about it. Alternatively you can obtain an attractive poster with the words already printed, from Dark Moon Designs (see Resources).

A Rite for the New Moon

You will need a white or pale green cloth for your altar; a silver vase; some flowers or greenery (preferably that you have gathered while the crescent of the new Moon is in the sky); lavender oil and some lavender water. Have some lemon juice ready in a white or silver chalice. Wear white clothing and silver jewellery (in the shape of a crescent if possible). You will also need three white candles in silver candle-holders, a silver pen and some thin card.

After casting your circle, light one of the candles. Raise your flowers or greenery to the Moon, if she is visible in the sky, or towards the lit candle. Say:

Lady most pure,
Princess of the dusk,
Lying fair over the Waters of the West,
Presiding over the waters of birth,
Let what is new come into being, and grow.
Let my creativity wax with your bright light
And let me be born again this month in new heart and vigour.
Blessed be.

Place the flowers or greenery carefully into their silver receptacle. Think about your plans and schemes and imagine them growing and coming into being as the Moon waxes. Light the other two candles, saying, 'Let the light become brighter.' Write three wishes or plans on the card with your silver pen. Ideally this should be one wish for you, one for a friend, and one for the world. Anoint the card with just a little oil of lavender – but be careful not to smudge the writing! Now, facing your candle, or the lunar crescent, anoint yourself on your forehead, saying, 'May the mind be free.' Splash your face with the lavender water, and rub it into your hands. If you are doing the ritual with friends share this with them – you can splash each other and have a giggle.

Sit and reflect once more, feeling hopeful and thinking positively. Drink some of the lemon juice in a toast and keep some to cast onto the ground after the ritual. Close your circle when you are ready and keep your card somewhere safe, or place it upon your lunar altar.

A Rite for the Waning Moon

You will need a purple or dark blue cloth for your altar; a white bone such as a chicken wishbone; a small square of black velvet; three candles in dark holders; a flat dark stone; incense or joss stick containing myrrh; a crystal or semi-precious stone that you particularly like; a black veil or scarf; and some red wine, stout, or dark-coloured juice.

If you wish to do this rite when the Moon is visible it will be after midnight. And please remember that it may be depressing! One of the purposes of the ritual is to honour all the processes of nature, including decay, and to value the inward time that is at hand. It can also be helpful if there are things we need to leave behind in life. However, be warned that if you are feeling low you could feel worse after this rite, unless you have some friends who will support you through it. But if you feel you need peace and rest, this can help you to let go of what is bothering you – think carefully!

Cast your circle after lighting the three candles. Go round your circle with the incense or joss stick, so that the rather bitter and solemn scent fills the space. Face the Moon or the candles and say:

Ancient Wise One,
Wayfarer of the night,
Take all that has to end, all that must disappear and die
With you into the darkness.
I welcome your peace, I welcome the stillness,
As you disappear into the dawn so I choose to go within.
Blessed be.

Put out two of the candles and place the black scarf over your head. Take the white bone and wrap it in the black cloth saying, 'All things must pass, all things must enter the caverns of night and be no longer seen in the world of humans.' Place the stone on top of the cloth-wrapped bone and pass the incense over it several times, saying, 'Let there be peace.'

Now sit quietly, meditating, holding your special stone or crystal. Ask the Great Mother for guidance, wisdom and serenity. Stay in this position for as long as you like. When you are ready, toast the Crone with the wine or stout to cheer her on her way, saying, 'Merry meet, merry part and merry meet again.' Close your circle when you are ready.

Dark Moon Rite
You will need a black altar cloth; your wishes from the New Moon rite; some black thread; a heat-proof bowl or cauldron; a seed (sunflower seeds are a good size and shape); a black or dark bowl containing some earth; one black candle; one white candle; oils of myrrh and sandalwood; a black scarf; and some red wine, stout or juice.

This rite should be performed when the Moon cannot be seen at all in the sky. This will be for about three days, when she is very close to the Sun. New Moon is marked in calendars and newspapers and this rite should be performed on that day or one of the days on either side of it. Cast your circle wearing the black scarf, by the light of the single black candle, which you have anointed with the oil of myrrh.

Sit quietly for a while and then say:

Darksome Mother,
Lady behind the veils, Priestess of the Mysteries,
I call to you. Hear me, in your temple beyond the stars.
Hear the voice of my soul.
Awaken in me the knowledge of all things
That I may come to know you, in truth
And find my way home.

Take the card on which you wrote your three wishes at New Moon and bind it round and round with black thread, reflecting on how much has come to pass, what needs to be done, what needs to be relinquished and what may need to be rethought. Don't work things out or plan, just let the images flow through your mind as you weave. Say, 'Things come and go and come again,' over again. When you are ready, you may burn the little package in your heat-proof dish or cauldron. In this way you are making room for things to move on and make way for the unknown. (You can miss out this part of the rite if you want simply to persevere, and you can re-anoint your card at the next New Moon. The black thread can simply be wound into knots as you chant, and burnt by itself, to emphasise passage.)

If you wish you can sit for a while as you did at the Waning Moon rite, meditating and going inward. You may use one of the Moon meditations (see Chapter 6) pre-recorded on a tape. You may choose the meditation for the sign the New Moon is in, which will be the current Sun sign (see Chapters 1 and 2) or the meditation for your own Moon sign.

Now stand and anoint the white candle with the oil of sandalwood. Say, 'This is the still time, the fallow time, the secret time. Soon it will be time for new growth. I prepare the way, in the name of the Great Mother.' Light your white candle and take the black scarf off your head. Pick up the pot of earth and push the little sunflower seed into it. Say, 'I plant this seed deep into the secret Earth. It has passed from my sight, and from the sight of the Sun, Moon and stars. May the Earth preserve, conceal and protect it until the time is right and the powers of light and life call unto it. Blessed be.'

Place your pot upon the altar and drink some of your wine, stout or juice as you contemplate the soft Earth. What magic there is within that simple pot of dirt! It is a marvel that a seed can simply be put in it and can grow unaided into a fine, golden sunflower. And so it is with all of Nature. Close down your circle when you are ready. Water the pot when the first sliver of the New Moon appears.

Spells and Charms

Magical Moons When the Moon is in a specific sign of the Zodiac, the time is better for certain spells. If you can combine this with the correct Moon phase, then your spell will wing on its way with extra power. However, do not be constrained by this! You will need planetary tables (see Further Reading) to be sure of the Moon's sign. These are the sorts of spells that can be undertaken with the different Moon signs.

Aries – Action, taking risks, independence, but watch for impulsiveness and running out of steam.

Taurus – Practical matters, permanence, sex, financial security.

Gemini	– Playing with ideas, learning, communicating, but this is not good for permanent changes.
Cancer	– Home, children and family – but watch for others' sensitivities.
Leo	– Vitality, the heart, strong feelings, entertainment, opportunity.
Virgo	– Organisation, detail, health, reaping just rewards.
Libra	– Contracts, partnership, love, charm, eloquence, friendships.
Scorpio	– Loyalty, ownership. Watch out for suspicion and anger.
Sagittarius	– Philosophy, adventure, journeys, study, honesty, imagination.
Capricorn	– Building, rules and regulations, discipline – this could be depressive.
Aquarius	– Inventions, social life, future goals.
Pisces	– Spiritual and psychic matters, but guard against confusion and deception.

Some Simple Spells

Lemon Charms: This spell should be undertaken with a Waxing or Full Moon. Lemons are ruled by the Moon and magically they are linked to cleansing and to friendship. Take a firm lemon with plenty of green in it, so it is quite unripe and hard. If possible, choose an organic lemon from a source you trust. Small lemons are best, about 3–4 cm in diameter. Now get some pins, preferably ones with coloured heads, but do not use black for that is too negative. You could name each colour for a specific quality – gold for prosperity, red for health, green for fertility and/or money, blue for tranquillity, silver for intuition, white for purity or for the interests of children, purple for learning, etc. Be inventive and go with what seems right to you. Sit quietly, preferably in your circle, sticking the pins in your lemon and stating the qualities you expect each time you pierce the skin. When you have finished thread a white ribbon through the top of your lemon. Now you can hang it in your hallway for good fortune or give it to a friend as a gift.

Lemon Balm Love Charms

Lemon balm (*Melissa officinalis*) is ruled by the Moon. At Full Moon simply soak a few leaves from the plant in wine. Best of all, leave the infusion out in the light of the Moon. Share the brew with your loved one, from the same chalice. This will make your love strong and true, but remember it is important to get the consent and co-operation of your partner.

If you are looking for a lover, bind a sprig of lemon balm with a silver ribbon by moonlight, saying three times as you do so, 'True love, sure love, enduring love, come,' and visualising the sort of person you would like. But make sure you don't aim this at someone specific! Carry the sprig with you until you are successful.

Lemon balm is healing and the oil can be burnt in healing spells.

Potato Spell to Guard Against Colds Potatoes are ruled by the Moon and healing is generally her province. To protect against colds, flu and illnesses involving excess phlegm, take a small, round potato and wash it carefully in water containing lemon juice. This spell is best undertaken early in the autumn, if possible under a Harvest Moon. Consecrate the potato (see the earlier instructions for consecration), then leave it out in the light of the Full Moon. Also (or alternatively, if the weather is bad and the Moon not visible) leave it upon your altar by your Goddess figure, for a lunation. Afterwards wrap it in green cloth and carry it with you all winter in your bag or pocket. The potency of the spell will only be affected if you persist in carrying the potato when it's become well and truly rotten – if it goes off, the spell can be re-done.

Cabbage for Luck Another Moon-ruled plant, because of its high water content, cabbage should be the first thing a couple plant in their garden after setting up home together. The time to do this is just before Full Moon.

Sleepy Lettuce Lettuces are soporific, as Peter Rabbit can tell you! They are also Moon-ruled. Crush a lettuce leaf against your forehead to ensure a good night's sleep. Plant lettuce seeds with a Waxing Moon to spell out the initial of the one you love, to ensure your love flourishes.

Cool as a Cucumber If you wish to be rid of a sexual desire that has become unhealthy or destructive, eat cucumber as the Moon is waning, saying:

> *Shrink, shrink lust,*
> *Go down to dust.*
> *This fruit of the Moon*
> *My desires will cool.*

You should be feeling free by New Moon and ready to seek a better object for your affections.

Camellia Money Spell These lovely Moon-ruled blooms are good for money spells. Just before Full Moon place a bowl of them on your altar and drop three silver coins in between the blooms, naming one for money to spend, one for a loved one to spend it on and the third for the wisdom to spend it wisely. When your rite is over, take the three coins and keep them in a piece of cotton. Press one of the flowers between two sheets of tissue paper and keep that with the coins as your fortune begins to grow.

Willow The willow's affinity for water ensures its connection to the Moon. Willow can be used in healing spells – salicylic acid from which aspirin is derived comes from the willow. A willow wand can aid you in Moon magic. Pick up some fallen wood or ask a friendly willow tree if it can spare you some! Bring an offering of crumbs for the birds as a thank you. You can make your wand as fancy as you like, perhaps attaching a piece of crystal or moonstone to the tip, engraving symbols upon it or anything else that appeals. If you want to keep things simple just make sure you oil the wand, to keep it supple. You can use it almost interchangeably with your silver knife (i.e. athame) but a wand, I feel, is better at conducting energy rather than 'cutting reality' – although opinions on this do differ. You could use your willow wand to direct lunar energies into a potion you are making, such as in the Lemon Balm love spell, above.

For protection, take some supple willow twigs and weave them into a circular shape to hang over your door or in your room. You may weave silver threads in and around the twigs, or choose three colours, one for Maiden, one for Mother and one for Crone and interweave these. Suggested colours are silver, white and black respectively, or white/silver, red and black. You can consecrate your wreath in your ritual circle.

To see spirits, burn willow bark as an incense at Waning Moon, mixed with sandalwood – and wormwood, if you can stand the smell!

Eucalyptus This healing lunar herb can be used in several ways, both magically and practically. A few drops of eucalyptus oil on a pillow case or handkerchief helps ease cold symptoms. Rub the oil into a green candle for a healing spell and burn this, saying:

> *Hale and hearty,*
> *By my spell*
> *[sick person's name]*
> *Is whole and well.*

You can do this spell at a Waxing Moon, imagining the person's health blossoming, or with a Waning Moon, imagining their illness shrinking. But remember that even for healing spells it is best to get the prior consent of the party involved. If this isn't possible, then try to concentrate on general wellbeing rather than actual health. The point is that we can never know what is right for another person and a cold now may give the person the rest they need to stave off something more serious in the future.

Dried eucalyptus leaves can also be made into a healing sachet. Choose green cotton and tie this up with green thread – you can consecrate it in your circle.

Turnip Another lunar vegetable, turnips used to be hollowed out at Hallowe'en and made into lanterns, although now we prefer the softer and larger pumpkin. The candle in such lanterns represents the life that endures within the root vegetables, hidden underground, during the darkness of winter. It also represents the light of the Moon that illuminates the night and this 'hidden' light also echoes the fact that the light of the Moon disappears for several days, only to reappear. Put simply, there is always light even when all is black.

If you want to get rid of an unwanted lover, cook them a dish of turnips! It isn't just the taste that will put them off, but the good old turnip has the magical ability to repel advances!

Poppy The drug opium is made from poppies, but poppies also have magical powers to induce dreams. Naturally they are ruled by the Moon. A Harvest Moon poppy spell can give you the answer to a question. Take an empty poppy-seed pod. Write your question on a small piece of paper and insert the paper into the empty seed pod. Place this under your pillow at the Harvest Full Moon and you will dream about the answer. This spell can also be undertaken at other times, but harvest is best.

Poppy seeds can be added to lovers' meals to intensify the passion and idealism of the union and to see the God and the Goddess within the other.

Grapes Grapes are special to the Moon. Obviously it is their healing qualities that make them such frequent gifts for the sick and hospitalised! Grapes make a wonderful addition to your lunar feast if you are doing a money spell. If you wish to become pregnant or increase your fertility, consecrate some white grapes as the Moon waxes and eat them in the two days coming up to Full Moon.

Lilies The heady, sensuous aroma of lilies links them with the love Goddess, but while they are indeed special to Venus, they are also ruled by the Moon. Lilies keep away evil spirits, and if you suspect that someone has put a love charm on you, wearing a lily will prevent you succumbing – but mind the bright orange stain from the pollen which could be a giveaway to those in the know! Because these flowers break enchantment they are, in fact, touching gifts from a lover for they speak of genuine feeling that does not wish to charm and seduce but to become truly close.

Jasmine The fragrant oil from these Moon-ruled flowers can be burned near the bed if you wish to have prophetic dreams. Try this at Full Moon and you may have many interesting dreams, but at the Dark of the Moon your dreams may be about deeper and more significant matters.

Honesty The pods of this lunar plant look like coins. Consecrate three in your circle when the New Moon first appears in the sky and keep them in your purse until Full Moon. Take them out and wrap them in a green cloth until the next New Moon and repeat – until you are loaded!

Full Moon Cleansing Spell This spell is good for cleansing your surroundings of all manner of subtle contamination, from hauntings to your own or other people's unpleasant emotions. It can be very good after a row and is excellent practice if you are moving in to a new house and you are not sure what 'vibes' have been left behind.

Wash your hands thoroughly in pure soap (not soap made from animal fat and/or synthetic perfumes). Natural lavender soap is excellent. Fill a bowl with water. Take three organically grown lemons and peel them over the bowl, letting the peel fall into the water. Squeeze the peeled fruits in your hand (it will sting any small cuts or sores you have, so take care) until they are as dry as can be. Keep the pith to bury outside later. If the moonlight falls on the water, so much the better, and stirring the mixture with a willow wand will add to its potency.

Scoop up a little of the lemon water in a cup or chalice and hold it up in a toast to the Moon, asking for her power. Now sip it saying, 'Let me be cleansed of all contamination so I am as pure as the white Moon.' Now take a clean white cloth and wipe it around all the doors, windowsills and skirting boards, and sprinkle a little of the lemon water over carpets and curtains. Go all over the house, flicking droplets and wiping. Remember, you aren't trying to scrub everything, by any means – just a symbolic touch will direct your intention and give your whole house a fresh feeling. Bless the Moon for the wonderful house-wife she is!

Simple Moon Phase Spells *Working with the New Moon:* When you first see the New Moon, turn over the money in your pocket or purse so that it will increase – and best to look straight at the Moon herself, not through the glass of a window (but your contact lenses can stay put!).

At first sight of the New Moon, make sure you are standing on earth or soft grass (not on tarmac). Bow three times or turn round, sun-wise, three times and make a wish.

When you first spot the New Moon, kiss the first person of the opposite sex that you see – without saying a word. Before the lunar month is out this will bring you a gift to treasure (but it may not be a material gift).

If you want to dream about your future lover, look at the New Moon over your right shoulder and say:

New Moon, New Moon, tell me true
When, where, what and who.
New Moon, New Moon, shining clear
Show my true love, drawing near.

A little jasmine oil on your pillow after this spell should make you dream about that special someone.

Waning Moon Spell to Get Rid of Negativity
Try this spell to banish grief, feelings of loss, feelings of inferiority, sorrow regret and ill-health. Find a black stone and obtain some white chalk. On a clear night as the Moon begins to wane, go to a stream, write something on the stone with the white chalk to represent the feeling you wish to be without. Throw the stone into the stream, saying:

Waning Moon wash away
All my sorrow of today
As your cycle starts anew
Bring me something fresh and true.

Walk away from the stream, take special care of yourself over the coming two weeks – pamper yourself, for you are not only recovering but incubating something new that will improve your life with the next lunar cycle.

Waning Moon Healthy Eating Spell
For this spell I'm avoiding the word 'diet' because it has such negative and unpleasant associations. Witchcraft is about enjoying life and loving yourself, so having food you like is, in fact, a ritual in praise of the Great Mother! Please never ever do a spell to get thin, because that result can come about in many ways, some of them horrid! You should instead work for health and wellbeing. However, having said this, if you are overweight to the point where it is a danger to your health, then a spell to get you on the right track will help, and the Waning Moon is the best time.

For this spell, you will need a little of the foods you wish to stop eating (this can be very general, for instance a small piece of chocolate can symbolise all the sweet things you want to cut down, a little butter can represent all animal fats, etc), a plant pot of a dark colour, some compost and seven garlic cloves.

Lie down and relax. Imagine that there is a table laid with all the foods that you do not want to eat any longer, then imagine all of them being bundled up and thrown away and the table re-laid with healthy foods. Describe all of this in detail to yourself. Describe foods you find delicious – there is no point trying to make yourself like stuff you hate. Choose from fruits, vegetables, wholemeal bread, yoghurt, lean meats, fish and all the things that we know are good for us. Tell yourself that you eat slowly, that you enjoy your food, that you can leave food on your plate, that you eat to satisfy your body and that you feel good.

Remind yourself of the good things you have done in the past and all your positive qualities. (This can be surprisingly hard because many of us have quite low self-esteem, so enlist a supportive friend to say some nice things about you to give yourself a boost!) Connect all these good qualities with the fact that now you are choosing to eat healthily and you will succeed with this as you have succeeded in the past. You can record all of this on a tape beforehand, if you wish.

After your 'pep talk' to yourself, get up and place the pieces of foods in the pot, place the soil over them and the garlic pods into the top of the soil. Garlic is a cleansing plant that will seal your spell. It is in fact ruled by the warlike and determined Mars, but is also associated with Hecate, Goddess of the Waning Moon, and so it is very suitable.

Perform this entire spell, including the part where you give yourself talking to, in your properly cast circle. Afterwards put the pot out in the garden and eat your way to health and fitness!

Moon Charms

Making a lunar charm will connect you to the tides of life and your own magical and instinctual self. You can keep it with you when you wish to use your sensitivity, open your inner eyes, or do divination, ritual or meditation. Your lunar charm can also help you sleep, have important dreams, attract love, and bring you peace and healing gifts. It can make you green-fingered and promote pregnancy, too. It is best to focus on one or two of these attributes for a single charm and make another for other purposes. For instance, if you want to get pregnant, focus your thoughts on that. If you want to become more psychic, concentrate on that and your charm will help with divination, meditation and ritual. Love is best kept as a separate charm. Peace, sweet sleep and dreams may be grouped together, and home and garden also form a comfortable duo of purposes for your charm. However, a single lunar charm will help you become more 'lunar' in nature and so can serve for all matters if you so wish. Go with what feels right for you.

Choose something small that you can keep with you. Any silver jewellery can suffice, especially if it is crescent-shaped. There are several Moon-ruled stones and you can choose from among these, consecrating and cleansing in the manner described earlier in the chapter. For a Moon charm, a wonderful extra touch is to immerse the object in water on which the Full Moon is reflected and then say the words 'I dedicate…,' etc. For objects that should not be made wet, use a silver dish on which the moonlight is falling.

Moon-ruled Stones

Crystal: There are many types of crystal (also called quartz) and these have been used by shamanic cultures for millennia. Believed by the ancients to be solidified water, crystal has been used in rain magic in dry parts of the world. In the Eleusinian temple quartz may have been used to generate fire from sunlight. (Eleusis was the site of the ancient mystery temple of Ancient Greece, over which was inscribed the words 'Know thyself'. The secret rites were designed to promote wisdom and awareness.) Crystals can be placed at the ends of wands, to conduct energy. Well-chosen crystals can be placed on your altar to represent Goddess and God, the former sphere-shape, the latter phallic. The familiar 'crystal ball' used for scrying is a well-known witches' accompaniment, although currently most 'crystal' balls are, in fact, glass, because crystal is so expensive. However, crystal does not have to be perfect to be used as a speculum, for the small 'impurities' can help in the formation of pictures. Your crystal ball can be placed underneath your pillow (unless it is too large and uncomfortable!) to make it more attuned to your subconscious.

Psychism is increased by wearing quartz crystal and it can be placed underneath the pillow to aid sleep and induce prophetic dreams. Crystals can take away headaches and toothache if placed against the affected parts and held in the palm to ease fever. Crystals can be used in healing any part of the body, and they should then be cleansed of the negative energies before being used again. Crystals are believed to help lactation. They can also be placed on the altar during ritual to increase the power, used as a focus for meditation and stored with tarot cards or runes to increase their divinatory properties.

There are several types of quartz crystal. Blue quartz generates peace, green quartz brings creativity and money, rose quartz encourages love, rutilated quartz increases magical power, and smoky quartz brings you down to earth and lifts your spirits.

Rose Quartz Love Charm   For this you will need a willow twig the size of your ring finger. (If you have to cut this from the tree, ask permission from the tree and cut it with a silver knife, or knife with a silver handle.) You will also need a silver ring, some lemon balm oil or jasmine, a piece of rose quartz (shaped like a heart if possible) and a rose-coloured cloth bag. Or you may use a piece of rose quartz set in silver, on a silver chain. Burn candles of rose colour on which you have inscribed a heart-shape with your silver knife (this doesn't have to be artistically exact!).

Do this spell at Full Moon, after cleansing your rose quartz in salt water and leaving it in the light of the Moon for the three days before your ritual if possible. Do the same with the ring.

Cast your circle. Anoint the ring with some oil and slip it onto the willow twig, passing it through the fragrance from the oil-burner. Say:

Sweet Lady Moon, I ask of you
Bring to me a love that's true,
Through sky, o'er land and over sea
His hand in mine, his love to me.

Imagine the love that you want, take the time to picture all his (or her) qualities, how close you will be, the things you will share, and so on. When you are ready, slip the ring on your ring finger and take up the rose quartz, which you should also anoint with the oil. Hold the rose quartz in your palm pressing against your ring finger. Once again imagine the love that you desire, and think of the things you will do together and of the happy times ahead. Pour all the love you can into the rose quartz.

Keep the quartz with you or wear it at all times, but take off the ring because you have not yet found the love that you want – when you do, he or she can put the ring back. Sleep with the ring beneath your pillow to dream of your love and plant the little willow twig near running water.

Please remember that this spell should not be aimed at a specific person because magic should not interfere with the will or life path of another person. Just think about the sort of person you want and let the Moon do the work – after all, as she looks down from the starry sky she can see everyone and look deep into their hearts as they sleep! She knows more than you do and will do a better job of picking Mr or Ms Right!

Beryl   This stone increases psychic awareness and is good for placing on the altar during Full Moon rites. Wearing beryl stops you being lazy. It is good for the liver, eases swollen glands and eye diseases. It aids study, attracts love and can help you to find a lost object if you hold it in your palm, close your eyes, still your mind and visualise the object. It is also a great protection for travel by sea.

Aquamarine   This is a semi-precious type of beryl. It helps psychism and may be rubbed on the body before magical acts to increase power. It brings peace and happiness. Aquamarine was traditionally cleansed at the sea shore in the shallows of the tide by Full Moon's light, but this can be emulated inland and indoors by using a blue bowl, filled with water to which a little sea salt has been added and leaving the stone in this all night in the light of the Moon. Aquamarine is worn for health, courage and alertness.

Mother-of-Pearl   This comes from the inner shell of sea creatures and is not strictly speaking a 'stone'. It is best not to use commercial mother-of-pearl in magical rites because the creatures have to be killed to extract it. It was used in money spells and to protect new-born babies.

Moonstone   This is a magical stone that comes in blue, white and pink and can be used to top wands. It attracts love. A Full Moon spell for love can be cast using a rose pink candle and surrounding it with pieces of moonstone, while strongly visualising the love that you desire. Lovers' quarrels can be healed by exchanging moonstones.

It is a great friend to gardeners and can be worn during planting or tending your plot, or even buried in the Earth in a small ritual, while you imagine your garden burgeoning into luxuriant growth. Trees will fruit, it is said, if a moonstone is hung from their branches.

Wearing a moonstone can help you keep to a healthy diet when trying to lose weight. As the Moon begins to wane, hold your moonstone as you stand in your circle and visualise your body the way you would like it – be realistic! Rub the stone over the parts of your body you would like to reduce – it is best to be naked for this. Then place it against your forehead, affirming that it will concentrate your mind. Keep your stone with you and hold it in your palm when you think you may be tempted to over-eat. This can be combined with the garlic weight-loss spell given above.

Pearl   Pearls are obtained by killing the creature and so their use in magic is not advised. However, if you are given pearls by a loved relative or friend you may feel more confident that their negative properties have been neutralised, although personally I would never use them in magic. Pearls can be worn to attract love and even 'thrown away' into a pile of rubbish as a magical act, presumably along the lines of 'where there's muck, there's brass'! Pearls also increase fertility.

Sapphire   This beautiful blue stone is very potent magically and can be used to increase power and open the psychic senses. It gets rid of envy and increases rapport between lovers. It can be worn for protection because it will deflect any negative 'vibes' back to where they came from. Sapphires can also be magically charged to attract wealth. If you are innocent and have to go to court to defend yourself, sapphire will protect you. It also promotes health, particularly of the eyes, reduces fever and stops nosebleeds if pressed to the affected part. Star sapphire is considered to be the most powerful.

Holey Stone   These are just ordinary stones that have acquired a hole in the middle through the action of water. They are most usually found on beaches, so for me they are allied to all things lunar. 'Holey stones' may have the hole right through, like a doughnut, and then they can easily be hung on a chain or thong around the neck. Some have only a cavity and these can be used for other magical work. It is nicest if you can find your holey stones yourself. Because they symbolise the vagina and womb, they are linked to the Great Mother and all things feminine. They can be charged up in a ritual and used for protection. Simply hold up the cleansed stone and dedicate it to each of the elements in turn, naming their particular form of protection – Earth: material and financial; Air: protection from gossip, bad thoughts, etc; Fire: courage, protection from negativity; Water: emotional protection and healing. If you have a specific thing or person from which you need protection, link this to the appropriate element and pay special attention in that quarter.

These stones can be cleansed in salt water and used to heal. They are traditionally used to heal children. Consecrate your stone by the light of the Full Moon and peer through it to see ghosts and spirits.

To get pregnant, select a stone with a hole right through it. The stone should be as womb-shaped as possible. Perform your ritual the day before Full Moon, or at the exact Full Moon. Consecrate your stone and insert through it a piece of green ribbon. Say:

Moon Mother, Moon Mother, give to me
Precious new life to be.

Ripe Moon, ripe Moon, swell my womb,
Bring a child to love into my home.

Wear the holey stone at all times but especially when you are ovulating. Alternatively you may take a stone that does not have a hole all the way through. Insert into the hole a grape seed or a grain of rice and wrap it up in a piece of green cloth. Leave this under your pillow when you make love.

Stones and charms make lovely and very personal, thoughtful presents, especially if you have imbued them with some positive energy of love and caring before you give them!

Lunar Divination

Different types of divination may be suited best to different phases of the Moon. Psychic senses are heightened at Full Moon and indeed at this time you may feel more like experimenting and experiencing. Full Moon is the time to abandon your conscious mind and let your imagination take shape, following your dreams. At Dark Moon you may prefer to go on inward journeys, reflecting, introspecting and withdrawing. At this time wisdom may be your goal, while at Full Moon it may be inspiration. Full Moon meditations may be colourful and inspiring, while the same one at Dark Moon may be more sombre yet more revealing. All this will only become obvious as you practise and find out your own skills and preferences.

Scrying This is the art of looking for 'pictures' in a crystal, dark mirror or bowl of water – each of these instruments is called a 'speculum'. 'Crystal gazing' is scrying, for instance, and the Mirror of Galadriel in *The Lord of the Rings* is a speculum, through which the elf-queen can see all of Middle Earth, and beyond. However, for the most part we have to be content with something a bit more modest!

Crystals can be very expensive, but results may be obtained with smaller, cheaper globes. Just hold the crystal, look into it and see how it makes you feel, before making your choice. You may also buy a 'dark mirror' which is a piece of dark glass, concave in shape – again, go by what you feel. Cheapest and easiest of all, take a dark, shallow dish and fill it with water. You may drop a silver coin or piece of jewellery into the water, if you wish. Moonlight is wonderful for scrying, or you can do so by candlelight – at all events, the room needs to be fairly dark.

Simply gaze into your speculum at first and see what happens. Sometimes it seems that nothing happens; if this is the case, stop after ten minutes and try again at another lunar phase or when you are in a different frame of mind. Burn incense if you wish to help induce the right state of mind. Just allow a dreamy feel to come over you; try not to tense up or concentrate too hard. Look for pictures of any sort forming in the speculum. Sometimes it goes milky and cloudy first. It may seem that you literally 'see' forms within the speculum or pictures may form in your mind's eye. Do not be too quick to jump to conclusions as to meanings – for instance, seeing a skull generally means change and ancestral wisdom rather than death.

When you feel you are mastering the technique, you can ask a specific question and see what appears. Don't forget to have a note-book handy because it's amazing how quickly those images fade when 'ordinary' consciousness returns. Also, symbols that are hard to identify or interpret may suddenly seem meaningful at a later time and you may find yourself saying, 'Ahah! – that's what it means!' Sometimes an event will take place and you will realise that something you saw, but couldn't interpret, in fact relates to it. Good gazing!

Dowsing Dowsing is best known as a method for finding water. The skilled dowser can detect its presence from the twitching of a hazel stick. However, the water doesn't make the stick twitch, but messages from the dowser's own intuitive mind. It is not only water that can be found by dowsing, but almost anything you wish – and a hazel twig isn't the only dowsing tool you can use. Many people prefer to use a crystal pendulum, and crystal is of course ruled by the Moon.

Dowsing takes many years of practice in order to experiment and refine your skills. However, some good and interesting results can be obtained immediately. Almost anyone can dowse, and those who 'can't' are probably blanking out their abilities through disbelief. Some sources state that almost anything dangling on the end of a piece of string or chain can be used in dowsing, but others say that crystal is best. I would agree with this, for crystal conducts energies in ways we don't fully understand. Besides, crystal is beautiful. You can 'make friends' with a crystal in a way that is just not possible with an old button on a string. White crystal on a silver chain is the perfect lunar dowsing tool.

Choose your dowsing crystal from one of the many New Age shops that sell them. You can make your own dowsing pendulum from a piece of quartz and some silver, if you are skilled. But at the time of writing (Beltane 2002), lovely crystal pendulums, ready-shaped, can be bought for about £12. If you use your intuition you can find one that feels wonderful, looks lovely and inspires you.

When you have chosen your dowsing crystal, cleanse and dedicate it as suggested earlier in the chapter. Leave it in the light of the Full Moon for one night if possible. Keep it in a pouch of dark, soft cloth. Take time to get to know your crystal by simply lighting a candle and sitting quietly with it, dangling it, watching it move and catch the light. Leave it beneath your pillow. Get to love it and feel close to it.

Now 'programme' your pendulum by holding it still and straight and saying, 'Show me yes.' Usually the pendulum will start to move sun-wise – i.e. clockwise in the Northern Hemisphere, anti-clockwise in the Southern Hemisphere. *It will move* – trust me! Just give it time. When you have established 'yes', do the same for 'no', which will naturally be in the opposite direction. Ambivalent answers are usually denoted by a swing from side to side. Test your pendulum by asking it some questions to which you already know the answer, so you are affirming and confirming the meanings.

Some dowsers consciously set the pendulum swinging before they start so it is going from side to side very rapidly before settling into clockwise or counter-clockwise circling. Others simply hold it steady. Most accept that involuntary movements of the hand actually cause the swing, but that is quite in keeping with the purpose of the pendulum – which is to access your own instinctual knowledge, bypassing your conscious mind. However, it seems to me that there is more at work than that on some occasions when the pendulum swings out almost horizontally. Whatever the case, the pendulum will give you answers you could not otherwise obtain.

What can you ask of your programmed pendulum? Almost anything! You can ask it what food is good for you; where is a good place to live, eat or sleep; when is a good time to get pregnant, buy shares or plant your cabbages! Lost objects can be found by holding your pendulum and turning round until you get a positive reading, moving forwards and letting the pendulum show you when you are 'getting warmer'. Skilled dowsers can even dowse with just a map, placing one forefinger on the map while they hold the pendulum in the other hand, watching for the swing. One of the favourite uses for pendulums is to assess the energies at ancient sites or to discover ley lines on the surface of the earth. When I do this I feel more in tune with the place and find it is a gateway to dreams and inner pictures – and sometimes to a gem of insight. But serious dowsers may uncover interesting information about such places, for example about underground passageways and similar. Dowsing can also be used in dealing with hauntings, to detect spirits and to find out how they may be laid to rest. One of the most useful things a dowser can look for is 'energy lines' or ley lines that run through a house and which may have effects on those who dwell there.

If you decide dowsing is for you this may be the start of a lifetime of exploration. Good journey!

Arianrhod's Silver Wheel Divination

For this divination you will need to be a bit creative. In making or finding your tools, however, you are imbuing them with your own special power and vibrations, and they will work all the better for this.

You will need a square of thick, soft cloth that does not fray, about a metre square. Within this you need to draw, mark or sew with tape, a circle, about 75cm in diameter. (You could draw around the top of a circular coffee table to achieve this.) You then need to quarter this circle. One quarter should be marked in the centre with a small black circle for Dark Moon, one with a silver semi-circle for Waxing Moon, one with a silver circle for Full Moon and one with a silver semi-circle for Waning Moon, in a mirror image of the Waxing Moon. These small circles can be about 1.5cm in diameter – you could draw around a coin. They need to mark the quadrants clearly and attractively. Now you will need three red stones, three green stones, three blue stones, three brown, dark grey or very dark green stones, and one black stone. These stones can be bought quite cheaply in many New Age shops and you can have fun choosing them. For instance, your brown stone could be mottled moss agate, your red stones carnelian, your blue ones lapis or chrysocolla, your green stones malachite and your black stone apache tear. An even cheaper and more natural option, probably in keeping with witches of old, would be to collect stones from your own locality, along lanes, woodland, parkland or beach. The stones should be of similar size and shape, slightly smaller than Brazil nuts is best. Keep the stones in a drawstring bag, large enough for you to insert your hand without seeing what you are picking.

The red stones represent the future, physical and mental energy, enterprises and career; the blue stones represent communication, thought, study and mental endeavours – they relate to the immediate present and close future; the green stones relate to love, healing, family matters and often to the past; while the brown stones relate to practicalities, to money, buildings, the physical body and the land. They may also relate to the distant past and to traditions. Naturally not all the meanings will be applicable – for instance timing may not be relevant to your question. The black stone relates to the unknown, mysteries, surprises and the unpredictable.

To make your divination, you should burn a silver or white candle. Burning jasmine oil or incense will help the process. Favoured times for Moon divination are on Monday, as this is the 'Moon's day' at the third hour after sunset (times for sunrise and sunset are given in newspapers). It is always better to have a salt bath before divination, to cleanse yourself psychically as much as physically.

When you are ready, formulate your question. Draw out a stone and hold it in your palm without looking at it. Hold your closed fist about 70cm above the exact centre of the circle and let the stone fall. Do this three times. If any stone falls outside the circle it doesn't count, and if it is the first stone, return it to the bag, shake and start again. If this happens three times in a row, leave your question for now because it is void. (However, be careful that you are not holding your fist too high above the cloth, or that your cloth is too thin, or uneven, for this may cause too many stones to slip outside.)

The first stone you draw defines the situation. For instance, your question might have been about love, but if the first stone is a brown one the conditions surrounding your question are financial or practical, in effect. So you might have asked 'Is my current relationship right for me?' and be thinking along emotional lines, although the true issues are in fact practical things, such as where you are living. The second stone indicates current conditions and the third stone gives the outcome. Where matters do not seem clear, a fourth stone can be drawn and dropped. The Dark Moon quadrant signifies endings and beginnings, the Full Moon quadrant things that are culminating either in achievement or 'too much', the Waxing crescent things that are growing and developing, or revealing themselves, and the Waning quadrant things that are winding down, or needing less effort and attention. Of course, all this is quite general and you will need lots of practice to feel confident of your interpretations. Learn to trust your intuitions and avoid the trap of equating Waning Moon and Dark Moon with 'badness' – they aren't the same!

An Example Tricia had been offered a new job, but she was afraid that this would affect her relationship as it would involve travel and her partner tended to be jealous. The first stone she threw, to her surprise, was a blue one, landing in the waning quadrant, indicating that the true issue was her boredom at work and need for fresh mental stimulation. A brown stone falling in the waning quadrant also indicated that practical difficulties could be resolved, and finally a red stone in the Full Moon area suggested creative fulfilment. 'But what about Richard?' she asked again. 'Will our relationship survive this change?' So another stone was drawn, this time a green one, landing on the Dark Moon quadrant, indicating endings and beginnings. As Tricia and Richard were very much in love and had, for the most part, an understanding relationship, the likelihood was that Richard would overcome his possessiveness and the relationship would have a new start on a different footing.

Of course, all divination is open to alternative interpretation. Remember, first thoughts are often best, and practice makes perfect!

CHAPTER 6

MOON MEDITATIONS

The purpose of a lunar meditation is to put you in touch with your instinctual self, to get in contact with that wise, but non-rational part of you that is obscured in the rough and tumble of the daylight hours and the demands of our schedule-driven lives. A meditation will also relax you and help you to expand your consciousness so that you know, at a deep level, that there is more to life in the great beyond. It may even give you the answers to some questions.

This chapter gives meditations for Dark and Full Moons, and one for the Moon in each of the signs of the Zodiac. While the Dark and Full Moon meditations are intended to be used at those phases, you can use the meditation for your own Moon sign at any time, wherever the Moon is by sign and phase, to get in touch with your own lunar nature. Or you could try the meditation that applies to the Moon sign of a friend, lover, child or family member, to help you understand them all the better. Another alternative is to use the Zodiac meditations when the Moon is in that sign, whatever her phase. Remember, Full Moon is always in the sign opposite the Sun sign, and New Moon is in the same sign as the Sun.

Another option you have is to 'journey'. This means going on an inward journey of your own, unscripted. To do this use merely the first part of the script, as indicated, and then see where you are taken. Remember to note down anything you see or experience immediately afterwards, before it fades. Challenge any creature you meet with the words 'Do you come in love?' Only if the answer is a clear 'Yes' should you have any more to do with them. 'Throwing' a quick circle around yourself before you meditate will act as protection. It may help you to play music of your choice. When you feel your journey is coming to an end, return to the place from which you started in order to come back to everyday awareness.

★ ⁂ ★ *Setting the Scene*

If you take a little trouble to prepare yourself and your surroundings, you are likely to slip into the necessary altered state of consciousness all the more easily. If you are busy and can only spend half an hour, that is fine for it is better to make your meditation manageable than not to do it at all. It may help if you can record the meditation on to a tape in advance, for that way you can simply listen and lose yourself.

If you have plenty of time, start by taking a bath containing a little jasmine oil (see the note in Chapter 5 about oils). Heat some of the oil in a burner and light candles. Make sure you are really comfortable and allow a pleasant, dreamy state to come over you, so you are as relaxed as you can be before you start. Make sure that you won't be disturbed by children, pets or phones. Lie on your bed, for that gives messages of relaxation to your unconscious, and let the Moon shine in if possible. Light candles – and you are ready to begin!

★ ⁂ ★ *Closing Down*

Occult tidiness is always a good idea whatever your working, and you should be careful to close down properly after your meditation. This should not disturb you too much if you want to go off to sleep, but get in the habit of doing it. When you have finished, put out your candles and remember to dismantle your protective circle. Pat yourself all over and have a bite to eat or drink – a sip of water will do. This will confirm to you that you have re-entered everyday consciousness.

★ ⁂ ★ *Full Moon Meditation*

It is night time and you are standing on the sea-shore. In front of you the Full Moon is hanging over the waters, white and beautiful. The breeze blows off the ocean, gentle and fragrant, bringing a tantalising scent of unknown places. The waves are pounding in a soft rhythm and you can feel a hint of moisture on your cheek and a faint tang of salt on your lips. Breathe deeply. Apart from the sigh of the waves all is still and peaceful. You can feel the softness of the sand under your feet. Around the glowing Moon, the sky is powdered with stars. *[Pause.]*

The Moon is casting a glistening reflection over the waves, tipping them with silver. In fact it is just as if the Moon is making a path over the water, a glittering, magical path to a mysterious and wonderful place. Wouldn't it be wonderful to be able to walk over the water, along the Moonpath, to find where it might lead? *[Pause.]*

You step over to the water's edge and find, to your delight, that something marvellous has happened. Where the Moon's reflection falls, the waters have turned solid. Now there is a silver path, rippled like the waters but smooth and still, leading towards the bright, shining Moon. Carefully you place your foot on its cool surface and look ahead. You are walking to the Moon! *[Pause. At this point leave the instructions and go alone if you wish to journey.]*

Slowly you tread the glorious Moonpath. On either side of you the dark waters heave, but the path feels good and ahead of you the Moon is coming nearer and nearer. How dazzling she is! You realise that she is encrusted with many fabulous jewels – crystals, opals, quartz, pearls and moonstones. You see that there is a silver staircase on her face leading to a jewelled door. Lightly you tread towards it. *[Pause.]*

Now the light of the Moon is overwhelming and you are at the foot of the delicate staircase. Slowly you go up it, admiring the jewels and precious stones around you. On the stairs there are many artefacts. What do you see? One of the objects is a large silver key. Pick it up and carry it to the top. *[Pause.]*

Before you there is a huge, arched silver door, marked by a circle with two crescents on either side. You put the key into the keyhole and open it. It slips open easily and you find you are in a large, cool enclosure. This is like an indoor garden, with many luxuriant plants. There are terraces and pools, and fountains playing. There is a sound of soft, strange music. *[Pause.]*

Ahead of you there is a path leading to a bridge over a small lake. On the lake lie water lilies like great white goblets. The light is clear and diffused and seems to be emanating from the opalescent walls. You start to walk along the path and notice that it is iridescent with millions of tiny jewels. *[Pause.]*

Now you have arrived at the bridge. It is made of silver. You walk upwards until you reach the level over the centre of the lake. The water lilies are thick and luscious. You look down and you can see there is a section of the lake that has been left completely clear. It is a perfect circle and it is immediately beneath you. *[Pause.]*

You stop and lean over the parapet, looking straight down into the water. You have never seen water so lovely. It seems to be a combination of many colours – purple, jade green, turquoise, deep blue. It is all those colours and more. You stare into it, mesmerised. *[Pause.]*

The water is becoming milky – how strange! You stare and stare, but it is opaque and clouded. Then the clouds form themselves into curtains, which slowly part and you find yourself looking deep into the lake. What do you see? *[Pause.]*

Take your time to look into the lake, staring deep within. You may see only water, you may see the bottom of the lake, you may see faces, landscapes, buildings. Take note of all you see for it is important. Note any events that are unfolding. *[Pause.]*

When you are ready to make your way back, you find a silver coin in your pocket and throw it into the waters as an offering. Make your way back down the side of the bridge, along the path and out, through the door, remembering to lock the door with the key and leave it where you found it. *[Pause.]*

Now you are on your way back. You go down the silver staircase and find your feet once more on the Moonpath. The brilliance of the Moon is behind you and around you the night is getting darker and darker as you move away from her light. The surrounding ocean is dim and restless. Soon you find your feet are once more on the sand. You turn to say farewell and find that the Moonpath has disappeared and now there is only moonlight on the waters. *[Pause.]*

Linger a while to give thanks for your safe journey and come back to everyday awareness when you are ready. Remember to make a note of what you saw in the waters.

★ ☆ ★ *Dark Moon Meditation*

Do this meditation in a dark room lit by a solitary candle.

It is the depths of night and you find yourself walking over rugged country beneath a star-spangled sky that has no Moon. Ahead of you there appears to be a building with high turrets and spires. As you come closer, you see it looks like a temple, built entirely of ebony. *[Pause.]*

You approach a great, black door, only just visible in the starlight. At first you cannot find the handle but once you do the massive door swings easily and silently inwards and you enter a huge, dimly-lit courtyard. There is a bitter-sweet scent of incense. *[Pause.]*

In the centre of the courtyard there is a wall with an archway in it. You realise that this is the entrance to a maze. You walk towards it curiously – should you go in? How will you find your way out again? Feeling that all will be well, you take your first steps into the maze. *[Pause. If you wish to journey, this is the point at which you may leave the instructions.]*

Within the maze it isn't as dark as you expected and you make your choices of directions with confidence, but you are not sure where you are going. Along one passage, through an opening, along another passageway, through a door, round a corner, the journey seems never-ending and you are sure that you cannot find your way back. *[Pause.]*

Now you are coming into a chamber and you realise that you are at the heart of the maze. There is an altar ahead of you, covered in black cloth. On the altar there is a mother-of-pearl box, a large white unlit candle and some matches. *[Pause.]*

You take up the matches and light the candle. Now you can see much better – the shadows seem to be fading. You open the mother-of-pearl box and you see three things – a seed, a book and a key. These are for you. You take them and put them in your pocket and give thanks. *[Pause.]*

By the light of the candle you find your way out of the maze and back into the courtyard. There you find a comfortable seat to sit down upon and con-template three questions. What will the seed grow into? What is the book about? And what does the key open? *[Pause.]*

Stay seated for a while until you are ready to come back to everyday aware-ness. Make sure you make a note of what these three items were for, because it will probably be different every time there is a New Moon. Bring yourself back to everyday awareness by the usual means, eating, drinking, patting yourself and dismantling your protective circle.

Zodiac Moon Meditations

Moon in Aries
You find yourself standing in a volcanic landscape. It is evening. Ahead of you the flaming sky is cut by the brilliant sickle of the New Moon. Hot pools are bubbling on either side of you and a stream of brilliant lava flows along in the distance. This is a beautiful, although challenging terrain. *[Pause.]*

You walk through the smoky air towards a castle you can see in the distance. The air is warm. Some of the stones beside the path are glowing with heat. Tough plants grow in the dry earth, their foliage strident in colours of red, orange and gold. *[Pause. If you wish to journey alone, leave the instructions at this point.]*

Determined to reach the castle ahead, you continue through the colourful landscape. The crescent Moon beckons. You feel it is important to get to your destination. However, the way is becoming softer and you see that there is a green patch of grass ahead with a small table laid for a meal. You walk over to the grass and realise that the most important thing is to look after your bodily needs. *[Pause.]*

Having nourished yourself, you continue on your journey. The castle is getting closer and you see flags flying from the ramparts, beside the crescent of the Moon. You feel excited by what lies ahead of you at the end of your journey. You realise how important it is to have goals in life. *[Pause.]*

The volcanic landscape gives way to rocky terrain and you are drawing close to the castle. Your feet clatter on the drawbridge as you cross it. You realise that this castle holds something important for you. But what are your real needs? You understand that it is important to keep asking yourself this question. *[Pause.]*

Ahead of you there is a dais and on it stands a two-handled silver cup with red ribbons attached. This trophy is for you. You approach it and see that within the cup there is a special treasure for you. You take this out and hold it – this is your real reward.

Come back to everyday awareness when you are ready, bringing with you the awareness of your gift. Make a note of your feelings and experiences.

Moon in Taurus   It is a warm spring evening and the new Moon is glistening in the pink sky. You are standing at the edge of a meadow filled with beautiful blue flowers. You are aware of their heady fragrance. You feel comfortable and secure. You want to hold on to this feeling and you breathe deeply of the fragrance. *[Pause.]*

A nightingale is singing with breathtaking sweetness. You are aware of the soft sensation of your clothes touching you and the firmness of the Earth beneath your feet. The flowers are blue as sapphires, swaying very gently in the evening breeze. You are aware of the devastating beauty that there is in life. *[Pause. If you wish to journey, stop the instructions a this point.]*

Ahead of you there is an especially large and wonderful flower. You are attracted by its remarkable brilliance. You go towards it and find that the centre of the flower is, in fact, an enormous jewel, sparkling and scintillating. This jewel is priceless. You become aware of the generosity and bounty of Nature.

Now you approach this flower and touch the jewel. You realise that this jewel is for you! It feels warm and smooth to your fingertips, so solid and perfect. It falls from the centre of the flower into your hand, like a ripe plum. You realise that nothing can take from you what is truly yours. *[Pause.]*

Now you take your jewel to the edge of the field. The blue of the flowers is echoed by the blue of the jewel. As you look into its azure depths you see a reflection of the crescent Moon shimmering within and you feel truly blessed and at ease. You realise that not only are you safe, you are surrounded by beauty.

Come back to the edge of the meadow. Look up at the crescent Moon in the sunset and at its reflection in the jewel you hold. This gift is worth a king's ransom, but it can buy you more than material goods. What do you wish for?

Come back to everyday awareness and record any thoughts or sensations.

Moon in Gemini The Full Moon is riding high and you find yourself on a hill above a magical moonlit landscape. All is silver – silver trees, silver birds and silver butterflies, bright under the moonlight, glinting and glittering as they move. *[Pause.]*

Beneath you, on the plains, there seem to be many fascinating buildings, also silver, with roads winding between them like white ribbons. You wish that you, too, were a bird with silver wings. You stretch your arms and to your delight you find you are rising from the ground! You too can fly! *[Pause. If you wish to journey alone, leave the instructions at this point.]*

Flying over the fields and towns, you realise how much variety and choice there is. There are so many interesting places you could land. You realise how wonderful it is to have choices as you hover and examine everything you see. *[Pause.]*

Below you there is an especially imposing building. You realise this must be a library of rare and special books. You decide that you will alight and enter it. Your feet touch down lightly in a moonlit square. You become aware that you have committed yourself and that this will improve your capabilities. *[Pause.]*

You see the moonlight playing upon a doorway and you walk towards it. You go in and find you are surrounded by ranks of books of all kinds. All the wisdom of the world is collected here. You want to explore, but ahead of you is a desk with a notepad and pen upon it. You approach this and realise that you need to write down your true feelings, for these are the most important information. *[Pause.]*

Getting up from the desk, you walk towards a large bookcase and select a book. You open the book and find that it does not contain written pages but a gift for you. Take this gift and treasure it.

When you are ready, come back to everyday awareness and note your experiences and your feelings.

Moon in Cancer   You are standing on a rocky beach at midnight with the Full Moon radiant overhead. The rocks glisten white in the moonlight and shimmer as though inlaid with jewels. You hear the steady swish-swish of the waves. Their crisp white edges fold gently, one over another, onto the shore. The rock-pools are patches of onyx, scattered about the beach. *[Pause.]*

You begin to walk along the beach. The taste of salt is on your tongue and the midnight wind stirs your hair. The sounds of the waves remind you of the gentle breathing of a sleeping person and the night air is warm and balmy. You feel at peace, yet you know you are seeking something. *[Pause. If you wish to journey leave the instructions at this point.]*

You find yourself close to an especially beautiful rock pool. The Moon lies within its surface as if it has been captured. You kneel down and cup the reflection of the Moon, feeling the cool water run through your fingers. The pearly reflection runs away with it, but is still there, rippled now, in the pool. You become aware that you do not always have to hold something to remain in contact. *[Pause.]*

You continue your walk along the beach. Ahead of you, lying on the beach but rising and falling with the waves that lap it, lies a small boat. You approach it and decide to get in. As you push off from the shore you become aware that you can direct the boat to wherever you wish. *[Pause.]*

Drifting over the smooth waves, the boat comes to rest on an island. You get out of the boat and walk up the shore. The sand is soft between your toes. You become aware that ahead of you, above the high-water mark, there is a cosy dwelling. You enter this and find it comfortably furnished and beautifully decorated, just as you would wish, with delicious food in the cupboards. You become aware that you can make a lovely home wherever you may be. *[Pause.]*

When you are ready to go, you walk back down to the little boat, get in and direct your passage over the moonlit tide, back to the original beach, where you began. The boat beaches itself gently and you get out. You find yourself standing next to a large white shell. Within that shell there lies a gift for you. Take this and treasure it.

Come back to the everyday, bringing your gift with you and be sure to note your feelings and experiences.

Moon in Leo   You find yourself at the head of a ceremonial path, flanked by burning torches. Overhead the waxing crescent gleams in the flaming sky of sunset. Banners wave in brilliant colours along the processional way and a red carpet stretches into the distance. *[Pause.]*

Ahead in the distance, something shines gold in the sunset, beneath the Moon's silver sliver. You decide that you want to walk towards it. On either side of you the torches are flaming and you hear the sound of trumpets in the distance. *[Pause. If you wish to journey alone, leave the instructions at this point.]*

As you walk along the carpeted path, you see that ahead of you a golden ball is rolling. You run after it, and it rolls more quickly. You run faster and catch it, throwing it up towards the Moon in the resplendent sky. You realise how wonderful it is to play. *[Pause.]*

You continue your walk towards the golden object. You become aware of a sound of chanting behind you. You realise that many people are following you and you feel justly proud. However, you do not turn around to see them, for you realise that you will go your own true way, whether you are followed or not. *[Pause.]*

The golden object is now closer and you realise that it is a gleaming throne, waiting for you beneath the Moon and the sunset sky. You approach it, and seat yourself upon it. You become aware that your heart is open and full of love. *[Pause.]*

Someone detaches from the crowd and comes up towards you. You notice that they are bearing a gift for you. You take it with gratitude and pleasure. This is something special and meaningful for you to treasure.

Come back to everyday awareness, remembering your gift and its meanings. Make a note of your feelings and experiences.

Moon in Virgo   You are standing in a golden wheat-field at dusk. The Harvest Moon hangs, lush and low, over the fruitful land. You smell the dusty, musty Earth and the warm breeze ripples the ranks of corn. *[Pause.]*

Beneath your feet is the solid Earth. You can feel the stalks brushing against your legs. Around you all is fertility and abundance. But what can you do with and within it? *[Pause. If you wish to journey, leave the instructions at this point.]*

By your feet lies a silver sickle. You pick this up and begin to harvest the wheat. How easily your blade slices through the dry stems! Magically, you soon find that the entire field is harvested and bound up into stacks. You become aware of how much you can accomplish if you simply get on with it. *[Pause.]*

You become aware that one of the stacks is larger than the other and appears to be quite smooth. The Harvest Moon crowns this stack and both seem to be made of pale gold. You approach this stack and find it has an opening in it. You become aware that all is not always as it seems. *[Pause.]*

You decide to enter the opening within the stack. You realise that you have come into a tent and before you there is a table laid for supper. You become aware that industry is always rewarded. By one of the plates there is a gift for you, in a pale gold wrapper. *[Pause.]*

Pick up your gift and take it out with you into the harvested cornfield. Look about you and see all the neat stacks of healthy corn – this is your work! Sit within the stooks and open your gift. It has special meaning for you.

Treasure this present for it has symbolic meaning for you. Be sure to make a note of it when you come back to everyday awareness.

Moon in Libra

You find yourself in a temple precinct. The Full Moon bathes some beautiful and graceful statues that flank it. In the pearly light the columns and carvings are entrancing and exquisitely beautiful. *[Pause.]*

You decide that you wish to enter this temple and you walk slowly up the marble steps. Your moonlight shadow is sharp and deep as onyx, and in the opalescent glow the statues seem to be dancing gracefully. All around you there is beauty. *[Pause. If you wish to journey alone, leave the directions at this point.]*

You come through an archway and find yourself in a walled garden. In the centre there is a fountain, crystal in the moonlight. By the subtle glow of moonlight, all is smooth and harmonious and you realise how priceless is the gift of peace. *[Pause.]*

Walking through the garden you come through another archway and find yourself in a gallery. Before you there is a giant statue of two Greek wrestlers, locked together, their mighty limbs shimmering under the Moon. You realise that there may be a beauty in temporary strife, if it leads to truth. *[Pause.]*

Proceeding through the gallery, you come upon an elegant lecture room. A lesson is in progress and you feel there is something you wish to learn. You take your seat among the audience, feeling delighted to be within this haven of culture and knowledge. You become aware of how important it is for you to develop your point of view. *[Pause.]*

The teacher is pausing, taking something up from the lectern, and beckoning you. Smoothly and happily you walk to the front of the hall. You take the gift that is being offered to you with a smile. This is means something very special to you.

Come back to everyday awareness when you are ready and make a note of all that you have learnt and experienced.

Moon in Scorpio

You are sitting beside a still pool. Around the pool you see there is a multitude of fragrant blooms growing luxuriantly. The atmosphere is sweet and magical. The Full Moon shines above you and you see her reflected in the pool. Take a deep breath and note how peaceful it feels. *[Pause.]*

You decide you will walk around the pool. You get up and move slowly. Your clothes brush against the flowers so they release their fragrance more strongly. All the while your gaze keeps returning to the Moon in the pool, held there, yet eternally free. *[Pause. If you wish to journey, leave the instructions at this point.]*

By the path you see an exceptionally strong and beautiful plant. You decide you want to pick this. However, the stem will not snap. You tug and tug to no avail. So you decide to pull gently. The plant comes up unbroken, root and all, fit to be replanted elsewhere. You realise that you can possess what you want, if you are gentle, and do no damage. *[Pause.]*

Your walk continues and you find yourself in the shadow of some tall trees. The light of the Moon flickers between the branches and the shadows are impenetrable, ebony. Ahead you see something large and black shifting about, and as you come close to it you realise it is a pony. You become aware that much that you fear is harmless, and can help you. *[Pause.]*

You climb on the pony and continue your steady exploration around the pool. Although you try to direct the pony, your mount has a will of its own. You want to return to your original spot, but the pony seems to be going elsewhere. Soon, however, you realise that your mount is taking the route most comfortable for you. You realise that you do not have to control everything in order to benefit. *[Pause.]*

Now you are back at your original spot. You dismount and thank the pony with a pat, and it disappears. You notice something glistening in the water near your feet. It is a bottle with a message in it. Pick it up and take out the message. It contains a gift for you.

Treasure the gift and return to everyday awareness. Make a note of all your feelings and experiences.

Moon in Sagittarius

You find yourself standing on a hilltop and ahead of you the sunset sky is breathtaking in shades of crimson and gold. The bright crescent of the New Moon hangs over the horizon. The balmy breeze blows fresh and gentle and there is a promise of adventure in the air. *[Pause.]*

In your hand there is a silver bow shaped like a lunar crescent and a silver arrow. You set the arrow in the string and pull it back. You feel a powerful twang as the arrow is released. The arrow arcs up in a silver flash against the evening sky towards the crescent Moon. Slowly and gracefully it comes down to Earth and disappears from your sight. You wish to follow it. *[Pause. Leave the instructions at this point if you wish to journey.]*

Now you are truly going to be going on a journey. It is exciting. However, you see that ahead of you there is a long, rough path with forests and hills to negotiate. For this you will need good shoes and provisions. You plan your journey. *[Pause.]*

Now you set off down the hillside, into thick forestland. Around you there are many wild deer and other animals. You feel conscious of them, their essence and their feelings. How aware they are of all that happens within the forest! They know all the secrets of thicket and coppice, and every scent tells them a thousand stories. You become aware of the breathtaking richness of life. *[Pause.]*

Following the forest paths you come out onto the plains. Soon you find yourself at a crossroads. You have a choice of three ways, but each of them is paved with gold. You become aware of the fact there are many possibilities, all of them promising. *[Pause.]*

Walking along this golden road, you meet three people, all of them smiling. One is a ragged child with a red balloon, another is a barefoot woman carrying a baby, and the third is a beggar-man with a book. You become aware that if one has a reason to live the conditions do not matter. *[Pause.]*

Now ahead of you, you see your silver arrow. As the Moon goes down and the stars come up, you pluck it from the soil to find that underneath the point there is something buried in the earth. Pull this out – it is a gift for you.

Treasure your gift for it has a symbolic meaning for you. Be sure to make a note of it as you come back to the everyday world.

Moon in Capricorn You are sitting on a mountainside at midnight. The Full Moon bathes the landscape for miles around. The rocks around you are ivory-white. They are all around you, holding you, supporting your back. You reach out and touch their smooth and surprisingly warm surfaces. *[Pause.]*

Looking upwards, you see that there is a path to the summit. It seems that the Full Moon is resting on the mountaintop. You feel a great urge to be up there, closer to the Moon and the purple, star-spangled sky. Slowly you begin to climb. *[Pause. Leave the instructions at this point if you want to journey.]*

The way seems long and arduous. You are encouraged by the bright and magical light of the Moon, but you are expecting that journey will be difficult. However, to your surprise, you feel light as a feather and you are almost gliding upwards. You realise that when things in life are right for you, they can be easy. *[Pause.]*

You are looking for the proper path, but it is hard to find. Often, what you thought was the beaten track turns out to be a dead end. You notice that there is a goat climbing nearby, its white fur silvered by the Moon. You follow its leaping and meandering trail and realise that the best ways are often the ones of instinct. *[Pause.]*

Now the summit is near at hand. You climb up over the crest and a wonderful, dusky panorama lies spread out before you. As you contemplate the sleeping world, blessed by the Moon, you realise that if you direct your efforts you can accomplish anything you choose. *[Pause.]*

Take your time to look around you, enjoying the feeling of achievement and the sweeping view that you have of the jewelled sky, the slumbering fields, and the Moon presiding over all of it. Beneath one of your hands a rock feels loose. You move it aside and beneath it there is a gift for you. *[Pause.]*

Treasure your gift and return to everyday awareness when you are ready. Make a note of your feelings and experiences.

Moon in Aquarius

You are walking eastwards through a group of beech trees, on a hill-top. Ahead of you, the Waning Moon appears in the in the sky, paling to a clear dawn. The wind is fresh in your hair and the trees are swaying and swishing in response. *[Pause.]*

Ahead of you there is an exceptionally tall, straight and powerful tree. You are drawn by its beauty and its suppleness. The Waning Moon is tangled in its branches. You notice there is a rope ladder dangling beside the trunk and attached to one of the branches. You feel drawn to climb it. *[Pause. If you wish to journey alone, leave the instructions at this point.]*

Steadily you climb the ladder. It feels firm and the footholds are strong and safe. Around you the wind sings and you feel exhilarated to be leaving the ground behind. Soon you find yourself in a small tree-house, perched on the roof of the world, and you realise how wonderful it is to be different. *[Pause.]*

Around you there are creaks and whispers as the wood responds to the wind. It is almost as if the tree is speaking to you. The trunk passes through the tree-house and you go up to it and touch it with your palms. You feel life-force within the tree, the depth of its roots, and how its branches embrace the winds. You become aware that you are in touch with all of life. *[Pause.]*

Looking out of the tree-house, you see the Moon like a fluffy cloud in the lightening sky. You see the vast panorama of wakening countryside spread out before you and you take a deep breath. You become aware that you are truly free. *[Pause.]*

You can see the Moon through the branches and as you gaze towards her wise face, you see that there is a package nestling in the crook of a branch, quite close to you. You reach out and take it. Within the airy tree-house you open it and find that it is a special and meaningful gift for you. *[Pause.]*

Look after your gift and return to everyday awareness when you are ready. Take note of it and any special messages for you.

Moon in Pisces   By the light of the Full Moon you find yourself beside a silver stream. Salmon are leaping in it, making glistening arcs that appear and disappear, sending up crystal droplets that splash back into the water. The moonlight plays on the stream and the shadows seem magical and mysterious. *[Pause.]*

You feel drawn to walk beside the stream, towards its source. You find your way along a Moon-bathed path as the stream tinkles and chatters. The sound of rushing water is getting louder and louder as if a thousand faery voices are calling. *[Pause. If you wish to journey alone, leave the instructions at this point.]*

Coming round a bend in the path, you find yourself confronted by a shimmering waterfall. Behind it there seems to be a cave. You feel the impulse to go through the curtain of water. Taking hold of your courage, you jump through, feeling the cool waters briefly over your body. You find yourself in an illuminated space. You become aware that there are many levels of reality. *[Pause.]*

Looking in front of you, you see there is a large expanse of cave wall, so smooth it could have been plastered. You feel that this should have paintings all over it and as you imagine them, they appear. You become aware that you can make your dreams real. *[Pause.]*

You walk more deeply into the cave and see there are many pools of still, clear water. You walk up to one of these and look deep within, at your reflection. You see your face mirrored many times, and then all the images combine into one. You become aware that you can feel many different things at once and accept them all. *[Pause.]*

Ahead of you the light seems to be catching an especially pretty rock pool. You walk towards it and see that its colours are changing from purple to turquoise, jade and indigo. As you approach, it you realise that beneath the water there is a gift for you. You reach in and take it, feeling the water run off it, as it dries in your hand.

When you are ready, come back to everyday awareness, treasuring the meaning of this gift. Make a note of what you have experienced.

CHAPTER 7

LUNAR LIVING

There is a tide in the affairs of men
Which, taken at the flood, leads on to fortune....
On such a full sea are we now afloat,
And we must take the current when it serves
Or lose our ventures.
WILLIAM SHAKESPEARE, *JULIUS CAESAR*

Getting Attuned

This chapter offers ways to tune in to the phases of the Moon and live more effectively in harmony with natural cycles. However, please remember that nothing can take the place of your own feelings and instincts. The exercises in Chapter 1 were intended to waken your instincts. The important point here is that however an influence is described, the way you react to it is individual and special to you. For instance, the effect of a Waxing Moon, generally, is to assist things that grow and increase. This may be considered a plus for most creative ventures, but with a Waxing Moon it is also possible to get carried away. Consider the analogy of cycling with a following wind – it is great for getting from A to B with more speed. However, if you are going down a steep hill and hit an unexpected oil-patch, that following wind could be just too much, pushing you that little bit too fast and meaning you come off the bike! So be aware, be observant, and check everything out with your intuition.

★ ☆ ★ *The Basic Lunar Cycle*

The lunar cycle can be divided and subdivided in a variety of ways because it is a cycle, and the different parts of the cycle naturally shade into one another. The usual way of considering the cycle of the Moon is to divide it into four – New Moon, Waxing Moon, Full Moon and Waning Moon. Naturally, within these four parts there is continual variation, as the energies involved are perpetually on the move, growing or decreasing. However, here we are going to look at just these four traditional lunar forces.

New Moon This is a wonderful time to make new beginnings of all types. It is especially favourable for getting rid of bad habits such as smoking or poor eating habits. Habitual ways of thinking that are harmful and negative can also be abandoned at this time. It is also a good time to start something creative such as a painting, dress-making or decorating the house. New projects at work can also be launched. Physically it is a beneficial time to start a detox diet or fast, because withdrawal symptoms or feelings of deprivation are at their lowest. Enthusiasm for new beginnings that will create a 'new you' will be highest now. However, if your new regime is going to make you feel deprived, you may find it harder as the Moon waxes. For a more thorough detox effect, the waning phase may be best, as the body eliminates toxins more successfully with a Waning Moon.

The first day of the New Moon is really best devoted to the planning stage of ventures for now the Moon is conjunct with the Sun and the 'energies' may be a little unpredictable. It is good to feel just a little excited and filled with anticipation, although your energy may not be at its highest. Many women start their period around now and may feel 'under the weather'. A day or two into the cycle is the time to take the initiative, apply for that job, start house-hunting or any similar schemes.

Waxing Moon Now your projects can get into their stride. Be aware, however, that over-strain is more likely at this time and that the body takes things in and absorbs them more readily with a Waxing Moon. Because of this, things like food-poisoning and insect stings may be worse with a Waxing Moon. By the same token healing remedies will be more readily soaked up. It is also a great build-you-up time if you have been off-colour. Absorbing, boosting your energy and taking up supplies are crucial now. You may also put weight on more readily now – in fact you may feel hungrier and thirstier. Vitamins and minerals are better absorbed by the body.

Go on an active holiday, get in touch with all your friends, plan a party, arrange meetings and increase communication. As Full Moon approaches, notice what isn't working and shed it so as to focus your energies more effectively. Have your hair cut, or have a manicure. Remind yourself to slow down a little and conserve your strength.

Full Moon Hold a party or event (but be aware that the energy level is likely to be high and anything troublesome is likely to surface). Cook for the freezer, and buy new paint, wallpaper or soft furnishings. Pay special attention to your creative ventures, and also to your dreams – let your imagination have free rein. Have a party or outing. Go for walks. Be prepared to work into the night if you are 'on a roll'. This is also a good time to try out forms of divination such as scrying or tarot. Reflect about your goals, feelings and matters to do with relationships and family – things may seem more highly charged, so be aware you may be more volatile and sensitive than usual. Make love! Get married!

The body is more susceptible to influences at this time so surgery should be avoided if possible, except for emergencies. Obviously with hospital waiting lists, this is not necessarily practical, but if your operation is privately funded and non-urgent you may like to bear this in mind. Haemorrhage is more common with a Full Moon. It isn't the best time for inoculation as the effects may be magnified. Special care should be taken with all wounds, lesions and swellings.

As the Full Moon just passes, the time arrives to put the finishing touches to what you have been doing and to get ready for the quieter time to come. Enjoy beauty and art, listen to music and appreciate landscapes. If you have argued with someone but do not feel the issues are really vital, make up now.

Waning Moon You do not have to be concerned so much about overdoing things now for the lunar rhythm will act as something of a brake. Now is a good time to have a sort-out, throw away your rubbish, and take old clothes to the charity shop. Consider how well things are working out, analyse and weigh up information. Some people feel more energetic with a Waning Moon as old things can be shed; others feel more supported by the strong take-up of Waxing Moon. Follow your own needs and reactions.

You may feel more like meditating and being alone. Clear spaces of all descriptions and make endings. In respect of your body, the Waning Moon flushes out the system, cleanses and detoxifies, so it is a good time to embark on a detox programme or to contemplate therapies such as colonic irrigation.

It is also a good time for an operation as bleeding is less and healing is quicker. The Waning Moon tends to 'dry things out' and scars are fewer. With a Waning Moon the tendency is to 'seal over' and shrink. Bear this in mind with your activities, bringing some things to a close or a fallow phase, until the New Moon once more appears.

Some people favour scrying and meditation with the Dark Moon, because it is a more inward time. The insights you glean now will have a deeper, more insightful quality, whereas at Full Moon they may be more obviously creative.

★ ⋆★ Gardening by the Moon

It is best to garden by organic methods and to avoid the use of anything unnatural such as pesticides or chemical fertiliser. This is because natural substances are more receptive to the lunar phases and generally more 'organically' a part of the natural world.

Here is a general run-down of gardening activities you can time with the phases. Basically anything that relates to growth and expansion, particularly in relation to plants that produce above the ground, is best timed for the Waxing Moon. Fruit for immediate consumption should be picked with a Waxing Moon. The Waning Moon is considered better for plants that produce below ground, such as potatoes. Also a Waning Moon suits pruning, trimming, weeding and harvesting produce that will be preserved.

★ Just after New Moon plant leafy vegetables and herb seeds.

★ At Waxing Moon lay down turf, sow large areas, pot cuttings, re-pot houseplants, water plants and lawns and pick herbs, fruits, vegetables and mushrooms that are to be used immediately.

★ Close to Full Moon plant 'watery' vegetables such as tomatoes, pumpkins, peppers and onions, and also raspberries and gooseberries. Check over your plants and water them for they will take up moisture best at this time. Fruit is often best picked now because of its succulence and instructions for harvesting herbs usually recommend picking with a Full Moon, likewise flowers, whose blooms will be at their most glorious. If the weather has been very dry, now may be a good time to plant seeds. Fertiliser should be added as close to Full Moon as possible.

★ Just after Full Moon plant tuber vegetables such as potatoes and carrots, raspberries, trees and flowering biennials and perennials.

★ At Waning Moon start a compost heap, get rid of weeds, cut and prune, mow the lawn, pick fruits, flowers, herbs and vegetables that are going to be stored or dried.

★ Close to Dark Moon cut timber and spray fruit-bearing trees.

Research bears out the traditional belief that seeds do germinate more quickly with a Waxing Moon. However, there is more to gardening than germination. The final yield of the plant is not necessarily better because it easily and enthusiastically broke the soil to the call of a Waxing Moon. The sign of the Zodiac the Moon is occupying when the seeds are placed in the Earth is also very important to the end product.

In Chapter 1 we discussed the difference between the ordinary Zodiac, i.e. the 'tropical' Zodiac, and the Zodiac of the stars, or the 'sidereal' Zodiac and explained that due to the phenomenon of Precession the two no longer coincide. While, in my opinion, the tropical Zodiac works very well for human beings, for plant life there are indications that the sidereal zodiac is the more important. (Instructions for converting tropical to sidereal are given in Chapter 1.) However, if you are serious about planting by the Moon, you will need planetary tables (see Resources) in order to check the Moon's exact position. Unless you have a market garden and your livelihood depends on the soil, experiment for yourself and see what works out best for you and your plants. Here are the appropriate signs for sowings.

Earth Signs (Taurus, Virgo and Capricorn) The days when the Moon passes before the stars of these constellations are called 'Root Days'. These are the days to select for sowing root crops such as radishes, potatoes, carrots, turnips and the like, when there is an 'Earthy' energy about. If the weather is unsuitable you only have to wait about nine days for the next run of Root Days.

Water Signs (Cancer, Scorpio and Pisces) The days when the Moon passes through these constellations are called 'Leaf Days'. Not surprisingly this is a favourable time for plants such as lettuce and cabbage for the water content of these is quite high and there is a 'Watery' energy around.

Air Signs (Gemini, Libra and Aquarius) These constellations relate to 'Flower Days', when it is a good time to plant flowering vegetables, such as broccoli and cauliflower, and flowering plants in general. Flowers flourish in the air and are more adapted to 'Airy' influences.

Fire Signs (Aries, Leo and Sagittarius) The days when the Moon passes by these stars are called 'Fruit-seed Days' and they are favourable for planting tomatoes, peas, beans and the like. The seeds contain the distilled essence of the plant, after the flower has dried away, which is why this is linked to Fire days.

Some Herbs to Grow You may enjoy growing your own herbs. Most of them are easy to produce, and if you do not have a large garden they can be grown in pots. Sow them just after New Moon, and re-pot them with a Waxing Moon. Here are some easy-to-grow herbs that can be used medicinally and in cooking.

Lemon Balm Lemon balm is ruled by the Moon and is easy to grow in temperate regions. It can be dried and used in healing incenses and sachets. It can be made into tea by using 2–4 teaspoons of the dried herb in ¼ litre hot water. Use this tea for chronic fatigue syndrome, one cup per day. It can also be used for colds and flu, stress, ear infections, herpes and insomnia.

Mallow This is another Moon-ruled herb with baby-soft leaves, the original source of marshmallow sweets that are now made synthetically. It is good for coughs, laryngitis, bronchitis, indigestion and urinary infections; use one teaspoon of the dried root, simmered in ¼ litre hot water for 15 minutes.

Mint Mint is ruled by Venus and is well-known for culinary uses. Peppermint is good for indigestion and morning sickness, but the essential oil should be avoided in pregnancy.

Sage This is ruled by Jupiter. Sage tea, as a gargle, is great for sore throats and mouth ulcers. It has antiseptic properties and so is good served with meat, to absorb the toxins. It should be avoided in pregnancy.

Parsley Parsley is ruled by Mercury. It is said to grow only for the true head of the household! Parsley can be chewed to allay bad breath, especially after eating garlic. It helps the digestion, but should only be taken in moderation if you are pregnant.

Rosemary Ruled by the Sun, rosemary is good for the circulation, also for treating hayfever, depression, anxiety and stress. Use one teaspoon of the dried leaves steeped in ¼ litre hot water for 15 minutes.

Thyme This is ruled by Venus, and is good for flatulence, coughs and diarrhoea. It is prepared in the same way as rosemary.

Lavender Ruled by Mercury, lavender is very soothing and easy to grow. For practical usage the essential oil is best, but the simple fragrance of lavender flowers will relieve stress and clear the mind.

A Little Hocus-Pocus! Some simple magic will help your plants on their way. If they are ailing, looking 'unenthusiastic', or if you have had to plant them at a phase not of your choosing, then you can give them a booster.

At Full Moon, stand your plant on the windowsill in the moonlight with the window open, if you can. If your plants are out in the garden, go out and stand in front of them. If the neighbours are watching, let them! Close your eyes and feel a connection with the Moon – you can do this even if it is a cloudy night. Draw the moonlight into you. Now feel your energy gather in your abdomen, just behind your navel. Be aware of that wonderful, gentle radiance! Feel the glow build within you, until you are ready to send it down your arms and out through your finger-tips. Raise your hands over the plants and feel the energy flow out of your finger-tips and into the plant and the surrounding soil. Form a five-pointed star in the air with your finger-tip (or your ritual silver knife) and say, 'I thank the Great Mother. Blessings of the Goddess, be with me and all I care for.'

It is amazing how plants pick up after this. Repeat this as often as you like or feel necessary.

★ ✦ ★ *Eating by the Moon*

We have seen that during the Waxing Moon substances are more easily absorbed by the body, with this process reaching a peak at Full Moon. With a Waning Moon, substances are more easily expelled. So if we wish to build ourselves up after a period of illness or an accident, the Waxing Moon is the time to concentrate on sustaining, vitamin-rich foods. If we feel we have been overburdening our systems or need to lose weight, we need to take advantage of the Waning Moon period to rid our systems of unwanted material. The Moon rules Cancer, which has long been linked to the digestive system, the liver, gall bladder and stomach (and in some systems the chest and lungs). All the signs of the Zodiac are associated with a particular part of the body, and therefore when the

Moon is in a particular sign, the associated limbs or organs may be especially susceptible to harming or healing. However, because of the Cancerian connection, digestion is especially sensitive to the phases of the Moon at all times.

Additives There is a multitude of research, counter-research and conflicting advice about additives to food. Where possible, choose food that is as natural as possible and leave it at that. Lunar living teaches us to respect nature and the simple needs of our bodies. Preservatives are not necessary in most foods – vinegar, salt and sugar are all natural preservatives; my home-made apple chutney, which remains, un-furred, in an un-refrigerated cupboard for many moons, testifies to this! Sugar is bad in excess but is a natural food and has been with us for centuries. Artificial sweeteners are all suspect; and why do we need colour and flavouring? Choose organic food wherever you can, because the 'organic' certification will extend to additives. Beware of the many unhealthy drinks that abound – particularly for children. And remember that there are loopholes to laws about foodstuffs and drugs because these serve big business. However, being obsessive about this will probably be far worse for you than absorbing the odd chemical! Just do your best and remember that substances are ingested more readily with a Waxing Moon.

Diets Dieting is a modern obsession. Because food of all types is readily and cheaply available and because methods of preparation – albeit synthetic and harmful – are highly sophisticated, food is plentiful. We do not have to worry about famine in the developed countries, so we worry about all those extra pounds, making ourselves miserable because we aren't slim and svelte. Perhaps in the Stone Age a spare tyre round the middle was considered gorgeous, as a sign of abundance and an insurance against hard times to come. Indeed, there are indications that this was the case, because ancient stone Goddess figures have been unearthed that are very rotund! Of course, it is more pleasant not to be carrying around too many excess pounds, and obesity is an acknowledged hazard to health. But, surprisingly, many adults find it very hard to put on weight.

Lunar wisdom teaches us to observe our own instincts, needs and reactions, and truly there is no substitute for this. Studies on people who live to be a hundred and over have not really revealed a common dietary factor, and in defiance of all current knowledge some smoke like chimneys and swill alcohol by the gallon! Of course, that certainly does not mean that such activities are 'healthy', but rather stresses the personal nature of diet, and the need to be in touch with our selves. Several months of self-observation, as outlined in Chapter 1, can get you in the right frame for making dietary adjustments. There are several factors to bear in mind if you wish to alter your weight.

Your weight and body shape are a product of your entire lifestyle, and even your attitude. To make lasting changes in your appearance, you will need to alter your habits and activities across the board; just changing eating habits is unlikely to work, or if it does, this may be only in the short term. Genetics are also a factor, but not so great as the habits you have learned. Whatever your genetic pattern, there is a way for you to adjust your habits in order to be the right weight and shape for you.

The way you feel also affects your weight. For instance, stress can make some people lose weight, but others might put it on, because the stress hormone cortisol, which is released by the adrenal glands (the 'fight-or-flight' glands), acts on certain fat cells around the abdomen. Unrealistic aims are a sure way to failure and a loss of self-esteem, which can lead to worse habits because you tell yourself, 'I'm not worth bothering with.' We cannot all have supermodel figures, and the truth of the matter is most supermodels can't either, which is why many of them live on drugs to cope with the famine conditions imposed by fashion! Food can be a substitute for love. This pattern is set in infancy when sweets are given as rewards and children are told 'Clear your plate, or Mummy will be upset,' etc. If you 'comfort eat', ask yourself what it is you really need, because unless you are honest with yourself you cannot meet your needs.

Your Moon Sign and Diet

Making changes is easier for some Moon signs than it is for others. Here are some guidelines for each Moon sign.

Aries

The thoughtless, impulsive qualities of Aries Moon mean they may embrace change wholeheartedly, but neglect to prepare for it. If this is your Moon sign, enlist the help of family and friends to plan your nutritious diet – and don't get mad at them! Sometimes Aries will not see that what they eat is important, feeling too impatient with such trivial matters. Realise that your engine can only run at full throttle on the right sort of fuel. Often you forget to eat and then grab any old thing and refuse to wait when you realise you are ravenous. Sorry, I know it's a pain, but preparation is better than perspiration!

Taurus

Of all the Moon signs, Taurus is the most difficult to change in the matter of habits, especially dietary ones. Changes that you make should be small, and based on simple logic that you can't dismiss when you get that craving for chocolate! Also it is important that any changes you make still leave you plenty of opportunity to have food you enjoy, because you can't do without this and will inevitably swing the other way and over-indulge if you try to deny yourself too much. Build plenty of sensuous delight into your life in addition to food – Taurean Moons will take to food as a substitute for love, fulfilment, sex and relaxation more readily than most of us.

Gemini You are willing to try just about anything in the way of diet as long as it can be logically justified. However, it must be interesting and varied. Of all the Moon signs, Gemini is the most easily bored. Moon Geminis are often the ones that have tried every diet in the book, but they rarely stick to anything. Because they fidget so much, they are less likely to have a problem with excess weight. Sometimes they may find it hard to put on weight. Relaxation techniques may ultimately be more helpful than dietary intervention. This is a very experimental Moon sign, but you may find it hard to see the importance of too much trying – the most important thing for you is to satisfy your curiosity. Have fun sampling lots of wholefoods, exotic vegetables and fruits and avoid committing yourself to too much preparation.

Cancer You find it easiest to make dietary changes if they are in someone else's interests, as you will happily go along with the needs of others. Sometimes you wait for them to notice yours, but this may not happen, leaving you with the scraps. It is important for you to understand that you have to look after yourself if you are to be any help to anyone else and make sure you prioritise your own needs. You may 'comfort eat' because that seems the only way to get your needs met. You may find you are more sensitive than most to the lunar phases, thus eating more with a Waxing and Full Moon, then being ready to cut down as the Moon wanes. Be especially prepared to listen to your own inner signals – and don't expect them to be the same every day!

Leo Let's be honest, you like to make a bit of a fuss about what you eat and you are very happy when other people make a fuss for you! You like a right royal helping and you may be dissatisfied with anything but the best! So when you decide to make changes, ensure that what you are moving towards is not only healthier but also of the finest quality. Ensure your large helpings are of nutritious foodstuffs, not 'junk'. Less impatient than the other Fire Moons, you may enjoy preparing your food and will change your diet if you can do it with a sense of importance. The love with which food is prepared means a lot to you, and you may be willing to accept changes made by others if you realise it is done from affection and respect.

Virgo You can be a little faddy on occasion, but you are fairly quick to embrace change, if it can be sensibly justified. However, you may find it hard to stick to a new regimen because you very quickly find something wrong with it! Your pitfall may be that you are more preoccupied with the little slugs on the lettuce than you are with its vitamin content, although you may be able to quote chapter and verse on the latter! If you decide your diet needs to change, give yourself time to research and experiment or you could become disheartened. Try not to expect too much too quickly from your diet – your skin, hair and silhouette may take some time to show improvement. Take comfort from the fact that your insides are benefiting. Many Virgo Moons have sensitive digestive systems and you should cater for this.

Libra This is often a sweet-toothed Moon and any changes you make should not deny you your sugar and spice. Libra Moons often find it much easier to make changes when their friends and family do it with them, for they like company when they eat. Care needs to be taken that you don't have too much of the wrong foods while you are engrossed in the dinner-table conversation! Often idealistic about food (e.g. possibly preferring to be vegetarian), Libra Moon needs food to have an aesthetic appeal too, so any changes made should not be in the direction of the tasteless and uninspired. Balance is important to this sign, so diets that call for the elimination of certain foodstuffs in preference for others (e.g. the high protein diet) are unlikely to be acceptable for long.

Scorpio You like to feel that you are in control of what you eat and this can sometimes mean that you punish your body in order to show it who's boss! If you decide to make a change, you are likely to be quite rigid about this and may fail to notice signs that your body is really under strain. Also you can become quite obsessive about your dietary decisions. Try to avoid any paranoia about food because it isn't possible to ensure that everything that enters your mouth is pure, organic, detoxified and uncontaminated by the modern world – trust your body to eliminate anything that does not support its wellbeing. You can make very radical changes and stick to them, but ensure these are for the right reasons and are truly to your benefit.

Sagittarius Life's a big adventure and food is just part of it. You probably can't see the need for a regular eating pattern. Sagittarius Moon should never be forced into any eating regime, especially one designed by someone else! You are capable of achieving long-term goals, but you may get bored along the way. Like Aries, preparation is the key and you need to get your food for the day sorted when you are in the mood – do not leave it until you are starving, which you are all too likely to do! It is best to have a variety of ready-prepared nutritious snacks for the time being. Sagittarius Moon easily becomes bored and impatient. You may also overdo things by bingeing, but the saving grace here is that you are quite capable of fasting and detoxing, because even excess can be boring! Like Gemini, this is a restless Moon and the fidgeting often ensures that the metabolic rate is high.

Capricorn You like to feel that you can take care of yourself and so any help or advice from others can be taken as interference. If you decide to make changes, they will be for a sound reason and you will need a definite structure and timetable – it will be hard for you to break with what you have grown up with. You are in danger of making things too complicated to work in an effort to cover all eventualities. You need to remind yourself not to be too stern with your body and to realise that its needs may vary. Any changes should include a feel-good factor, however hard you may find this. For any changes to succeed, they need to fit in to your work timetable, or you will disregard them.

Aquarius Your eating habits may be quite erratic, and while you may think you are happy to change, actually doing it isn't easy. You may change your diet often; in fact, the many changes you make reflect the fact that you are not readily prepared to give your body due attention – you have more important things to do. It may keep your interest if your chosen diet has an abstract quality, such as focusing on the 'life energies' within foodstuffs. Occasionally you may be attracted by a 'faddy' diet, and you are keen to experiment, although things other than food are usually a priority here. Like Libra (and, to some extent, Gemini), you can be idealistic about food. And like Aries and Sagittarius, it is all too easy for you to overlook food, so preparing ahead and having something quick and nutritious available to eat as you go out of the door is very important.

Pisces You rather like the idea of a change – in fact you rather like the idea of lots of things! The problems for you are firstly making a decision, and then sticking to it. You can see things from so many different angles that it is hard to focus on what you are doing. If results do not come quickly, you are quite likely to try another route without giving things time to work. Also it is hard for you to remain moderate and you may binge at times. At others you may be in another world and feel the whole thing is unimportant. Any changes you make should still leave you with plenty of scope for variety, and opportunities for self-indulgence. You are not likely to be contented with your changes, either in what they achieve or in how you enjoy them, but try to be realistic and have plenty of interests that absorb you, so you do not turn your attention continually to food.

Moon Menus

A totally lunar meal may be very gentle and, while somewhat bland, it can be soothing and nourishing. Lunar foods include pale vegetables such as cabbage and white meats such as chicken and fish, the latter living in the waters ruled by the Moon. A simple menu might therefore be as follows.

★ Starter: melon balls
★ Main course: fresh salmon or trout served with steamed potatoes and broccoli
★ Dessert: ice cream.

Starters A richer menu could start with garlic mushrooms, watercress oysters or a haddock pate.

Watercress Oysters Oysters are rich in zinc and there is some truth that they can act as an aphrodisiac if your zinc level is low. Casanova allegedly used to eat 40 oysters a day! Here is a recipe for two people.

You will need: 1 large bunch of watercress, 12g (½oz) butter, 2 medium potatoes, 300ml (½ pint) water, 24 oysters, 2tbs thick Greek yoghurt, seasoning, chives as garnish.

Wash and chop the watercress, then cook two-thirds of it gently in a pan with the butter. Peel and dice the potatoes and add to the pan with the water and a little salt. Simmer for a quarter of an hour, then add the remaining watercress. Place in a blender on full power until smooth. Shell the oysters and put them with their juice in a pan, heating them for just under a minute. Pour off the remaining liquid into the blended mixture and add the yoghurt, with a little black pepper and extra salt if needed. Place the oysters in bowls, pour over the sauce and garnish with the chives. Serve with a little white wine to make a light and tasty meal for lunar lovers.

Garlic Mushrooms

Succulent mushrooms, which love the shady places and nestle in the compost, are like little Moons come to Earth. Choose button mushrooms and leave them whole if the Moon is full, or halve them for Waxing or Waning Moons.

You will need: as many mushrooms as you think you will be able to eat, garlic, seasoning, butter or oil, soy sauce, red wine (or grape juice), parsley.

Fry the mushrooms in the oil or butter with garlic to taste, for a couple of minutes. Season with black pepper and a little naturally fermented shoyu (soy sauce) – you probably won't need much salt with the shoyu. Add red wine (or red grape juice) and let it bubble for a couple of minutes. Now add a few teaspoons of chopped parsley. Remove the mushrooms and simmer the wine or juice until it is reduced by about half. Pour over the mushrooms and serve with brown bread – and more red wine, of course!

Haddock Pate (serves four)

You will need: 175g (6oz) smoked haddock, 25g (1oz) organic sunflower margarine, plus a little extra to cover, 6 tbs double cream, 1 tsp lemon juice, ½ tsp Shoyu sauce, lemon slices and parsley to garnish.

Poach the fish gently for about ten minutes, drain and place in blender with the margarine. Whip the cream and add carefully and gently – do not beat. Add the lemon juice and Worcester sauce, then place in the fridge until the pate is firm, then pour a little melted butter over the top. Serve with water biscuits, for a tasty lunar starter.

Main Courses

Chicken and Mushrooms (serves four)

You will need: 4 large (or 8 small) chicken pieces (choose free range, organic, skinless and boneless, if possible), 30g (1¼oz) seasoned flour, 50g (2oz) butter, 1 tbs oil, 100g (4oz) button mushrooms, 200g (8oz) can evaporated milk, 2 tbs red wine or red grape juice, 200g (8oz) cooked carrots, parsley.

Fry the chicken gently in the oil. (You may coat it in seasoned flour and use butter too, if you wish, but the lower fat option is quite acceptable and can be obtained with just a little oil in the pan to stop the chicken drying out.) Fry the pieces very gently in a covered pan until they are almost cooked through – this takes about half an hour. Pour off any excess oil. For the last few minutes of cooking, add the mushrooms and cook till tender. Make the evaporated milk up with water to at least 1/3 litre. Blend this with 25g (1oz) flour and cook gently in a saucepan, stirring all the time, until it thickens. Transfer the chicken and mushroom to an oven-proof dish. Remove the sauce from the heat. Drain the sweetcorn and add it to the sauce along with the sherry or wine and seasoning to taste. Pour the sauce over the chicken and cook for about 15 minutes (more if the ingredients have cooled) at 180° C, 350° F. Serve with creamed potatoes and peas/broccoli.

Cauliflower Cheese/ Pasta Cheese (serves four)

You will need: 1 large organic cauliflower, 800 ml (1½ pints) semi-skimmed organic milk; 125g (3–4 oz) organic white flour, 50g (2oz) organic butter, seasoning, garlic powder, English mustard powder, 220g (8oz) grated cheese (you can vary the amount of cheese, depending whether you want an economical, low fat dish or a rich one. Cheddar cheese is the usual choice, but most cheeses work in this recipe and you can use up scraps of cheese that are becoming a bit stale and dry – blue cheeses are tasty), breadcrumbs, slices of cooked potato, sesame seeds.

Prepare the cauliflower, using the leaves if they are in good condition, as well as the florets. Wash, cut into pieces of the desired size and drop into boiling water for three to five minutes. Check during the cooking time – the cauliflower should be just tender or 'al dente', and not soggy. Alternatively, steam the cauliflower.

Melt the butter in a pan, stir in the flour, garlic powder and mustard powder and then slowly add the milk, stirring all the time. As the mixture begins to thicken, add seasoning. Add 110g (4oz) grated cheese – let this melt but do not let the sauce boil after the cheese has been added, or it may curdle.

Place your cooked cauliflower in a heat-proof dish, and pour the sauce over it. Top with a sprinkling of breadcrumbs, sesame seeds or sliced, cooked potatoes, then sprinkle on top of this another 110g (4oz) grated cheese. Place under the grill until golden.

If you do not like cauliflower, substitute 225g (8oz) cooked pasta shells or any pasta shapes.

Chestnut- Stuffed Cabbage (serves two)

This recipe cheats a bit because chestnuts are ruled by Jupiter. Chestnuts are traditionally used in love-spells, so feed this dish to your lover.

You will need: half a small cabbage (choose one with firm, clean leaves, organic is best), 50g (2oz) dried chestnuts (fresh ones may also be used but dried are better), 12g (½oz) butter, 1 clove garlic (or use garlic powder), 50g (2oz) mild onion, 50g (2oz) mushrooms, 1 tsp lemon juice, half a finely chopped celery stick, 1 very small free range egg, a generous pinch of freshly ground black pepper, salt to taste.

Prepare the chestnuts as stated on the packet – they will need to be soaked and then simmered for at least half an hour. Drain them and chop them finely.

Take four large leaves from the cabbage, remove the centre of the stalk and drop them into rapidly boiling water for just two minutes. Finely chop the remaining cabbage. Gently fry the onions, mushrooms, chopped cabbage, celery and crushed garlic (if using) until the onions are translucent. Add the chestnuts, juice and powdered garlic (if using). Cool slightly and add the beaten egg and remaining seasoning.

Line a 0.7 litre (1 pint) oven-proof pudding basin with some of the cabbage, fill the centre with the mixture and top with remaining leaves. Cover with an oven-proof plate and bake for one hour. Then turn out to serve.

A cheese sauce similar to the one used for cauliflower cheese goes well with this dish, or a tomato sauce made from tinned tomatoes, finely chopped onions and garlic – or even good old ketchup!

Desserts

Economical Cheesecake

You will need: 150g (5oz) digestive biscuits, crushed or crumbed in a food-processor, 50g (2oz) melted butter, 50g (2oz) halved glacé cherries, 225g (8oz) carton cottage cheese, 150g (5oz) plain organic yoghurt, 40g (1½ oz) golden caster sugar, 1 free range egg, 1 tsp natural vanilla essence, kiwi fruit or grapes to garnish.

Melt the butter in the microwave, stir in the biscuit crumbs and spread on a greased 18cm (7–8 inches) pie dish. Pack down and leave to chill, if possible. Arrange the cherries on the biscuit base. Simply mix together the other ingredients, reserving half the yoghurt and vanilla and a tablespoon of the sugar. Spread the mixture over the biscuit-crumb base and place in the oven, at 160° C, 300–325° F, for about 20 minutes till firm. Remove from the oven and turn the oven up to maximum. Mix together the remaining yoghurt, sugar and vanilla, spoon carefully over the top and return to the very hot oven for five minutes. Take care that it does not burn. When the pie has cooled, slice kiwi fruit and/or grapes or more cherries for the top. Serve with fresh cream for a richer lunar pudding.

Moon Cakes

These are cakes for sabbats (major festivals) or for esbats (the minor ones). They are especially good for your lunar rituals – you can cut them to the shape suitable to the phase of the Moon, if you wish, and for Dark Moon, sprinkle them with chocolate powder.

You will need: 110g (4oz) butter – softened, 225g (8oz) golden granulated caster sugar, 2 free range eggs, 275g (10oz) organic plain flour, 1 tsp baking powder, 1 tsp salt, 1½ tbs organic honey, 1 tsp vanilla extract (natural), 1 tsp white wine or white grape juice, 2 tbs quick oats.

Mix the butter, sugar, eggs, honey, vanilla and wine thoroughly together. Blend in the flour, baking powder, oats and salt. Cover and chill for an hour, to make the dough easier to handle. Pre-heat the oven to 400° F, 200° C. Roll the dough out to the thickness of 5cm and cut into shapes with a pastry cutter. Bake for 6–8 minutes, until pale gold in colour.

Drinks and Sundries

Banana Milk-Shake Full of Moon-ruled substances, this is a great build-you-up to take with a Waxing Moon. Bananas are rich in potassium, which regulates blood pressure and is vital for muscle and nerve functions.

You will need: 1 large banana, ½ litre (about ¾ pint) of semi-skimmed milk. The shake can be made from these ingredients alone, but you could also add a raw free-range egg (but be sure it comes from a reputable source to avoid infection), golden granulated castor sugar to taste (but many people find bananas are sweet enough), a few drops of natural vanilla essence, 1 tbs vanilla ice cream.

All you do is place all the ingredients in a blender and mix on full power for a few seconds – delicious! You can experiment with combinations until you find one that suits you. For instance, for a thicker shake, use two bananas.

Nettle Tea This is excellent for detoxification during a Waning Moon. It can help all the digestive organs, the bladder and kidneys, and gives the body many minerals and vitamins. However, be sure you are healthy before taking it as it can be rather strong. (Also, if you have been feeling under the weather with aches and pains, etc, be prepared for this to get worse before it gets better – this is a good sign.) Nettle is ruled by Mars and has a powerful effect! Combine this with a general detox diet for maximum effect. Usually two periods of 14 days (Waning Moon) is enough to detox most people. This recipe is enough for a day's dosage.

If you are picking your own nettles, try to find some which you can be sure haven't been exposed to pesticides. Choose only young ones and pick, dry and store them when the Moon is on the wane. Avoid washing them if you possibly can before drying. Crush the leaves with a rolling pin to eliminate the stinging hairs. Use the purest water you can – preferably fresh spring water. Hard water may prevent the release of certain ingredients. A china, glass or enamel pot should be used.

You will need: 75g (3oz) of fresh herb, 570ml (1 pint) of water, honey or brown sugar (optional). Use a third of the quantity of herb if it is dried.

Boil the water, wait for it to cool for 30 seconds, then sprinkle the herb onto it and allow it to steep for ten minutes, stirring from time to time. Strain the tea into a mug and drink it at intervals during the day, especially between three and seven in the afternoon. According to traditional medicine, the period between three and five in the afternoon is when the bladder works particularly well, with the time between five and seven being best for the kidneys. The mixture can be gently reheated, but do not boil it or use a microwave. You can sweeten the tea with a little honey or unrefined brown sugar.

Nettle juice (available from healthfood shops) can be used as a substitute – take three tablespoons, or follow the directions on the packet.

Yoghurt Cooler To bring a little lunar softness to a spicy meal like curry, use two cups of organic plain yoghurt, stir in a brimming teaspoon of honey and two teaspoons of dried mint. Now add half a diced cucumber, complete with skin, and garnish with a little paprika. Children often like this on its own and it makes a welcome change from very sweet flavoured yoghurts.

Exercise by the Moon

It is best to start new routines of all descriptions with a New Moon and build up as the Moon waxes. However, be careful that you do not overdo it, especially at Full Moon. As the Moon wanes you may feel less energetic, although the water-retention factor at Full Moon may make you feel sluggish in itself – so the Waning Moon can also feel like a release. It is less likely that you will overdo things as the Moon wanes. At Dark Moon you may feel like staying in and giving up, especially if you are menstruating. Give yourself a few days off, in the knowledge that the Moon will take you forward again, with renewed vitality.

Your attitude to exercise will vary according to your Moon sign. Here are some tips for each of the Moon signs.

Aries You like a challenge and can easily overdo it. Be careful of accidents and strains, especially if you are competing with others. You like to do things fast and furious, so you may like running or games like squash.

Taurus You get going slowly and are almost impossible to stop once you have started. But, let's face it, you can be lazy! Having a reward at the end of it will keep you on track. Your advantage is stamina and persistence and you may enjoy sports such as weight training. Walking is also good.

Gemini Lots of things attract you, but you are easily bored. You need variety and company. Sports that involve lots of light movement, such as fencing or dance may appeal, also badminton.

Cancer Your moods change from day to day so it is best to have several different forms of exercise available. Something you can do at home may appeal, for those times when you want to lock the door and hide! Moonlit walks are your favourites and swimming is a classic Water sign sport.

Leo Pick something at which you stand a fair chance of being 'the best' and you will be unstoppable! Be honest, you're a bit of a show-off and you don't mind having that wonderful body on display! You may enjoy going to a trendy gym, and you can have staying power.

Virgo You tend to worry about sprains and injuries, and you probably can never get trainers that are really comfy. Walking is your best bet and you may be good at precision sports such as archery. Like the other Earth signs, gardening may appeal.

Libra Elegance is your middle name so you avoid anything sweaty. Wearing your designer gear may inspire you! You will enjoy sports where you have a partner, like tennis doubles. Like Gemini, you need company, and dance is ideal.

Scorpio You can be very intense and have to be careful that you don't get into a 'do or die' mindset. You need a challenge but may prefer to battle against your personal best or the elements rather than another person. Hill-walking, long-distance running and weight-training may appeal.

Sagittarius You'll try anything twice but after that you may forget about it. You're easily bored so exercise has to be varied. You will do better if you have a distraction, such as music or television, while you exercise. Horse-riding is a traditional Sagittarius sport, and you may like things like yoga, because they operate on an abstract level.

Capricorn You find exercise more emotionally satisfying if it dovetails with your work and so the golf course could be a favourite! Once you get into a routine, you stick to it, however. You like a challenge and may enjoy climbing.

Aquarius If it's high-tech it's more likely to appeal, so book yourself into one of those gyms where you can monitor your heart rate, breathing and body fat/mass ratio. Company should be available to you, but sometimes you will like to be alone, and the open air will appeal.

Pisces You could sit and watch other people exercise all day long! You aren't all that energetic and if you are under-the-weather or upset then you feel especially tired. Exercise should be gentle, with friends and family preferably, and dancing and swimming may be favourites. Disciplines like T'ai Chi may strike a chord.

★ ·★· ★ Lunar Healing

Lunar healing is all about getting in contact with your instincts – a favourite theme. However, please remember that none of the information in this section is meant to take the place of qualified medical advice, so if you are worried consult a professional. If you are pregnant take special care, for research on many herbs is incomplete or inconclusive. Do not ingest herbs or use aromatherapy oils in pregnancy without first consulting a professional. (The exception here is lavender oil, to which there are no specific contra-indications, although allergy is still a possibility.) It is best to test all oils for allergy by dabbing some on the inside of your wrist to see if there is a reaction.

Modern medicine is a wonderful thing and none of us would wish to be without it – it saves lives. However, the drawback with current medical practice is that it treats the disease, not the patient. Drugs intended to zap the illness unfortunately tend to zap the rest of the body too! In the UK in 2001 it was announced that the number of deaths from infections caught in hospital outstripped road death statistics, so modern medicine is far from having all the answers. Many people are aware of the undesirable side-effects of drugs, and the undesirable power that resides with drug companies, into the bargain! Drugs often use a 'sledgehammer to crack a nut' approach. It is a pity that so many GPs do not feel more able to liaise with alternative practitioners whose approach strengthens the patient and has fewer side-effects. Having said this, I must stress that herbs are far from harmless and some dosages can kill, so take care. Certain herbs can reduce the effectiveness of some medication, for instance St John's Wort, which is used to treat depression. Moreover, the Association of Natural Medicine points out that some herbs, such as garlic and gingko, are inadvisable in the lead-up to surgery.

There is no definitive answer to resolving this dilemma. If you are fortunate to have a GP who is well-informed and positive about alternative therapies then they will be able to advise you. If not, then you may need to take responsibility for your own health by becoming as well-informed as possible and, most of all, listening to your body and its responses. The lunar cycle is a start in this attunement.

Two Examples from my own Life

As the mother of four children, health is one of my preoccupations and I have plenty of experience of sick children! I steer clear of drugs such as antibiotics and steroids wherever I can because of the side-effects. It is important to me that, in their developing years, children's sensitive bodies should be supported, not assailed.

My son Jonathan had never taken antibiotics since infancy, when he was hospitalised for a condition called pyloric stenosis, which required surgery. When he was ten he became poorly with a sore throat. He didn't seem too ill, but when he described it as 'a bad neck' I panicked. We were all down at Casualty at ten o'clock in the evening because I feared meningitis and wanted him to have immediate treatment. When the doctor saw him, it transpired that all he had, in fact, was a streptococcal infection of the throat. Along came the inevitable antibiotic prescription. 'What will happen if he doesn't take that?' I asked. The doctor, to my surprise, looked relieved! 'Most people expect a prescription,' he said, 'but actually he should be okay. The infection could spread upwards into the sinuses, mastoid bone and ears, but keep an eye on him, and hang on to the prescription in case.' This was fine; I knew what I was dealing with. I made an infusion from home-grown sage, did a little hocus-pocus and gave it to Jon to gargle. In two days he was better. Had I not done this he would have been on antibiotics for ten days, quite unnecessarily, so destroying the benign bacteria in his body and possibly causing a spiralling into other conditions.

When my third son, Adam, was four, he had a sore throat with a fairly high temperature. I kept an eye on him, going up to him every 20 minutes to touch him and get a feeling about what was happening inside him. He felt strong and resilient, although he was very hot. I gave him lots of love and attention, that's all. In a couple of days he was better. However, a week or two later he developed a rash on his back which turned out to be a form of psoriasis, called 'guttate psoriasis'. The doctor said it followed a streptococcal infection and gave me a funny look, possibly because he hadn't seen us at the surgery! At this point I became alarmed at the possibility of steroid creams and went off to do some research. This yielded coal tar as a likely cure but the chemist told me that the preparation I needed was only available on prescription. Back to the surgery I went and asked for the coal tar cream, which the doctor obligingly looked up and prescribed. Adam's skin was back to normal in a few days.

I give these examples to show how instinct and common sense can so often be your friends – but get your diagnosis also. Here is a selection of herbs to back up your intuitions.

Your Lunar Medicine Chest

Lavender Oil This lovely oil is a 'must have' for magic, healing and general domestic atmosphere. In an oil burner it creates a fresh and calming fragrance if you are stressed. A few drops on the pillow will help you sleep. It also eases headaches. It is the one oil to which there are no contra-indications (except possible allergy) and I know one masseuse who never uses any other oil. It can be put neat onto the skin for minor burns, cuts and stings, acne and blisters. For the latter, dilute in a carrier oil such as sweet almond, one part of oil to five of carrier. To treat stress, place 10–15 drops in a bath (natural lavender soap will also help). I used it to treat two of my children, when small, for wasp and bee stings, and it stopped them crying immediately.

Echinacea This comes in tablet form, principally. Some people take a course of tablets in the autumn as a prophylactic, to boost the immune system. Others take sizeable doses as soon as they feel a cold coming on.

Goldenseal This can be used instead of antibiotics for many infections from pneumonia to vaginal problems. Obviously serious conditions may need medical intervention, but if you are allergic to antibiotics, goldenseal is a good alternative. Choose cultivated goldenseal as it is endangered in the wild.

Eucalyptus This essential oil is linked magically to healing, and is ruled by the Moon. It can be rubbed on a green candle for a healing spell and placed in an oil burner in the sick room. It helps to ease congestion when inhaled. It can be placed on the pillow of a patient suffering from bronchitis (but keep it away from their eyes).

Arnica This is conveniently available in creams and gels. It is antiseptic and anti-inflammatory. Use it for bruises and sprains. Arnica should not be swallowed.

Clary Sage	This oil is great for menstrual cramps. Dilute in a carrier oil as instructed for lavender, to use for massage, or place a few drops in your bath.
Bach Flower Rescue Remedy	Bach flower remedies use tiny amounts of oils distilled from flowers in order to treat a wide variety of emotion-related conditions. These remedies are a subject in themselves (see Further Reading). However, the Rescue Remedy can be used any time you are traumatised and upset, and a few drops placed on the tongue are effective. This is a useful addition to your lunar medicine chest.
Calendula	This is widely available as a cream. It can be used for cuts, inflammation and abrasions. Calendula tea can be made into a compress for tired and 'computer' eyes.
Witch Hazel	This can also be used for skin problems and distilled witch hazel can be applied to haemorrhoids to shrink them and control bleeding. It should not be taken internally.
Aloe Vera	This comes in a gel and eases eczema conditions that do not respond to other treatments. It can also be used to ease cracked and dry nipples, after breast-feeding.
Cranberry	Cranberry is excellent for preventing that women's bane, cystitis. It can be taken as a juice, and is also available as tablets.
Cantharis	This is a homeopathic remedy, as distinct from a herbal remedy. Homoeopathic remedies work on a different principle, using very minute dosages of substances that could cause the condition, in order to stimulate immune response. Some people find this hard to accept – but these remedies usually work. Use cantharis for cystitis.
Pads, Dressings and Plasters	Always include a good supply of these in your lunar medicine chest.
Analgesic Drugs	Include Ibuprofen, paracetamol and/or aspirin in your lunar chest for they are invaluable in quick pain relief – and work all the better the more infrequently they are taken. Include a paracetamol syrup for children.

This selection is designed to cover a range of family ills. However, if you have a specific requirement or condition to treat do a little research on herbal/

natural remedies and add your choice to your lunar 'chest'. If possible choose an attractive wooden box for your medicine chest. When you have assembled all your ingredients you can infuse them with extra healing energies in a short ritual. Natural substances conduct these energies more effectively, but love finds its way through anything!

A Healing Consecration Ritual

When you have gathered together all your healing materials, you will then be able to do a ritual to consecrate them and to pour all your own healing energies into them. Natural substances such as herbs absorb healing energies more easily because their organic nature means they more readily harmonise with your own frequency. However, it is your intention that is of paramount importance! You can empower a special remedy for someone you love in an individual ritual, but this consecration exercise will do for your entire supply – meaning that you also can benefit when you feel poorly!

Choose Full Moon for your ritual and place green candles on your altar (green being traditionally considered a healing colour). You may like to rub eucalyptus oil into them and/or surround them with green leaves. Choose an incense from the selection on pages 234–5, or burn a joss stick. Have also a large silver candle to take the place of moonlight if the Moon is not visible. Your favourite Goddess-figure should be on your altar.

Cast your circle and invoke the elements as usual. First place your medicine chest in the North, then lay your hands on it and call for the strength, protection and solidity of the Earth element to enter it. Take the time to describe any other healing quality you associate with Earth and imagine it flowing into you and through you, into the chest. Now move to the East and do the same with the Air element, asking for the freshness and ever-renewing attributes of that element, and any other qualities that seem important. (Naturally, if anyone you know has respiratory problems you can visualise the clean, clear unobstructed flow of Air.) Next move South to Fire and ask for energy, vitality, and strong powers of recovery, and then to West and Water, where you should ask for comfort, cleansing, calming, soothing, understanding and healing itself. Now face the Moon (or your substitute candle), close your eyes and feel the lunar energy building up in your solar plexus. Feel the light grow, gentle, powerful, and all-pervading. When you are ready, send this healing glow down into your medicine chest. Do this for as long as you like. When you have finished take a good drink of spring water, close your circle down in the usual way and leave your chest out in the light of the Full Moon for a night or two if possible.

Psychic Healing

Psychic healing can give a lot of relief and support to people who are ill and you can use a similar method to the one suggested for boosting your plants given on page 199. Here are some simple steps. Remember that it is easier to build up the body when the Moon is Waxing, so this is a good time to send healing energy. With a Waning Moon, this is a good time to take away negativity. However, you will need to judge what the person most needs and they may well be able to tell you.

Check the Moon phase, and form as clear an idea as you can of what you are trying to do – are you trying to ease pain, increase energy, heal? (Pain can often be eased by visualising an appropriate colour, usually green or blue, in the affected area.) Take the time to centre and ground yourself. Heat some lavender oil in your oil-burner to calm you, and light a candle. Be careful – you need to protect yourself. Visualise a thin blue membrane around yourself and affirm that while you may send out healing energies, nothing may come back at you through the membrane. Take a minute to visualise this before you start and call on the help of your favourite Goddess to support you.

Now feel the build-up of energy behind your navel. If you are sending simple healing and pain relief you can send the energy down your arms and out through your finger-tips when you are ready. If you are removing negativity, use your energy as a temporary magnet to draw out what is harmful, which you can then flick away with a gesture of your wrist, into the body of planet Earth where it will be easily neutralised. Do not take this negativity into you. Visualise it dispersing in small sparks.

Always be sensitive to your feelings and reactions and to those of your patient. When you have finished – this will probably only take a few minutes, but judge the duration using your intuition – then ground yourself by touching the floor and patting yourself. Take a drink of spring water and dab a little lavender oil on your forehead to seal and cleanse your subtle energies. Re-absorb your protective membrane.

These are very simple instructions and you will find your abilities develop with practice. More complex methods exist that involve opening the chakras (energy centres in the spiritual body). You can find these instructions in several other books such as *Witchcraft, A Complete Guide* and *Wheel of the Year; Myth & Magic Through the Seasons* (see Further Reading). However, even without specific knowledge healing can work. There are many routes in the subtle realms and the map is not the country! As an example, I thought I had a very clear idea of what I was doing when I opened my chakras for healing, etc. When I did this in front of a clairvoyant he could see it happening very distinctly, but while the description of what he saw fitted what I was 'doing' in essence, the details were different. Which one of us was right? Both or neither – it doesn't really matter. In our material state the subtle realms are not easy to grasp, but you can still get results with your healing if you experiment carefully and respectfully and find what works for you.

The Moon and the Body Tradition states that the signs of the Zodiac are related to certain parts of the body. Here are three general rules:

★ Anything done for the wellbeing of the body parts ruled by the sign through which the Moon is passing will be even more beneficial, with the exception of surgery.

★ Any illness or strain in the parts ruled by the current Moon sign will be more unfavourable.

★ The phase of the Moon is crucial – building up the body part ruled by the Moon's sign is best with a Waxing Moon, while anything that cleanses or flushes out will be best with a Waning Moon.

So, a headache or injury to the head is likely to be worse when the Moon is passing through Aries, while a massage of the shoulders will help even more when the Moon is in Gemini. Of course, the dividing lines are not exact and it is not possible to pinpoint the exact place in the head and neck where Aries gives way to Taurus, for instance. In the same way it does not matter too much about the exact position of the Moon as it passes from sign to sign. At certain times of the year the Moon will always be waxing in a certain sign and at other times it will be waning. For example, from the end of March to the end of September the Moon in Aries will always be waning, because the position of the Sun means it is not possible to be waxing in Aries. This can only take place after the Sun has passed through the opposite sign of Libra. Refer back to the diagrams on pages 4 and 28, bearing in mind the positions of the Sun through the summer months, to get a more visual idea of this.

Obviously in these times of long hospital waiting lists it is very hard to refuse surgery, and indeed this should not be contemplated if it will be detrimental to your health. Emergency surgery must obviously be carried out when needed. But if you are paying privately for a hip replacement, for instance, it is best to avoid the Moon in Libra, Scorpio and Sagittarius. You can also avoid dental surgery, fillings, etc, when the Moon is in Aries or Taurus. However, the Waning Moon in these signs is great for a visit to the oral hygienist!

Naturally it is not possible to structure your life completely by Moon sign. For instance, if completion on your house purchase cannot be avoided for a Capricorn day, you will have to carry boxes and move objects on that day. However, you can try to be especially aware that you need to lift things carefully, take plenty of rest and have a massage lined up for next day!

Aries   Upper part of the head, eyes, nose. There may be a greater risk of migraine, nosebleeds, sinus and eye problems on Aries days, so treat these areas with respect. A great day for a peaceful sit-down with cucumber-slices on your eyes! – but don't sit for too long or you'll become restless.

Taurus   Neck and jaws. Take care of your throat and teeth on Moon in Taurus days. Wear a thick scarf if the wind is cold. Give your teeth a special floss and clean.

Gemini   Shoulders, neck, hands, arms and lungs. Rheumatism in these joints could be worse when the Moon is in Gemini, making it a great day for a massage or to burn special oils in your burner to inhale.

Cancer   Stomach, gall bladder, liver, and some systems include lungs for Cancer. (Please note, the sign Cancer has nothing to do with the disease Cancer and those with the Moon in Cancer are not more likely to get it!) Take special care of your digestive system on these days.

Leo   Heart and circulation. Stimulate blood-flow with gentle walks, be loving, and avoid anything that strains the heart on Moon in Leo days.

Virgo   Intestines. Take special care of your diet and eating habits. Eat plenty of fibre. Avoid heavy or spicy foods if you are 'delicate'. Drink lots of water.

Libra   Kidneys and bladder. (Some systems also include the hips.) Take care of your bladder and kidneys. Avoid excesses of caffeine and alcohol, drink plenty of water.

Scorpio   Sexual organs. Pay attention to your sex life and your deepest emotions, and address any sexual dysfunction. Avoid sexual 'marathons' or anything too challenging to the emotions and desires (e.g. situations of sexual jealousy).

Sagittarius   Hips and thighs. Gentle exercise is beneficial. Avoid strain or very demanding walking or climbing. Massage of the hips and thighs is beneficial.

Capricorn   Knees, skin and skeletal system. Take special care of the skin, cleansing, moisturising, etc. Avoid irritants. Consider certain gentle types of massage but any heavy manipulation of the skeleton is best left for other times. Avoid carrying heavy weights when the Moon is in Capricorn.

Aquarius   Lower leg. Take special care of any varicose veins. Gentle walking will be beneficial, but long walks that cause strain should be avoided. Leg massage will help particularly, especially with 'restless legs'.

Pisces   Feet. Be careful what shoes you wear on Pisces days and do not make your feet uncomfortable. This is a good time for reflexology, foot massage and a pedicure.

★ ⁂ ★ *Women's Special Times*

Menarche   When the periods start is a very special time for a young girl and should ideally be marked by some form of ritual. This feminine passage is honourable and valuable. Societies that honour the menstruation of women are less violent. It is sometimes said that men are more aggressive because they do not menstruate – they do not have that compelling connection to Nature, the Moon and cycles, they do not shed the wise blood. The horrible rite of subincision (where the penis is slit), practised by some tribes, has been described as an emulation of menstruation. At puberty boys sometimes seem to be on some sort of quest to get wounded! Native American males go on a vision quest, a journey that is both physically and spiritually demanding. However, young women receive their initiatory experience with their menstrual bleed and do not have to face the same gruelling rites as the males. Menstruation is not simply being 'on the blob', but a time of many meanings, where the young girl becomes fertile, is able to be a mother and take part in the sequence of life – and the knowledge that comes with that is profound and inexpressible.

So, realising this, older women need to welcome the newly-menstruating young woman into their company. It is good to have a special meal, either at home or out, with a red candle on the table, and a present, such as a red scarf (or pair of red knickers!) is good. Affirming passage in a ritual will make this really a time to remember. This ritual should be carried out when the Moon is new, preferably when the first sickle is in the sky.

You will need a luxuriant bouquet of red and white flowers, preferably roses, a large red candle, some white candles to place round and about and on

your altar if you have one, a Goddess-figure in a place of honour, a present for
the newly-menstrual girl wrapped in red, a large chalice, some red wine and a
plate containing sweets and pickles (such as pickled onions or gherkins) and a
bowl or cauldron as a symbol of change and rebirth.

The older women (sisters, aunties, friends of the family, etc) should be
assembled in a circle, around a bowl or cauldron, holding hands, while someone goes to fetch the girl. As the young woman is brought in, they should open
the circle, admit her and close it up again with her in the centre. Now they
circle, chanting, 'She changes everything She touches; everything She touches
changes,' three times. The older woman who is leading the proceedings now
takes one white flower from the bouquet and gives it to the younger woman,
saying, 'This is the flower of innocence.' The young woman places this in the
bowl/cauldron and the older woman takes up a red flower and gives it to her
saying, 'This is the flower of experience.' The young woman now also puts this
in the bowl/cauldron. At this point a big red candle is placed in the cauldron
and the young girl lights it. The older woman chant, 'We celebrate your life-
giving power. We celebrate your blood-flow. We welcome you to womanhood.'
She is now offered the plate and told to take a pickle, with the words 'Life can
be bitter.' Then she takes a sweet with the words 'Life can be sweet.'

The young woman now joins the circle, everyone holds hands and circles
once more, saying again, 'She changes everything She touches; everything She
touches changes.' Offer the chalice of red wine to the Goddess as consecration,
and pass it round in the chalice. The young woman is now given gifts, e.g. a
special pouch for sanitary protection, essential oil such as clary sage, jewellery
made from rubies or garnets, etc. Now follows a relaxed time of womanly chat
and feasting.

This ritual was adapted from my book *Spells and Rituals, a Beginner's
Guide* (see Further Reading). It can be performed in a magic circle if you wish.

Pregnancy Pregnancy, as we are always told, takes an average of 40 weeks from the date of
the last period. Actually, if we reckon from the probable date of conception two
weeks later, this amounts to exactly nine lunations, i.e. nine passages of the
Moon through her phases – nine 'Moons'. There are many theories about how
the phase and sign of the Moon at conception tie up with those at birth, which
signs produce a male child and which produce a female one, etc. It is not my
intention to cover this here because this is a complex and unclear area.
However, for a pregnancy close to the average duration, birth will take place at
the same phase as conception.

During pregnancy, take the time to meditate at each Full Moon, contemplating how your baby has grown during the previous month. If possible sit in the light of the Full Moon, or meditate by candlelight. Burn lavender oil or ylang ylang oil in your burner. Send all the love you can to the precious little foetus growing inside you. Place your hands on your swelling belly, talk to the little one, imagine golden light coming from your hands and going into your womb where the baby can feel its warmth, welcome and encouragement. Imagine it making your baby strong, helping it to grow beautifully. Ask the Great Mother to show you how you can be the best mother possible and how you can best take care of yourself, for you are vital in this process and deserve some extra love.

The following guided meditation can be pre-recorded onto cassette tape, with pauses left where indicated, for use at your Full Moon meditation.

Imagine that you are walking slowly along a moonlit beach, listening to the soft swishing of the waves, seeing their silver ripples and smelling the fresh and salty fragrance. Feel the peace that surrounds you. Be a part of the relentless and reassuring cycles of the Moon and the heavens. *[Pause.]*

The night is balmy and warm and you feel caught in its embrace. The moist sand is soft between your toes. You feel safe and very special – it is as if the entire cosmos knows that you are carrying a treasure. *[Pause.]*

Ahead of you there seems to be something shining faintly as if a piece of the Moon has come to Earth. Drawing closer you see a basket nestling by some rocks at the high-water mark. Slowly you approach this basket – it is woven of silver strands and it has a faint glow around it. When you eventually come to the basket it has the answer to your question in it, symbolically. Treasure this, and come back to everyday awareness.

You can do this visualisation for questions about your role as a mother, what you should do and anything else you want to know. Extend the walk along the beach as much as you like.

Something you need to remember, especially if this is your first baby, is that birth changes you completely. Nothing will look the same, and nothing will feel the same. You will look different in your own eyes, your ideas about your parents and the world in general will change. This profound change is rarely spoken about in ante-natal classes and is one of the reasons why some women find adjustments after the birth so hard – this is connected to more than stitches and sore nipples! Subconsciously you will be realising this and so what you see in the silver basket can sometimes be scary. You should not be scared or jump to negative conclusions about the birth or anything else – this is your subconscious mind preparing you for an exciting and challenging life passage. The more time you take to rest, to watch the Moon and to reflect on your internal changes, the better you will adapt. Pregnancy should not be spent working in hectic fashion, in order to get as much done as possible before the birth. I know this is hard, especially in today's world, but take as much time as you can off, to bask in the moonlight!

Losing a Baby   Miscarriage, abortion and the loss of a baby are tragic times in a woman's life. This also applies if you are trying for a baby and not succeeding, when each unwanted monthly period can feel like a 'death'. I have had three miscarriages and know all too well that awful feeling, not only of loss, but of worthlessness. If you have chosen an abortion, then you will have had your reasons, and they are to be respected; but at some level you will still feel loss.

Do this ritual at Dark Moon or when your bleeding is beginning to subside a little.

Take an egg-cup and fill it with water. Add to this some dark food colouring (red or black will do) and some drops of myrrh oil. Take the egg-cup to the side of a running stream. Hold it in both hands and feel all your hurt and loss, pouring into the liquid. When the time feels right, empty the egg-cup into the stream, saying, 'My loss is returned to the Goddess. It shall become a part of the cycle of life.' Say (or sing, if you know the tune):

We all come from the Goddess
And to Her we shall return.
Like a drop of rain flowing to the ocean,
All that dies shall be reborn,
All that dies shall be reborn.

Probably you will feel like a good cry; if so, let your tears also flow into the stream. Take your empty egg-cup home, fill it with wine or fruit juice and light a white candle. Visualise all the creative things you can and will do, including having a baby in the future if that is appropriate. (Sometimes it is hard to do this positive bit immediately and you may like to wait a day or two, or until you see the crescent Moon in the sky.) Drink the contents of your egg-cup and have as many refills as you like! Trust in the Goddess that things will get better, because they will.

This ritual is much better done with one or more trusted women friends who can support you.

Menopause It is hard to think of a natural condition that receives as much medical intervention as the menopause! This is the 'hormone hell' dreaded by women, with its hot flushes, mood swings, palpitations and many other grim symptoms! Often it is treated by HRT, and 'menopause clinics' are held at surgeries to help the many sufferers. Yet the menopause happens to all of us when we are 50 or so. We would not dream of trying to halt the progress of the menarche, although its symptoms can be just as bad, with sore breasts, cramps and 'flooding', all of which are very bewildering to a young girl. The menopause, on the other hand, spells 'the beginning of the end'.

But is this really the case? Women currently experiencing the menopause can expect to have one third of their lives ahead of them, at least, and this time-span is growing all the time. No more bleeding, no more PMS – a time of peace and creative activity. It isn't my intention to brush off the very real and acute suffering of a definite physical nature that many menopausal women experience. However, I do wonder if this is mostly due to psychological causes. Certainly in my practice as a hypnotherapist I have been able to help considerably women who are experiencing all the usual menopausal symptoms.

Our culture does not prize the older woman and her wisdom. Many older women feel they are on the scrap-heap, no longer attractive and fertile, no longer interesting and vital – in short, no longer relevant. Issues about creativity, how the earlier years have been spent, relationships and, of course, children, all surface. It seems that women who have not had children may have more troubles at the menopause and this may be because they feel they have missed their chance. If this is the case, counselling may needs to be sought.

However, it's worth considering these snippets of information. Women in their fifties and sixties now frequently appear in lists of 'The Hundred Sexiest Women' and similar – that can't be all down to cosmetic surgery! The French find women over 'a certain age' fascinating, and much sexier than inexperienced younger women. Women who have honoured their periods and who have created menstrual diaries and mandalas, as suggested in Chapter 1, tend to have an easier menopause. After the menopause, many women say that sex improves. The menopause is part of normal ageing and many of the conditions associated with it are just that – getting older, and there are ways to minimise the effects. After the menopause you need something to be passionate about, whether it's a person, a profession, a cause – or all three! The hormone changes at the menopause do not redistribute fat, cause wrinkles or make your muscles lose their tone – if this happens, look for other causes. Observing and adjusting to the cycles of the Moon keep you in touch with a menstrual rhythm.

The menopause is less of a cessation, more of a completion. It is your grad-uation into the class of Wisewoman. You have served your apprenticeship in your many menstrual bleeds, your ups and downs, your cramps and exhaustion and you can now move into a time that is more free, that offers you scope as your wise wound heals and your personality deepens. You have so much expe-rience and richness to offer – society is lucky to have you!

Regular exercise where you work up a sweat can help reduce hot flushes. Several herbs and dietary factors can help the menopause. Again, please exer-cise caution when using herbs; as already noted, herbs are far from harmless, so please consult a qualified herbalist if in any doubt. Here is a list of some herbs and supplements that can ease the effects of the menopause.

★ *Agnus Castus (Agnacast):* This acts on the pituitary gland and stabilises hormones.
★ *Black Cohosh (Squaw Root):* A very effective herb, this has received official recognition in Germany. It eases hot flushes, vaginal dryness and depression.
★ *Dang Gui (Angelica Sinensis):* A traditional Chinese herb, it mimics the effect of oestrogen.
★ *Vitamin E:* This eases symptoms and calms anxieties.
★ *Vitamin C with Bioflavonoids:* These can ease leg discomfort and flushes.
★ *Calcium and Magnesium:* These help bone density, and can be used in order to offset the osteoporosis to which some women are prone at menopause.
★ *B Complex Vitamins:* These help with a variety of related conditions.
★ *Selenium:* This is helpful for hormones.
★ *Acidophilus:* This helps keep the natural bacteria in the body in good order (it is also a useful supplement if you are taking antibiotics), and wards off vaginal problems.

A menopausal woman's diet should include plenty of nuts and seeds, oily fish containing Omega 3, fruit, vegetables and garlic. Eating soya has been recom-mended but this is highly debatable, and should probably not be taken in its commercially prepared fashion – instead naturally fermented soy products like shoyu may be considered. Animal fats, sugar, red meat, alcohol, caffeine and nicotine can make menopausal symptoms worse, so go easy.

It is worthwhile using natural methods to deal with symptoms, as HRT may well significantly contribute to the risk of cancer and other diseases, while having fewer of the vaunted positive attributes. Criticism of the use of HRT and the clinical trials surrounding it and evidence against it is given at length in *What Doctors Don't Tell You*, Spring 2002 (see Further Reading).

A Menopause Ritual Such an important passage is best confirmed and celebrated in a ritual. This should ideally be an 'exoteric' ritual, not performed in circle, but as part of a community celebration. Here is a simple rite you can do alone. It should be done when you have not had a bleed for a year. Choose Full Moon for this rite, as it feels more cheerful and we are marking menopause as a culmination. This is purposely slightly up-beat to offset the negative attitude of the culture in which we live.

You will need: three candles (one white, one red, one black), a black veil, some incense containing frankincense (because it is majestic and uplifting, and relates to achievement) and cypress (because that is about passage), paper, pen, silver ribbon, cake, wine, your favourite Goddess-figure, flowers for your altar, a cassette-player with some of your favourite music, a small gift for yourself, preferably contained in a small cardboard egg of the sort that tend to be available for gifts around Easter time.

Place the candles in a row from left to right, with the white one on the left. Light the white one first, saying, 'I light this for my Maidenhood.' Then light the red one, saying, 'I light this for my Motherhood.' Now light the black one, saying, 'I light this for my Wisewomanhood.'

Extinguish the white candle, saying, 'My Maidenhood is completed.' Move the white candle to the right of the black one. Extinguish the red candle, saying, 'My motherhood is completed.' Move this candle to the right of the white candle. (Please note that even if you have had no children, the phase of your life where you have had to cope with the possibility of motherhood is complete – and anyway you are sure to have had to work very hard at other creative projects, to which you are 'mother'.)

Place a black veil over your head, saying, 'I enter the still time, the time of knowledge, the time of wisdom.' Contemplate this for a few minutes. Draw the veil from off your head and state: 'My time of greatest creativity is before me.' Light the white candle from the black one and the red one from the white one. Say, 'The Wisewoman contains the Maiden and the Mother. Blessed be in the Goddess.' Make an offering of incense.

Now write down three things you are proud of achieving, three things you like about yourself and three things you will do with your life in the future, free from your bleeding. Role these up into a scroll and tie it with a silver ribbon. If you are helped in this rite by other women, they should take part in the 'three nice things' and the 'three achievements', writing down what they see in you and presenting it to you rolled up in a small scroll as a gift.

Dance, if you wish – you are free, free as a bird! Make an offering of incense, enjoy some cake and wine and plan what you're going to do with the extra money now you do not have to buy tampons! Now open your gift and consecrate it as part of your rite. Your eggs have all been released and now a new and abstract 'egg' can be laid! So much the better if you have friends to give you gifts, too! Follow this up with an outing of your choice the next day. Enjoy!

★ *The Gift of Poetry*

Lunar Knowledge, Lunar Poetry The poet and author Robert Graves identified two types of knowledge – solar and lunar. 'Solar' knowledge is rational and logical, whereas 'lunar' knowledge is the knowledge of the subconscious and the intuition. In his book *The White Goddess* (see Further Reading), Graves links poetry not only with the subconscious mind but also with ancient cults of the Moon Goddess, which were later banished by the light of 'pure solar reason'. There exists a powerful school of thought that argues that humans were once instinctual, Goddess-worshipping creatures and this was superseded by rational thought, allied to worship of a Sun God and all that was light, bright and reasonable. This, however, does not harmonise with what we know about the many Sun Goddesses, and there are those who argue that Graves' theories have been discredited. Whatever the exactitudes of history and deity-gender may be, however, much of what Graves describes is compelling, suggesting it contains a truth, if not the whole truth – perhaps it is a 'lunar truth'.

Graves tells us that there are two types of poetry, 'muse poetry' and 'Apollonian poetry' (Apollo being the Sun god of the Classical Greeks). The former arises from inspiration and is checked by common sense while the latter is a product of the intellect. If you wish to write poetry to the Moon or use the Moon as inspiration, here are some hints.

★ Jot down any ideas about the poem/s you want to write as they run into your mind and do not attempt to order anything.

★ Write down any words, combinations of words, rhymes, descriptions, feelings about rhythm and length, as they occur to you.

★ Never fear being silly, crass, obvious, soppy or childish – you probably won't be, but even if you have been that 'common sense' can check everything over later.

★ Keep all your scraps of paper in a special folder, perhaps decorated with lunar stickers and designs.

★ Sit by moonlight and let your imagination wander.

★ Sit by candlelight and do the same.

★ Note your dreams as a basis for poems.

★ Contemplate using your Moon sign and/or phase at birth, or that of a child or lover as a basis for a poem.

★ Contemplate setting a strange or intriguing story you have heard to verse.

★ Strong feelings, whether of joy or sorrow, sometimes can be well-expressed in poetry, and this may be very therapeutic.

★ Use the mythology of a favourite Goddess or God to inspire you, especially if they are specifically 'lunar'.

★ Conduct a little ceremony to a lunar Goddess or God asking for inspiration. Simply have a representation of the deity nearby, burn some incense or a joss stick, light a candle and visualise the deity being present, showing you words and objects. Don't forget to say 'thank-you', ground yourself, close down your circle and then make a thank-you offering, which could be just watering your plants to creating the poem itself.

Here are some examples of poems.

Whimsical/ Nonsensical

Nursery Rhyme

Hey diddle-diddle, the cat and the fiddle
The cow jumped over the Moon
The little dog laughed to see such fun
And the dish ran away with the spoon.

This is full of lunar symbols actually, because cows and dogs are both associated with the Moon, and so is food/feeding, especially of children.

Emotional

Hag

I whisper of the darkest hour
Followed by no dawn
I sigh of blindness, barren, bent,
The Undead and Unborn.

I weave the great black spider's spell
In caverns underground
Clothed in loss and long-gone lives
I haunt the barrow-mound.

I am coal and I am bone
Grey drizzle on cold stone
Come to me in your despair
Naked, broken and alone.

I cackle, mock and turn my back
I jab you with my claw
Clasp to your skin my hackles dire
– I throw wide the bright door.

This poem was first published in *The Wheel of the Year, Myth and Magic Through the Seasons* published by Hodder & Stoughton 1997 and now re-issued by Capall Bann. I wrote it as a result of a miscarriage – it is a Dark Moon poem.

Goddess Poem

Rhiannon

Bloom of thorn and flight of dove
Wild heart-beat with thoughts of love
Bewitching calls of birds, above
Rhiannon

Sweet sleep weights the waking eye
Surrender, with a long, last sigh
Yet stir the pale dead where they lie
Rhiannon

I come now on the high moon-tide
Hooves drumming, as the night-mare rides
Brave soul, let me be your guide
Rhiannon

Hot limbs entwine in ecstasy
In love, death, wakening, there find me
In lover's eye your deep self see
Rhiannon

This poem is about the guises and inspirations of the goddess Rhiannon, whose story is given in the Mabinogion (see Further Reading), but she is much more than that. She may be allied to the Waxing, Full and Waning Moons because she is both a love Goddess and an Underworld Goddess. Now, if you like, make up your own poem, bit by bit. Don't expect it all to come together at once.

★ ∴ ★ *Lunar Crafts*

Timing your Craftwork by the Moon — All of the things we have said about living by the lunar cycle can also be applied to crafts. However, as always, your best bet is to tune into your own responses, so that you are aware of the fluctuations in your own creative urges and are able to work with them and take advantage of them. Here is a general summary of the lunar cycle.

New Moon — This is the time for new ideas and inspirations, and is full of energy. It is the time to gather the bits and pieces that you need for your project, to make plans and prepare.

Waxing Moon — This is the time to see your project growing and developing as you work steadily on it.

Full Moon — Now you may want to work long and hard at what you are involved in. You may not want to sleep much because you feel 'full of it' and want to make the most of your creativity. You may want to finish your work at this time. You may also feel inspired with many ideas for other creative work. Lots of images may rise up in your mind. Make a note of these and remember that you can't do it all at once! Occasionally you may see your current project more clearly and totally, and find that you are dissatisfied with it. This can be very frustrating, but try to remember that all has not been wasted and this is part of a process. With your clearer realisations, you will now be in a better place to do something more fulfilling and satisfying.

Waning Moon — This is the time to put the finishing touches to your project, to wind down, and maybe prune and discard. If your type of craft involves stripping down, removing old paint, etc, this is the time to do it in preparation for the next New Moon when you can begin to get into your stride.

Dark Moon — For the three or so days when the Moon is invisible you may feel more like having a 'fallow' time. Meditate, relax, get more sleep, in preparation for the

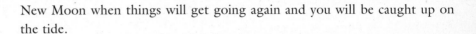

New Moon when things will get going again and you will be caught up on the tide.

A Selection of Lunar Crafts

All crafts are 'lunar' crafts because everything swells and ebbs with the phases of the Moon. However, here are some that are specifically lunar in character.

Moon Candle-Making

It is possible to buy kits for candle-making, and if you can find one that includes crescent-shaped moulds you have all you need. (You can make crescent-shaped moulds from margarine or yoghurt pots, by placing a smaller pot inside a larger one to leave a crescent-shaped space for the wax in the larger pot. Experiment with several shapes and sizes until you feel satisfied, and then glue the pots together with strong glue.) However, if you are collecting your own 'kit', you will need: an old saucepan, wax (left-over candle stubs are ideal, and you can buy stearin dyes from craft shops if you wish to add colour), wicks, moulds, a wax thermometer, a piece of wire, a bowl of cold water, a metal button for each candle.

Gently heat your wax to about 90° C. Weight or fix your mould in a bowl of cold water to help the wax to set – the water-level should be at the finished height of the wax in the mould. Tie one end of the wick to a piece of wire and the other to a metal button. Rest the wire across the open end of the mould so that the wick dangles down, weighted by the button. Pour in your wax very slowly and carefully and let it set. Gradually add a bit more wax as it cools, because it will shrink as it sets. Let it set completely – be patient! When it is totally hardened, remove it from the container. It should come out fairly easily, but if not, transfer the mould to the fridge for a while. After the wax has become even colder it should be easier to remove the candle.

Here are some suggestions for decorating your candle.

★ Paint on designs in non-flammable glue, then sprinkle on some glitter.
★ If you have made a thick candle you can paint it with natural shellac-based paint (painting thinner candles isn't advised because the paint may disturb the burning of the candle).
★ Use stickers on your candle – crescent moons are easy to find in craft and stationer's shops.
★ Melt left-over wax crayons to make decorative designs.
★ Grease the inside of your mould and stick sand to it, so the outside of your candle is cased in sand.

However amateurish your finished article appears to you, the fact you have made it will enhance your lunar rituals. Candles you have made yourself also make great presents because you have put love into them.

Decorated Eggs This is traditionally an Easter craft. However, decorated eggs may feature in Moon celebrations, placed upon the altar to symbolise the fertility of the Moon. The symbolism of decorated eggs is suitable for both menarche and menopause, for in each case creativity, of a different character, is being honoured.

Soak the eggs you wish to paint in a solution of water mixed with equal amounts of vinegar for 24 hours and then make a tiny hole at each end. Use a straw at one end to blow out the white and yolk. Do this very steadily and patiently, and save the white and yolk for use in cooking. Rinse the shell under the cold tap, dry it carefully, then leave it on the windowsill or near a heater so that the inside can dry out. Now you can paint anything you like on the eggs, depending on your imagination and skill. Eggs can be covered in glue and rolled in glitter, like candles. You can put stickers on them or draw designs with felt-tipped pens. An ankh, for instance, would be easy to draw, and hearts and stars are simple and evocative.

A Lemon Pomander In Elizabethan times pomanders were very popular with the nobility who had to travel through the poorer quarters of London and couldn't stand the smell! Today a pomander can be used to scent a wardrobe or cupboard. Lemons are ruled by the Moon, and are a good choice for a lunar pomander.

Choose a firm-skinned organic lemon and make your pomander when the Moon has started to wane. You will also need plenty of dried cloves, some orris root, cinnamon and allspice. Push the cloves into the skin of the lemon until it is completely covered. (You can use a knitting needle to make holes first.) Then roll the lemon in the herbal mixture, wrap it in tissues and leave somewhere warm and dark to dry out for at least a lunar cycle. When it has dried out, tie it up with white or silver ribbon and hang it up where required. Your pomander may keep for years.

Lunar Lantern Cut some thick but bendable card to approximately 40cm by 15cm. Cut crescent shapes out of the cardboard and cover these with coloured tissue paper. Roll up the card to make a cylindrical lantern shape and glue the edges together so that the tissue paper is on the inside. Then cut a circular base from card. This circle needs to be larger than the bottom of the cylinder so that it can be folded up inside and glued in place. Add a handle made from a pipe-cleaner or a strip of cardboard. Place a tea-light inside – these are fairly safe as they tend to go out when tipped over.

Your lantern can form a decoration for lunar celebrations and rituals and if you look after it, it can be used several times. However, be careful with this lantern because it is very flammable! Do not leave it unattended.

Moon Mobile   Make a circle of thick wire and cover this in silver paper. Fasten three equal lengths of silver thread at equal distance around the circumference and tie these together at the top, making a loop from which to hang the mobile. Now, on your silver circle you can hang anything that you wish to remind you of the Moon – a circular silver shape for Full Moon, perhaps flanked by cut-out animal shapes such as wolves or dogs, or dried flowers, crystals, etc. The Waxing and Waning crescents can be placed at 90° to the Full Moon, with a round black disc for the Dark Moon. In the Waxing Moon quadrant you may like to place seeds, such as sycamore wings, and in the Waning Moon quadrant maybe the figure of an owl, or a witch on a broomstick. Around the Dark Moon would be an appropriate place to hang silver stars, for these shine brighter when the Moon is absent. Experiment with ideas that make this special to you. Again this makes a lovely menarche or menopause gift.

White Rose Necklace   Garland yourself for your lunar rituals with a necklace made of dried white roses. Use flower heads that have not fully opened and pick them when the Moon is waning, taking them off the stem 75mm below the flower. Thread through the flower heads with a needle and allow them to dry. You may like to alternate them with silver charms and crystals. Dab rose oil, or Moon-ruled jasmine oil on the dried flowers to renew their fragrance.

Flower Pressing   This is a simple craft that is best done when the Moon is waning, because the moisture-content of the flowers will be lessened. Pressed flowers can remind you of all sorts of occasions and they can be used as bookmarks for your lunar journal or you can frame a pressed flower and use it as a focal point in your meditation. For instance, a pressed rose whose petals are dark to the point of being almost black would be excellent at Dark Moon.

All you need are two sheets of tissue paper. Lay one flat on a surface you will not be needing for a while, or on a tray or a piece of cardboard. Place your flower on top of it, then place the other sheet of tissue paper on top of the flower. Then place a weight over the top, such as several heavy books, and leave until Dark Moon, by which time it will be dried out and ready to use.

Making Incense

Incense is mentioned in several places in this book. You can easily obtain incense blends (see Resources) but it is also possible to make your own, even from ingredients bought in the supermarket. Where possible, however, buy your incense ingredients from reputable suppliers who use ethically-farmed and even organic resources, because this is important for the energies you generate.

All plants have a planetary ruler, and you will not want to stick merely to lunar herbs for most of your lunar incenses. With a little imagination you can adapt other planetary rulers to the lunar phases. For instance, which lunar phase best fits Venus, the Goddess of love? (Probably the Full Moon.) Sombre Saturn feels more like Waning or Dark Moon, while lively Mercury is appropriate for the Waxing Moon. Go with what you feel to be right.

Incense is simply a combination of any combustible plant material, dried leaf, root and bark. Essential oils can also be added. Gum resins are what give most incenses their intensity and these are more pricey but worth the investment. These include frankincense, myrrh, benzoin and copal, although frankincense and myrrh are also obtainable as essential oils. You can make incense from plants or bark that you gather, but some will stink! Pick them when the Moon is waning and dry them in an airing cupboard. Be aware that some plants are highly toxic and inhaling the fumes is not to be recommended. So be careful! When you have chosen your ingredients (which should be broken or chopped into small pieces), place them in a large jar and shake them all together, adding essential oils one drop at a time. Then transfer the incense to a clean jar and label.

Here is a list of some substances with their rulers and characteristics. Many of these you can find in your corner store. Some are easily obtained as oils, e.g. lavender, jasmine, frankincense and myrrh.

Lavender	Mercury. Cleansing, purifying, clears and strengthens the mind, promotes a feeling of peace.
Cinnamon	The Sun. Spirituality, psychism, healing, attracts money.
Bay	The Sun. Prophecy, meditation, protection.
Thyme	Venus. Love, courage, psychism, health, sleep.
Sage	Jupiter. Money, protection, longevity, granting of wishes.
Rose Petals	Venus, but also linked to Isis and Demeter. Love, healing, divination, psychism, protection, luck.
Rosemary	The Sun. This herb is akin to frankincense. Sleep, eternal youth, remembrance, love, lust, mental acuity.

Parsley Mercury. Protection, lust, purification. (But also associated with Persephone and the Underworld, for Mercury was an ambiguous God who could travel into and out of Hades.)

Lemon Balm (Melissa) The Moon. Love, healing, success, fertility.

Fennel Mercury. Purification, protection, healing.

Basil Mars. Love, wealth, exorcism, protection, assertion.

Mint Venus or Mercury. Travel, exorcism, protection, money, lust, healing.

Marjoram/ Oregano Mercury. Used for love spells.

Ginger Mars. Use for some extra oomph!

Benzoin The Sun. Success, energy, magical power, astral projection, purification.

Frankincense The Sun. Protection, purification, spirituality, exorcism, courage.

Myrrh The Moon. Passage and 'laying to rest', purification, exorcism, spirituality, protection.

Sandalwood The Sun or the Moon. Purification, healing, exorcism, spirituality, protection.

Cumin Mars. Fidelity, exorcism, anti-theft.

Copal The Sun. Protection, spirituality, love, purification.

Mace Mercury. Sharpens the intellect.

Coriander Mars. Love, health, healing.

Eucalyptus The Moon. Healing, protection.

Jasmine The Moon. Love, money, prophetic dreams.

Lemon The Moon. (In incense use grated, dried peel.) Purification, longevity, friendship, love.

Patchouli Saturn. Money, fertility, lust.

Here are some suggested combinations for different kinds of magical work.

★ *Full Moon (Motherhood):* Frankincense, sandalwood, rose petals.
★ *New Moon (Menarche):* Jasmine, lemon, lavender.
★ *Dark Moon:* Myrrh, bay, frankincense.
★ *Menopause:* Myrrh, copal, patchouli.
★ *Love:* Rose, jasmine, copal.
★ *Healing:* Lavender, sage and eucalyptus.
★ *Money:* Cinnamon, sage, basil.
★ *Fertility:* Patchouli, lemon balm, frankincense.
★ *General:* Frankincense, myrrh, cinnamon.

Here we just touch on a vast subject. You may like to explore further, starting with *Herbs for Magic and Ritual, a Beginner's Guide* (see Further Reading). To burn your incense you will need a censer or a special container that is strong and heatproof. You will also need the small charcoal discs obtainable from suppliers and many New Age and alternative shops. Some tongs will also be useful. Store the charcoal in a dry place, ignite one side of the 'wheel' until it sparks and starts to go grey, then lay it flat and sprinkle on the incense. Then watch as the magical vapours spiral up towards the Moon!

CONCLUSION

And Finally...

This book has contained many suggestions for linking your daily life to the Moon and thereby making your days more balanced and creative. Use the Moon in spells, honour her on your altar, observe how the position of the Moon at your birth effects you and start – just a little at first – to use lunar wisdom in ordinary life. The Moon is 'sister-planet' to the Earth, there to remind us of our natural cycles and the importance of just 'being' with things as they are. With this sense of 'beingness' comes development of the instincts and the intuition. Let yours develop with each cycle of the Moon and let your night-sight grow. Happy Moon-gazing!

FURTHER READING

★⋰★ *Books by Me*

Witchcraft, A Beginner's Guide (Hodder & Stoughton, 1999). A basic guide to working rituals, plus general information on the Craft.

Witchcraft, A Complete Guide (Hodder & Stoughton, 2000). This is a witch-craft training manual, in essence, which will give you more in-depth information.

Herbs for Magic and Ritual (Hodder & Stoughton,1999). You will find this useful for learning more about incense recipes, the magical use of herbs etc.

Spells and Rituals, A Beginner's Guide (Hodder & Stoughton,1999). More spells and rituals for you to try out.

The Wheel of the Year, Myth and Magic Through the Seasons (Capall Bann, 2002). Co-written with Jane Brideson, this suggests lots of ways to celebrate the eight seasonal festivals.

Spellbound, The Teenage Witch's Essential Handbook (Rider, 2002). A fun and factual guide for teenagers, and even older people, too!

The Moon and You, A Beginner's Guide (Capball Bann, 2003). This is a more complete guide to your Moon phase at birth.

Vampires, A Beginner's Guide (Hodder & Stoughton, 2000). Are you afraid of the dark? Find out more about these creatures of the night and the Moon.

Faeries and Nature Spirits, A Beginner's Guide (Hodder & Stoughton, 1999). Who's at the bottom of your garden? Find out – one moonlit night!

The Goddess, A Beginner's Guide (Hodder & Stoughton, 1997). Simple guide to the Goddess in Her many forms.

Other Works

Graham Boston, *Astrology, A Beginner's Guide* (Hodder & Stoughton, 1998) Lesley Bremness, *The Complete Book of Herbs* (Dorling Kindersley, 1994). Fully-illustrated guide.

Zsuzsanna Budapest, *Grandmother Moon* (HarperSanFrancisco, 1991). Lunar wisdom and magic.

Adrienne Clarke, Helen Porter, Helen Quested and Patricia Thomas, *Living Organic* (MQ Publications, 2001). Thorough, revealing guide to a natural way of life.

Nancy Cunningham, *I Am Woman By Rite* (Weiser, 1995). Recommended for inspirational feminine rites.

Scott Cunningham, *The Complete Book of Incense, Oils and Brews* (Llewellyn,1991) —*Encyclopaedia of Magical Herbs* (Llewellyn, 1994) — *Crystal, Gem & Metal Magic* (Llewellyn, 1994). All three books by Scott Cunningham are good reference works.

Mark Evans, *The Guide to Natural Living* (Lorenz Books, 1999). Comprehensive fully-illustrated guide.

Janet and Stewart Farrar, *The Witches' God* (Phoenix, 1989). Comprehensive guide to the many masculine forms of deity by these two respected Wiccans.

Janet and Stewart Farrar, *The Witches' Goddess* (Phoenix, 1987). The many forms of the Goddess thoroughly described and listed, with rituals.

Robert Graves, *The White Goddess* (Faber & Faber, reprinted 1988)

Nick Kollerstrom, *Gardening and Planting by the Moon* (Foulsham, 2001). Handy, with some interesting snippets of information.

Gwyn Jones and Thomas Jones trans., *The Mabinogion* (Everyman, 1989). Stories from ancient Welsh myth.

The Lunar Almanac (Piatkus, 1991). Packed with lunar lore.

Tracy Marks, *The Astrology of Self Discovery* (CRCS Publications, 1985). An insightful work, especially in regard to Moon Signs.

Jeff Mayo and Christine Ramsdale, *Teach Yourself Astrology* (Hodder & Stoughton, 1996)

Lynne McTaggart, *What Doctors Don't Tell You* (Thorsons, 1996). The Newsletter 'What Doctors Don't Tell You' and its accompanying publication on alternative medicine 'Proof!' is available from 4, Wallace Rd, London, N1 2PG England.

Claire Nahmad, *Fairy Spells* (Souvenir Press, 1997). A charming little book.

Nexus Magazine, nexus@ukoffice.u-net.com

Naomi Ozaniec, *Dowsing, A Beginner's Guide* (Hodder & Stoughton, 1999)

Johanna Paunger and Thomas Poppe, *Moon Time* (C.W. Daniel, 1995). Guide to lunar living, especially in regard to health.

Danielle Ryman, *The Aromatherapy Handbook* (C.W. Daniel, 1991)

C. Norman Shealy MD, PhD, *The Illustrated Encyclopaedia of Healing Remedies* (HarperCollins, 2002). Comprehensive guide, including sections on Bach Flower remedies.

Penelope Shuttle and Peter Redgrove, *The Wise Wound – Menstruation and Everywoman* (Harper Collins, 1994). Definitive work about menstruation, its hidden meanings and its links with psychology, legend and anthropology. *Alchemy for Women* by the same authors (Rider 1995) follows on from this and gives practical advice on experiencing the cycle.

Dr Linda White and Steven Foster, *The Herbal Drugstore* (Rodale, 2000). Full information on herbal cures.

Denise Whicello Brown, *Teach Yourself Aromatherapy* (Hodder & Stoughton, 2001)

Gail Wood, *Sisters of the Dark Moon* (Llewellyn, 2001). Lunar rituals.

RESOURCES

Planetary Tables Neil Michelsen, *The American Ephemeris for the 20th Century* (Astro Computing)
— , *The American Ephemeris for the 21st Century* (Astro Computing). The address for Astro Computing Services is Box 16430, San Diego, CA 92116, USA. These give you the position of the planets and the Moon, day by day.

Herbs and Oils Herbs and oils can be ordered worldwide from the following, but sometimes you may have to send a small sum for a catalogue:

Starchild, The Courtyard, 2-4 High St Glastonbury, Somerset BA6 9DU, UK. Tel 01458 834663. Catalogue £1.50.

The Sorcerer's Apprentice, 6-8 Burley Lodge Road, Leeds LS6 1QP, UK. Tel 0113 245 1309. Send two first-class stamps or international reply coupons.

Enchantments, 341 East Ninth St (Between 1st & 2nd Avenue), New York City, NY 10003, USA. Tel 212 228 4394. Catalogue $3 USA, $5 elsewhere.

Mystery's, 386, Darling St , Balmain, NSW 2041, Australia.

Eye of the Cat, 3314 E Broadway, Long Beach, CA 90803, USA. Catalogue $10, $5.50 refundable on first order.

Lunar Calendars and Artwork For calendars and artwork, including cards for the four major phases, contact: Dark Moon Designs, e-mail morrigan@mac.com. Or write, enclosing suitable International Reply Coupons or SAE, to 'Rainbow Cottage', Clonduff, Rosenallis, Co. Laois, Eire.

Associations

The Pagan Federation
BM Box 7097, London WC1 N 3XX, UK
The PF have a branch called 'Minor Arcana' for young people:
PO Box 615, Norwich, Norfolk NR1 4QQ, UK
Website: www.members.tripod.com/-Minor

The Children of Artemis
BM Artemis, London WC1N 3XX, UK
Website: http://www.witchcraft.org
This is a dynamic association for those interested in witchcraft, with a lively web-site that is monitored and so is as safe as it can be made, particularly for young people.

Other sites www.witchvox.net/links/webusa-w.html
www.bookofshadows.net

Contacting the Author

You can e-mail me on undines@freeuk.com. I try to give a brief reply to all correspondence but I cannot answer detailed enquiries or help with specific problems – sorry! But anything you say will be borne in mind for future books and will be treasured.

To have your chart drawn up or for any astrological work please e-mail me on the above address. I offer a variety of astrological services from full private consultation to simple information on your Moon phase and sign, etc. Price list available on request.

INDEX